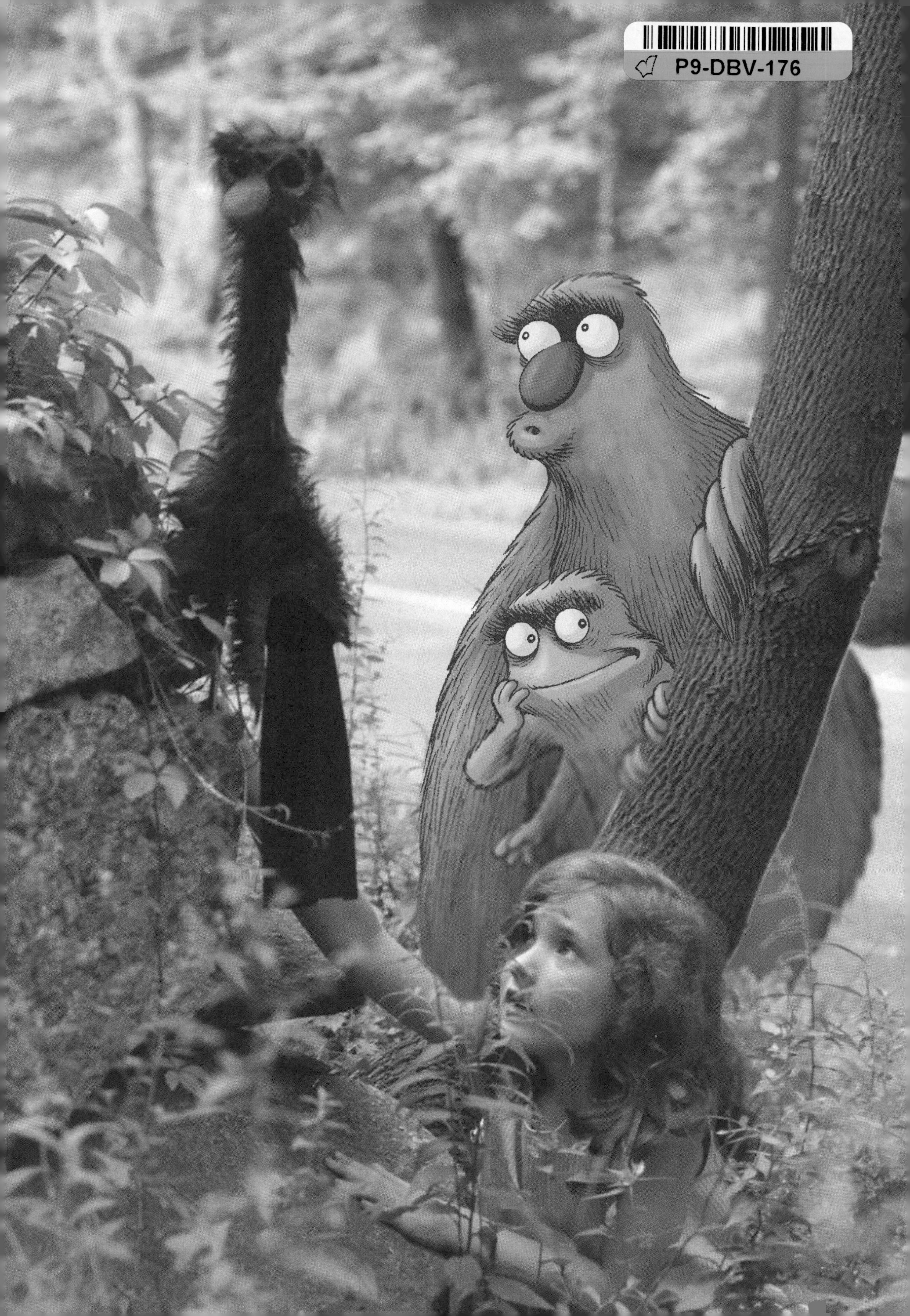

# Jim Henson's™
# THE MUSICAL MONSTERS OF TURKEY HOLLOW™

THE LOST TELEVISION SPECIAL
BY JIM HENSON & JERRY JUHL
ADAPTED BY ROGER LANGRIDGE

Published by
ARCHAIA™

# Jim Henson's
# THE MUSICAL MONSTERS OF TURKEY HOLLOW

## THE LOST TELEVISION SPECIAL BY
## JIM HENSON & JERRY JUHL

### ADAPTED, ILLUSTRATED & HAND-LETTERED BY
## ROGER LANGRIDGE

### COLORS BY
## IAN HERRING
#### WITH COLOR ASSISTS BY JUL MAE KRISTOFFER

### DESIGNER
## SCOTT NEWMAN

### ASSISTANT EDITOR
## CAMERON CHITTOCK

### EDITOR
## REBECCA TAYLOR

I'D LIKE TO THANK SYLVIE, TAMSIN AND THOMAS FOR PUTTING UP WITH MY STRESSED, OVER-TIRED BEHAVIOUR AND MY PROLONGED ABSENCE FROM BASIC FAMILY ACTIVITIES WHILE I WAS WORKING ON THIS BOOK. SAINTS, ONE AND ALL.

—ROGER

SPECIAL THANKS TO
BRIAN HENSON, LISA HENSON, JIM FORMANEK, NICOLE GOLDMAN, MARYANNE PITTMAN, CARLA DELLAVEDOVA, JUSTIN HILDEN, JILL PETERSON, KAREN FALK, THE ENTIRE JIM HENSON TEAM, CRAIG SHEMIN, FORREST LIGHTHART, AND STEPHEN CHRISTY.

ROSS RICHIE CEO & Founder
MARK SMYLIE Founder of Archaia
MATT GAGNON Editor-in-Chief
FILIP SABLIK President of Publishing & Marketing
STEPHEN CHRISTY President of Development
LANCE KREITER VP of Licensing & Merchandising
PHIL BARBARO VP of Finance
BRYCE CARLSON Managing Editor
MEL CAYLO Marketing Manager
SCOTT NEWMAN Production Design Manager
IRENE BRADISH Operations Manager

CHRISTINE DINH Brand Communications Manager
DAFNA PLEBAN Editor
SHANNON WATTERS Editor
ERIC HARBURN Editor
REBECCA TAYLOR Editor
IAN BRILL Editor
CHRIS ROSA Assistant Editor
ALEX GALER Assistant Editor
WHITNEY LEOPARD Assistant Editor
JASMINE AMIRI Assistant Editor
CAMERON CHITTOCK Assistant Editor

KELSEY DIETERICH Production Designer
JILLIAN CRAB Production Designer
DEVIN FUNCHES E-Commerce & Inventory Coordinator
ANDY LIEGL Event Coordinator
BRIANNA HART Executive Assistant
AARON FERRARA Operations Assistant
JOSÉ MEZA Sales Assistant
MICHELLE ANKLEY Sales Assistant
ELIZABETH LOUGHRIDGE Accounting Assistant
STEPHANIE HOCUTT PR Assistant

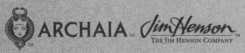

BOOM! Studios, 5670 Wilshire Boulevard, Suite 450, Los Angeles, CA 90036-5679. Printed in Italy. First Printing. ISBN: 978-1-60886-434-8, eISBN: 978-1-61398-288-4

# CREATIVE HARMONY

## THE MUSICAL MONSTERS OF TURKEY HOLLOW

As the pages of ***The Musical Monsters of Turkey Hollow*** outline emerged in rapid succession from Jerry Juhl's typewriter in 1968, Jim Henson would have heard the frequent "ding" of the carriage return — a signal representing the countless ideas erupting from their creative partnership. First joining forces in August 1961 during the final months of Jim's Washington, DC five-minute television series, *Sam and Friends*, Jim and Jerry found an easy rapport. They shared literary influences and comic inspirations, laughed at lowbrow slapstick and enjoyed sophisticated political humor. Both relished wordplay, invented languages and puns and recognized the easy relationship between music and poetry.

In the early days, Jim and Jerry worked in lawn chairs under the trees behind Jim's Bethesda, Maryland home and then, starting in 1963, moved to a two-room office/workshop over a bar on East 53rd Street in Manhattan. Sometimes laughing until they cried, they sketched out everything from two-minute comedy bits to feature-length films, dreaming up humorous television programs, and settings and situations that would challenge and entertain. Jim and Jerry were eager to develop live-action projects geared toward adult audiences, like Jim's Academy Award nominated short, *Time Piece*, or their teleplay for the surrealistic drama *The Cube*. At the same time, the Muppets they had invented offered a joyful creative direction. Accessible to wide swaths of the television audience, these characters were popular guests on the major TV networks. Jim and Jerry set their sights on getting long-form programs on the air and began working on various specials based on fairy tales or, like ***Turkey Hollow***, linked to holidays. A 1965 pilot evolved into the television special *Hey Cinderella!*, taping in 1968 and airing in 1970. *The Great Santa Claus Switch*, developed from an idea dating to 1963, became the first Muppet Christmas special to air when it was produced in 1970.

On their own, in short pieces on variety shows, the Muppets were engaging and hilarious, but when they interacted with humans, something magical happened — they became real. The warmth and spontaneity of Rowlf's banter with country music star Jimmy Dean each week made viewers believe Rowlf was a living, breathing celebrity. This was not lost on Jim and Jerry, and for the most part, their fairy tale and holiday special concepts featured human leads. This interaction was to be a defining element in ***The Musical Monsters of Turkey Hollow***.

The "Note of Introduction" that starts the ***Turkey Hollow*** outline describes a New England location that would "take full advantage of the fall colors" and puppetry techniques that allow the characters to be seen, "scampering across the country side, just as a real animal would." This autumnal setting, placing puppets in the real world for the first time, and the centrality of music to the story, may have been inspired by a short film Jim made in 1965 called "Run Run." That October, in the woods behind his Connecticut farmhouse, Jim had filmed his young daughters scampering through the trees. He set the colorful footage to a playful musical track written by a young composer, Joe Raposo. The result was a lovely and evocative combination and would have lingered with potential in Jim's mind.

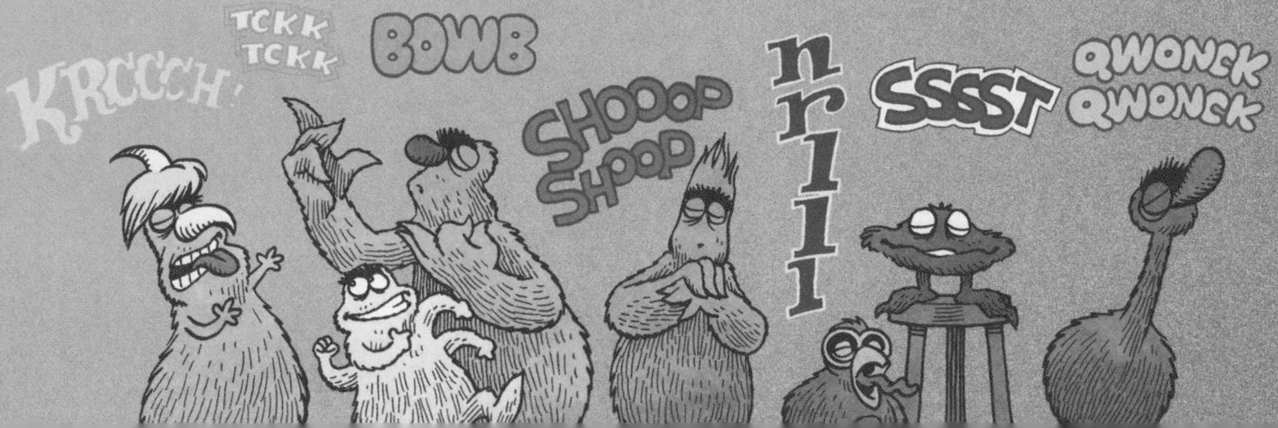
KRCCCH!
TCKK TCKK
BOWB
SHOOOP SHOOP
nrlll
SSSST
QWONCK QWONCK

While Jerry was the wordsmith, Jim often utilized sounds to illustrate an idea. The storyline of **Turkey Hollow** relied heavily on audio elements to help portray the characters. The folk songs and score, to be written by Joe Raposo, gave viewers a sense for the human roles. Jim and Jerry envisioned the musical monsters, however, as communicating in unique, otherworldly music. To be created on an electronic synthesizer by Raymond Scott, the monsters' unique tones were meant to harmonize, indicating their communal nature. Jim had been working with Scott on several projects, employing the distinctive sounds from Scott's synthesizer for commercials, experimental shorts, and an abstract puppet called Snerf whose up and down movement was accompanied by the sound of an electronic slide whistle. Jerry and Jim seemed partial to this character, using him as a comic foil for Kermit on *The Hollywood Palace* and other variety shows, and Snerf was included among the monsters of **Turkey Hollow**.

Several of Jim and Jerry's ideas of the period had sci-fi themes, allowing for a range of abstract puppet designs. In preparation for **Turkey Hollow**, master puppet builder Don Sahlin, with his knack for translating Jim's brief sketches into expressive characters, made four friends for Snerf (called Qwonck in the outline). Expert in creating a visual connection between puppet and audience, Don used a variety of taxidermy eyes for the first time, focusing on their shape and placement. Discovering a new material that could make the creatures more lifelike was exciting for Jim, opening up new avenues for exploration. Don gave each alien monster a unique silhouette and a fur color within a specific mossy palette. Like their sounds, the distinctive looks of these musical monsters harmonized into a unified group.

After Jim and Jerry finished their outline and Don finalized the puppets, they returned to the leafy woods behind the Hensons' house to see how the puppets would look in the natural world. They posed the monsters among the trees, atop small boulders and peeking into windows. Jim's daughters Lisa and Cheryl, who had scampered through the trees three years earlier, held the furry creatures for their father. Jim snapped photographs, illustrating the group's effort. **The Musical Monsters of Turkey Hollow** was ready to share, and Jim arranged to send the concept to potential television producers. While there were no takers at the time, there is no statute of limitations on a good idea. More than forty-five years later, Jim and Jerry's original outline has been rediscovered along with the original puppets. With this volume, audiences of all ages can finally enjoy this charming story.

**KAREN FALK**
*The Jim Henson Company Archives*
*July 3, 2014*

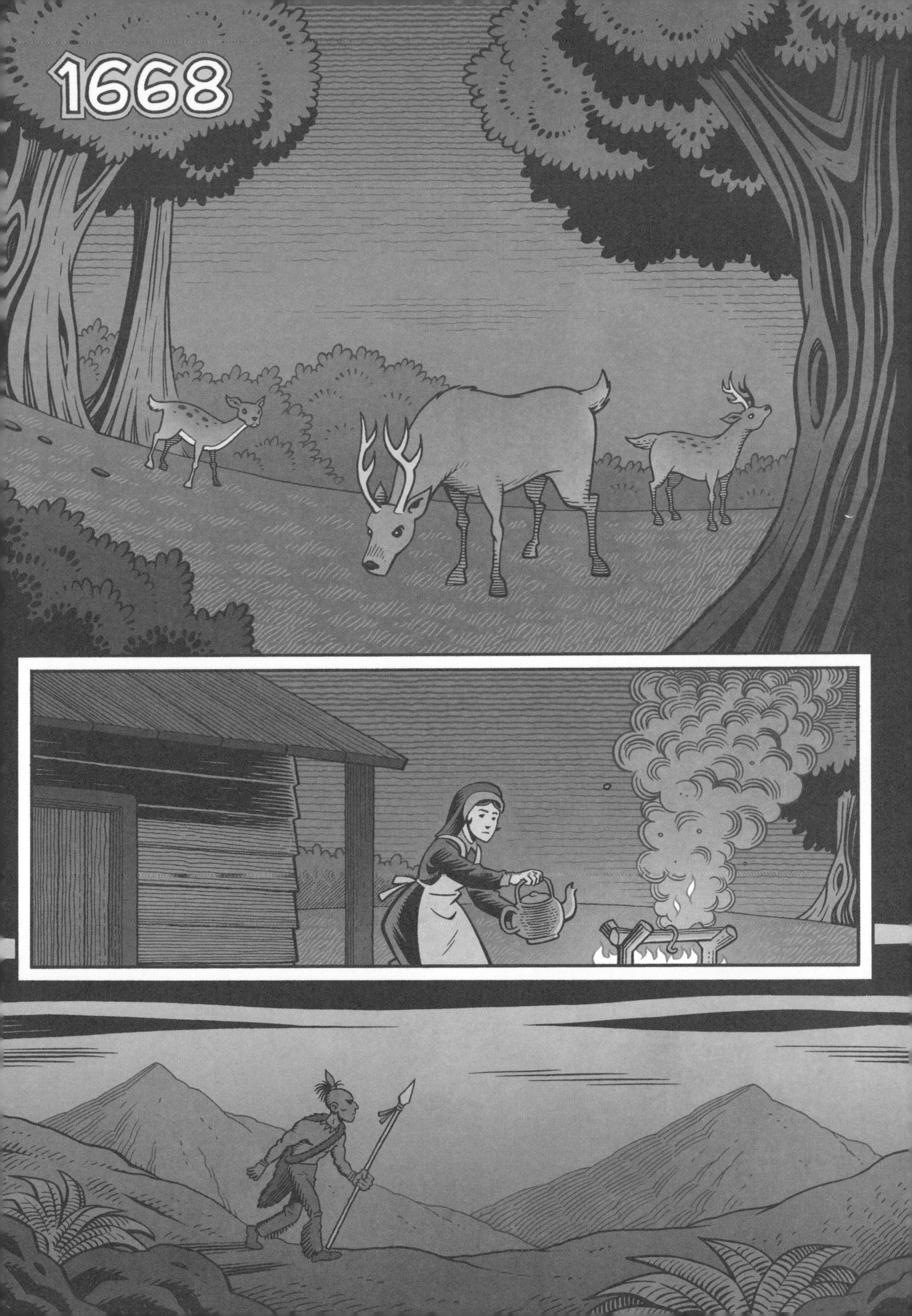
1668

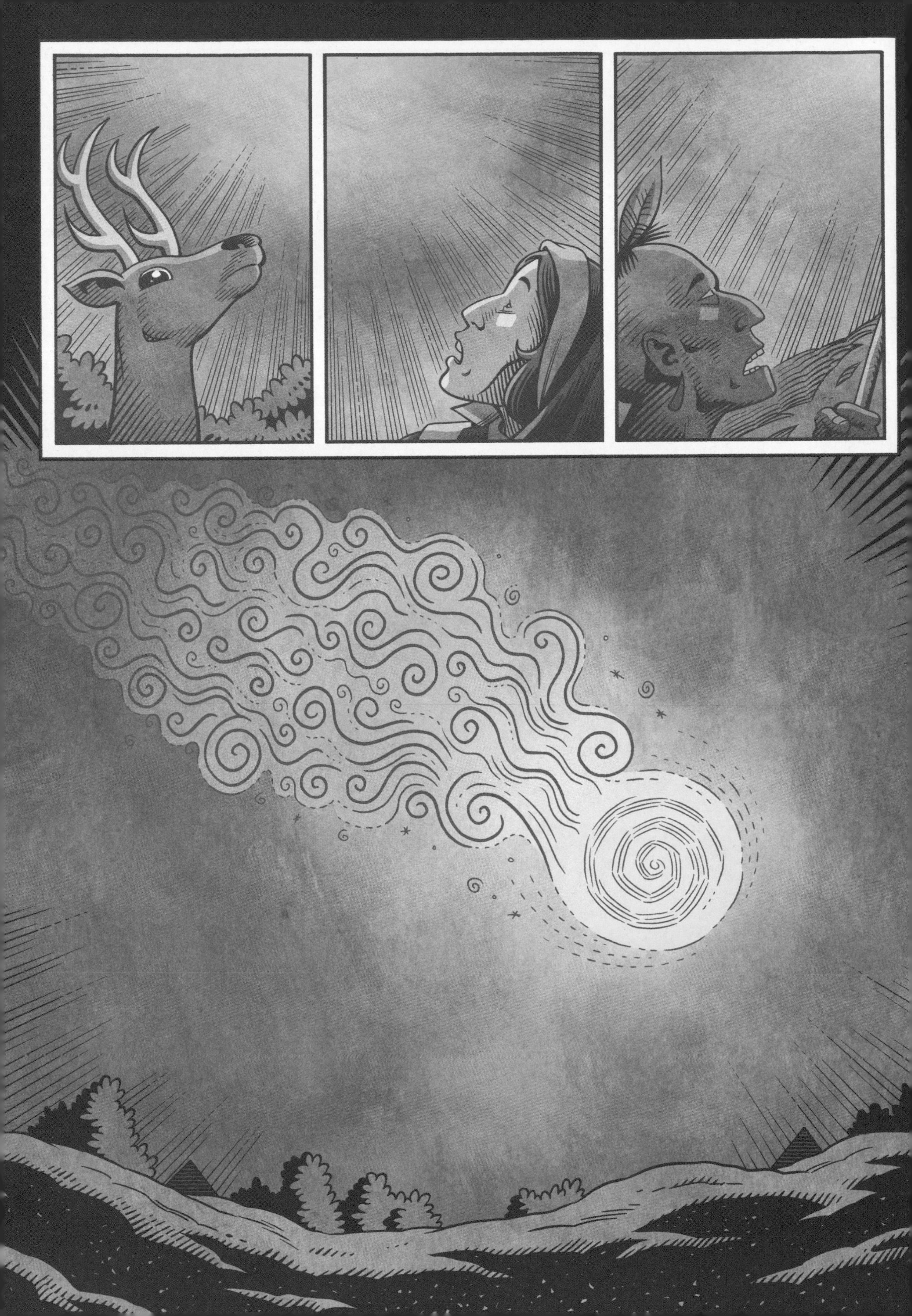

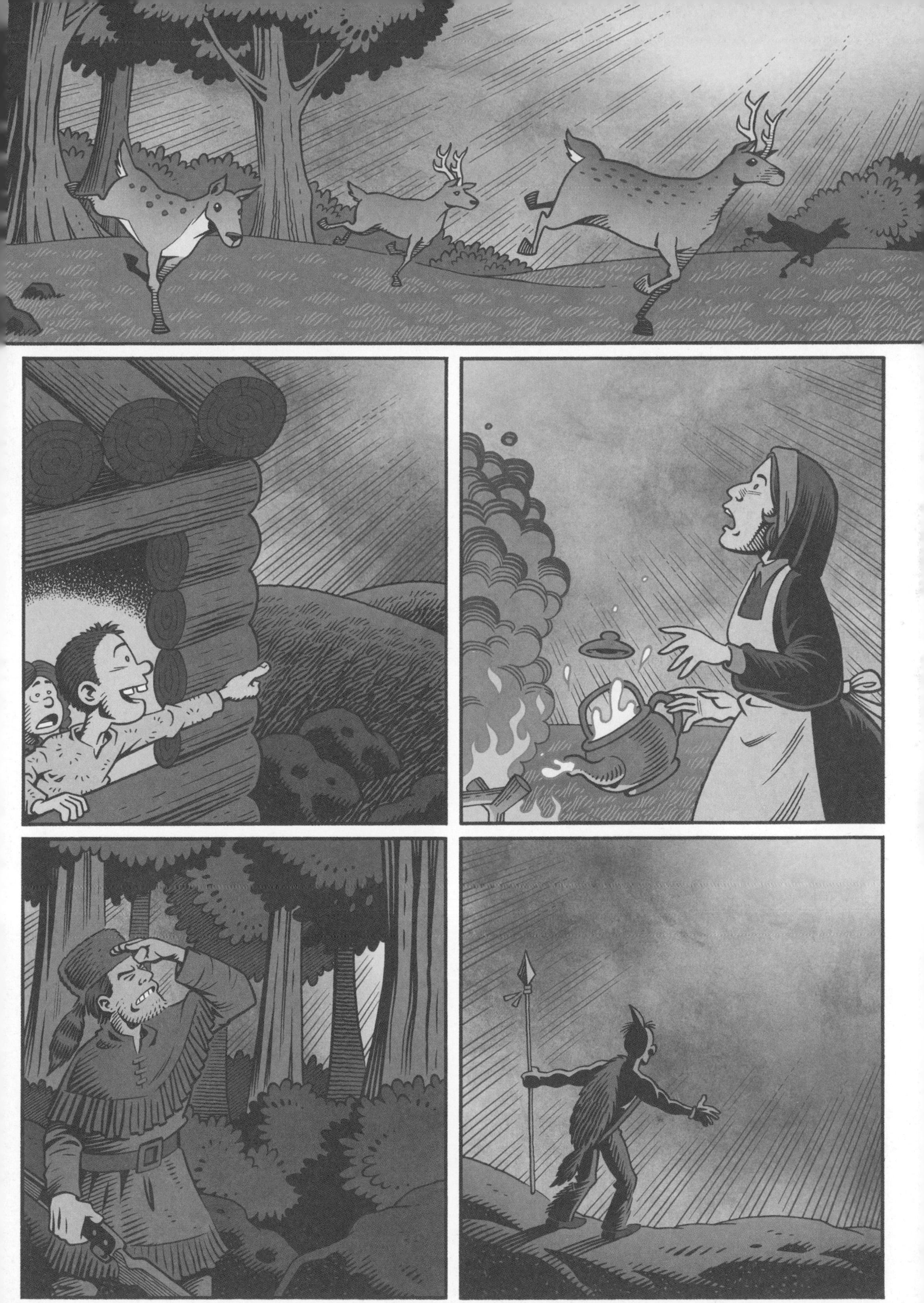

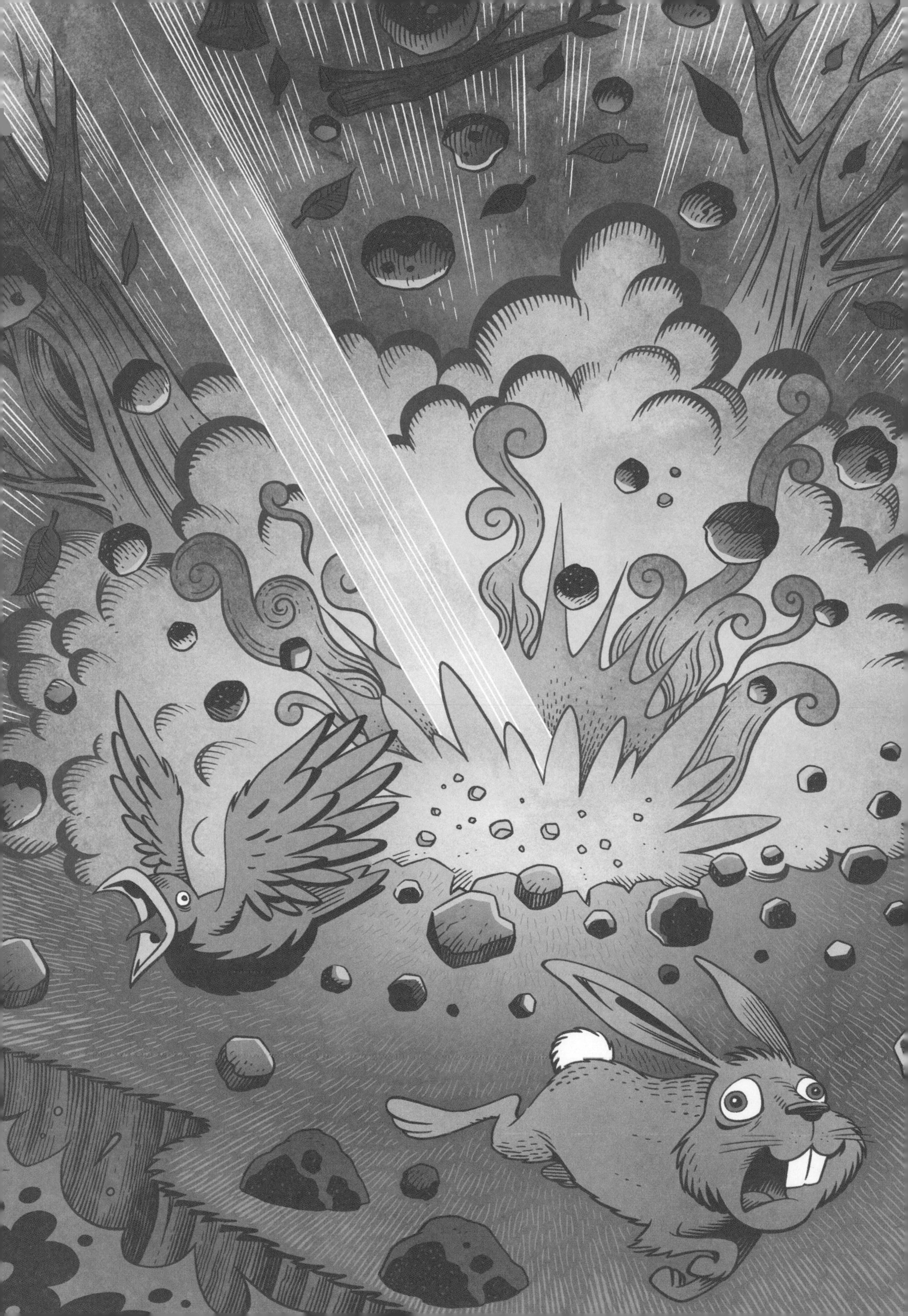

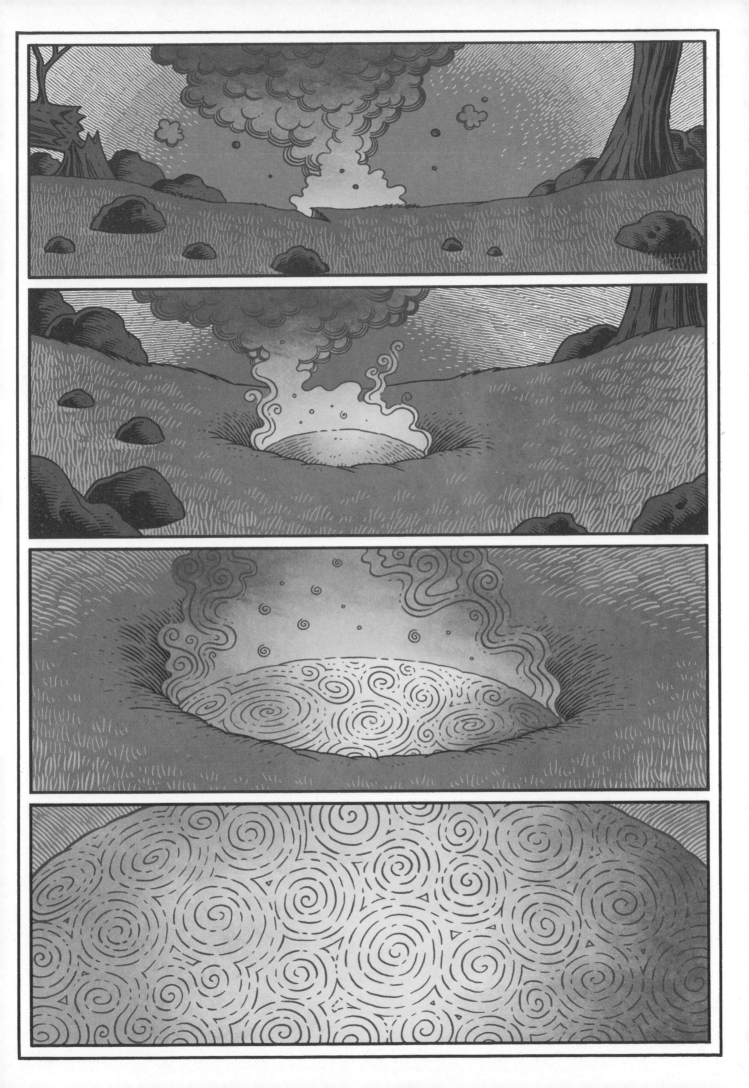

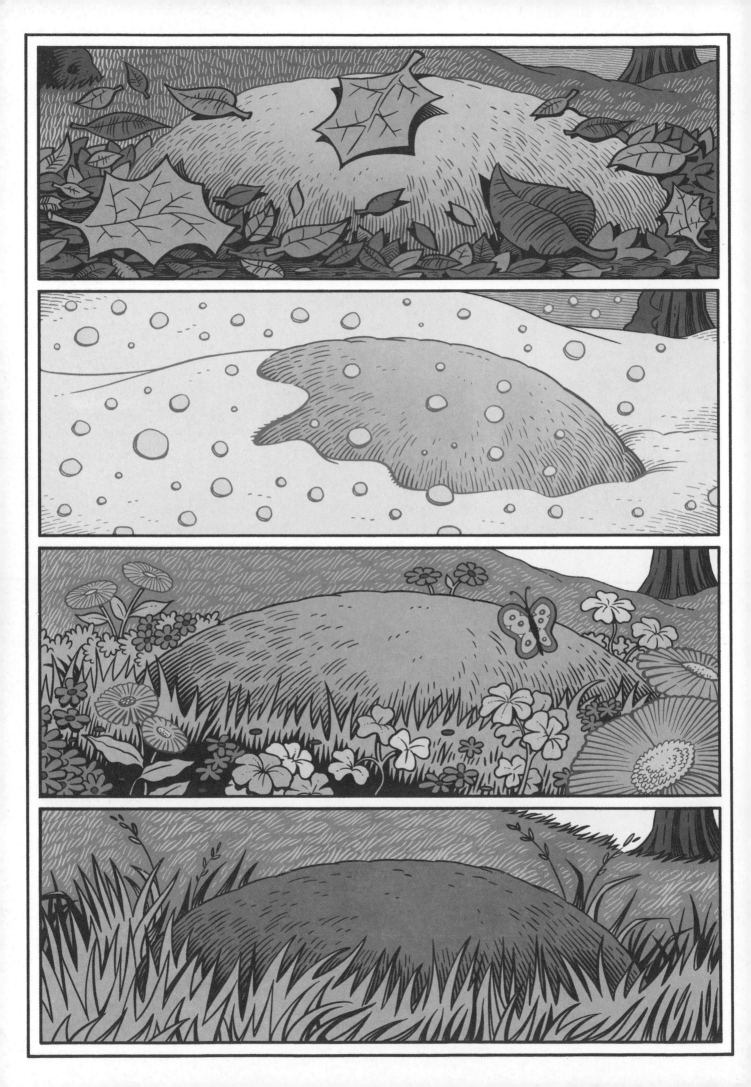

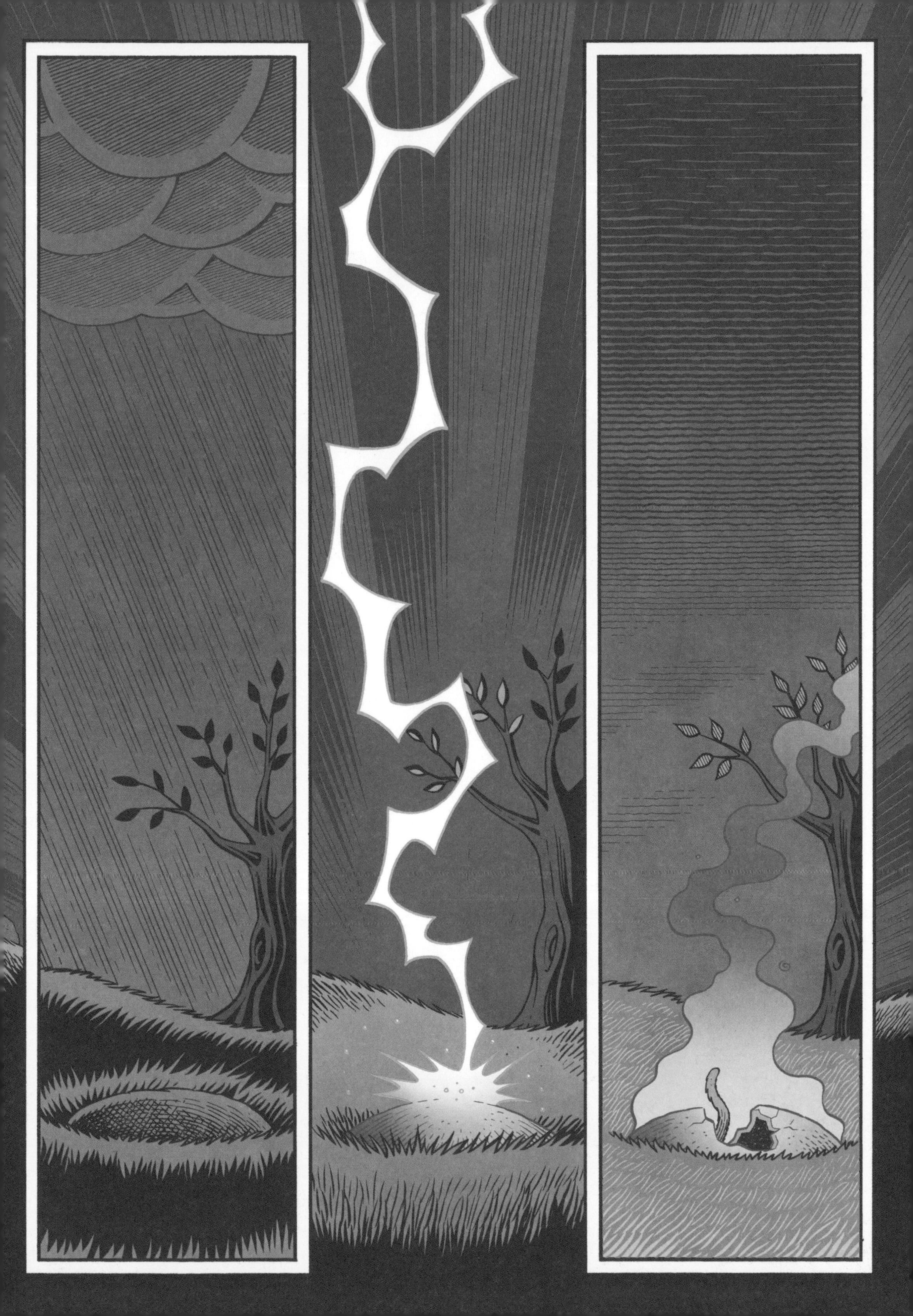

Jim Henson's™

# THE MUSICAL MONSTERS OF TURKEY HOLLOW™

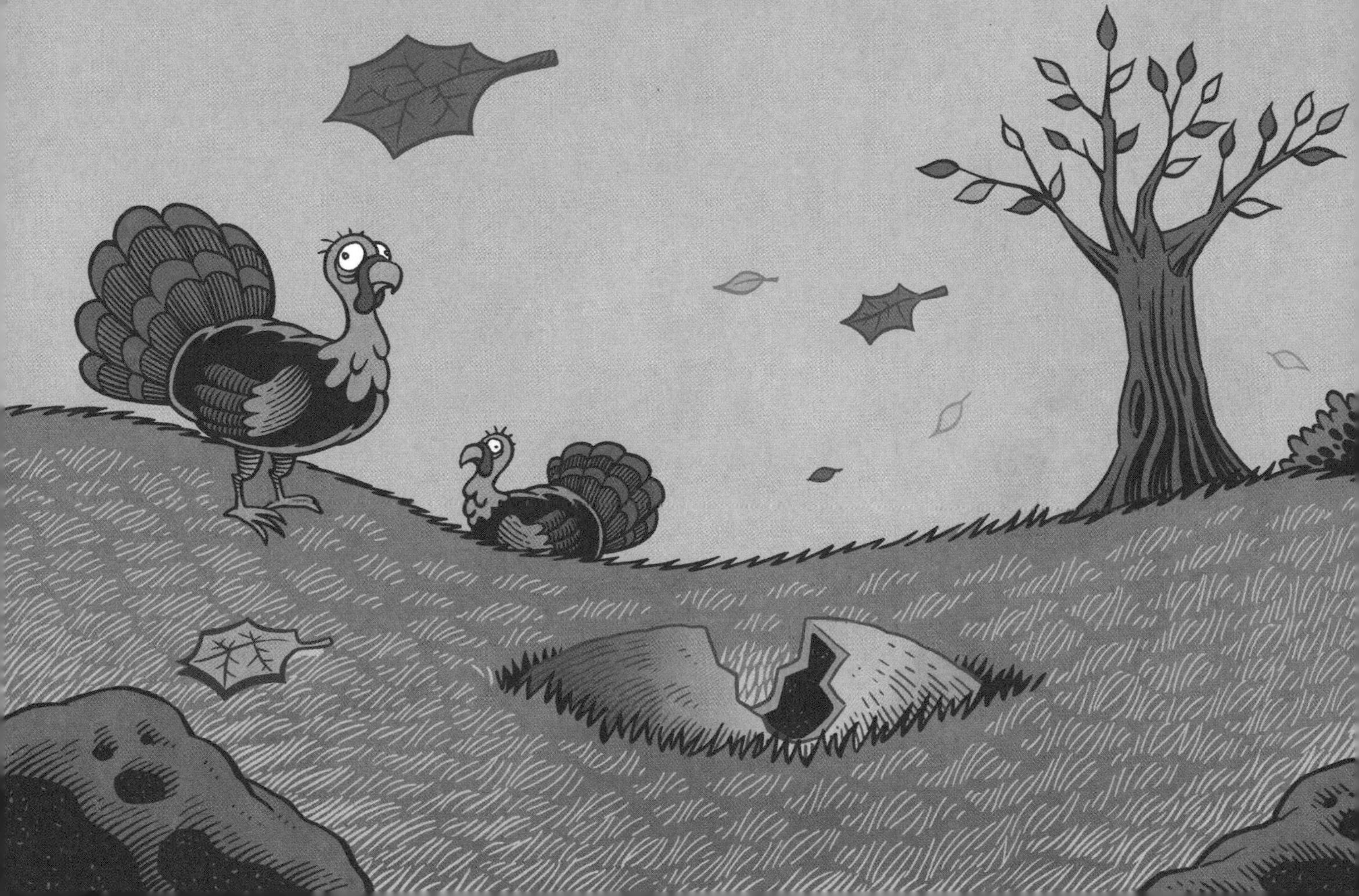

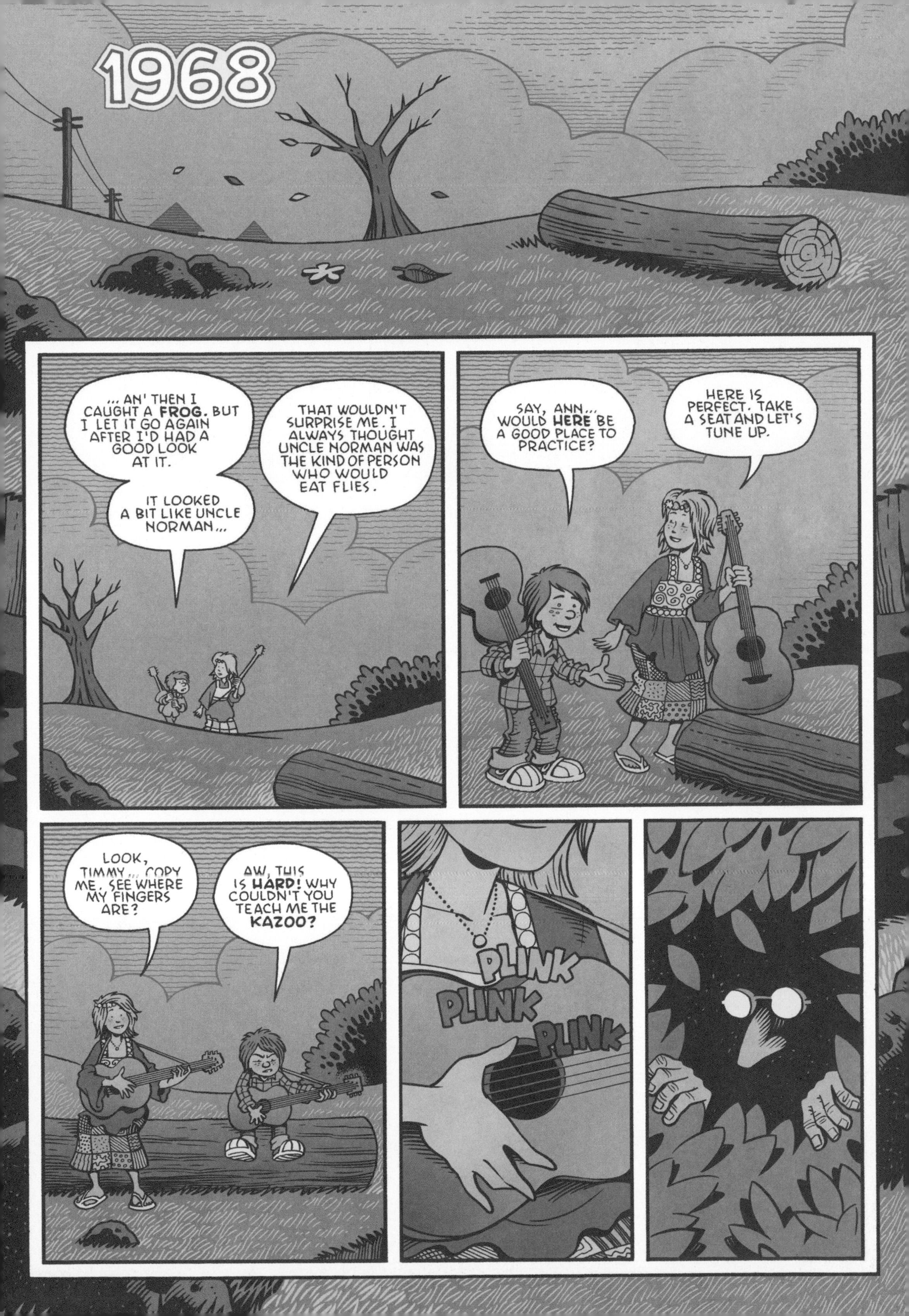
1968
... AN' THEN I CAUGHT A **FROG.** BUT I LET IT GO AGAIN AFTER I'D HAD A GOOD LOOK AT IT.
IT LOOKED A BIT LIKE UNCLE NORMAN...
THAT WOULDN'T SURPRISE ME. I ALWAYS THOUGHT UNCLE NORMAN WAS THE KIND OF PERSON WHO WOULD EAT FLIES.
SAY, ANN... WOULD **HERE** BE A GOOD PLACE TO PRACTICE?
HERE IS PERFECT. TAKE A SEAT AND LET'S TUNE UP.
LOOK, TIMMY... COPY ME. SEE WHERE MY FINGERS ARE?
AW, THIS IS **HARD!** WHY COULDN'T YOU TEACH ME THE **KAZOO?**
PLINK
PLINK
PLINK

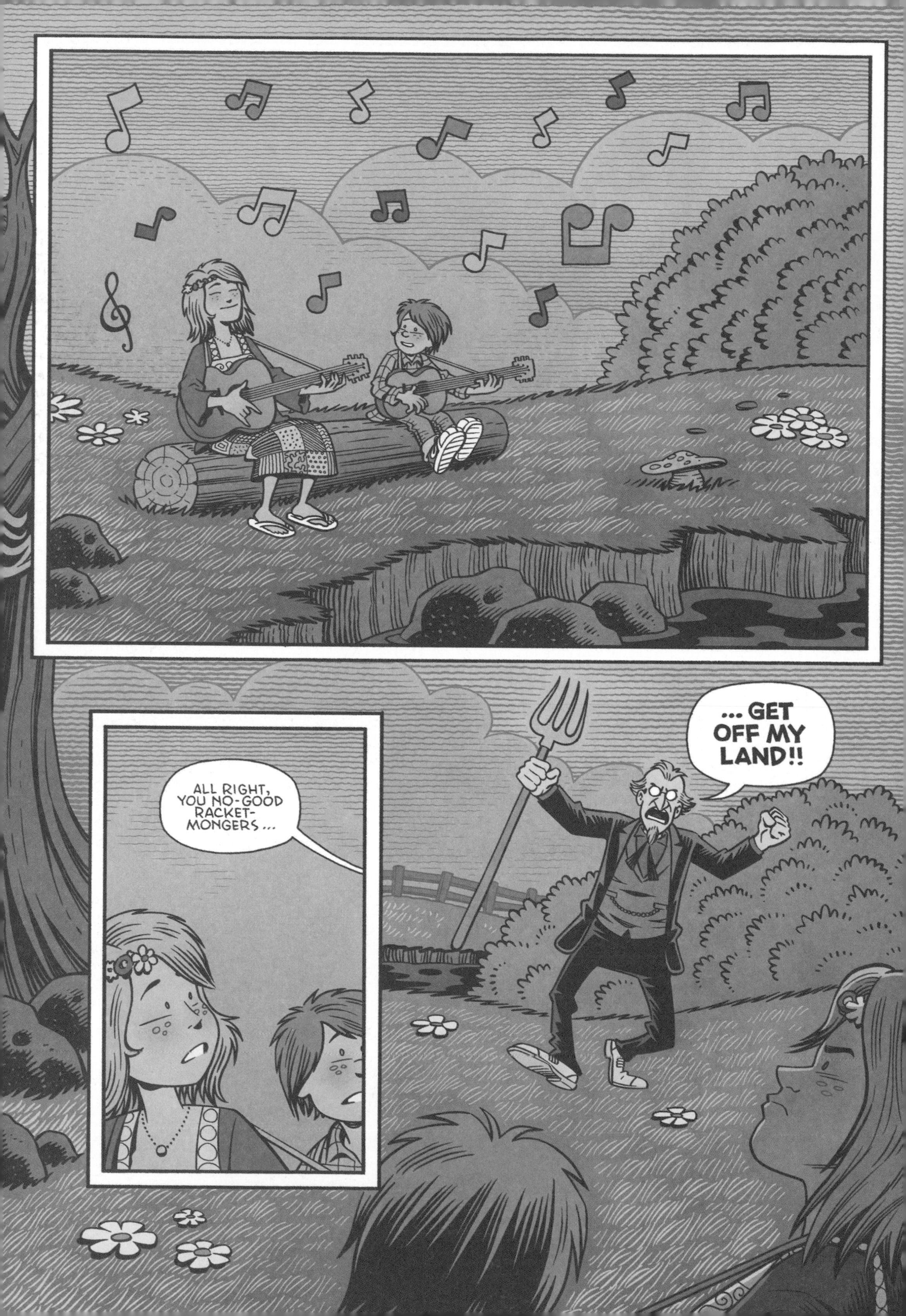
ALL RIGHT, YOU NO-GOOD RACKET-MONGERS...
... GET OFF MY LAND!!

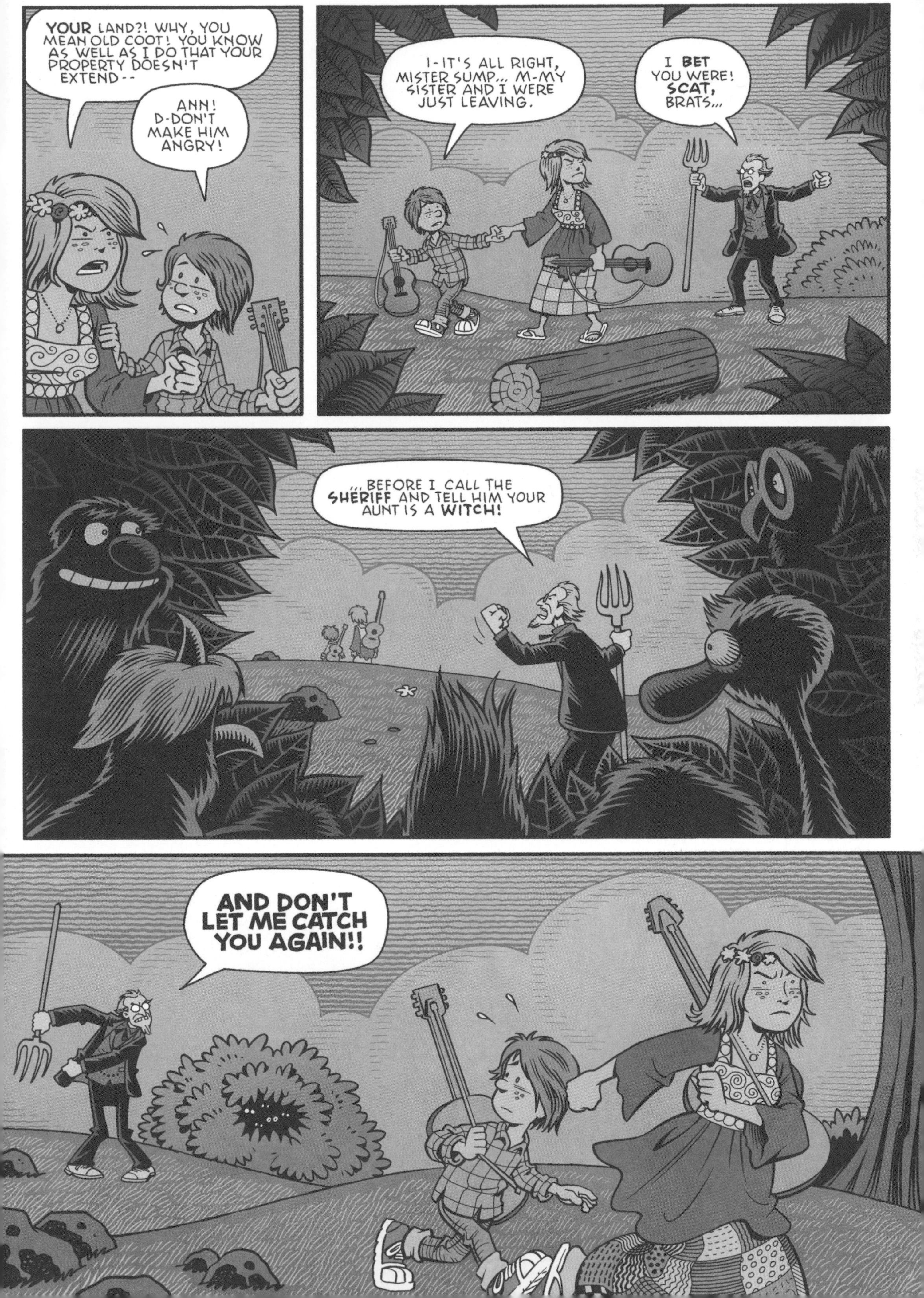
YOUR LAND?! WHY, YOU MEAN OLD COOT! YOU KNOW AS WELL AS I DO THAT YOUR PROPERTY DOESN'T EXTEND--
ANN! D-DON'T MAKE HIM ANGRY!
I-IT'S ALL RIGHT, MISTER SUMP... M-MY SISTER AND I WERE JUST LEAVING.
I BET YOU WERE! SCAT, BRATS...
...BEFORE I CALL THE SHERIFF AND TELL HIM YOUR AUNT IS A WITCH!
AND DON'T LET ME CATCH YOU AGAIN!!

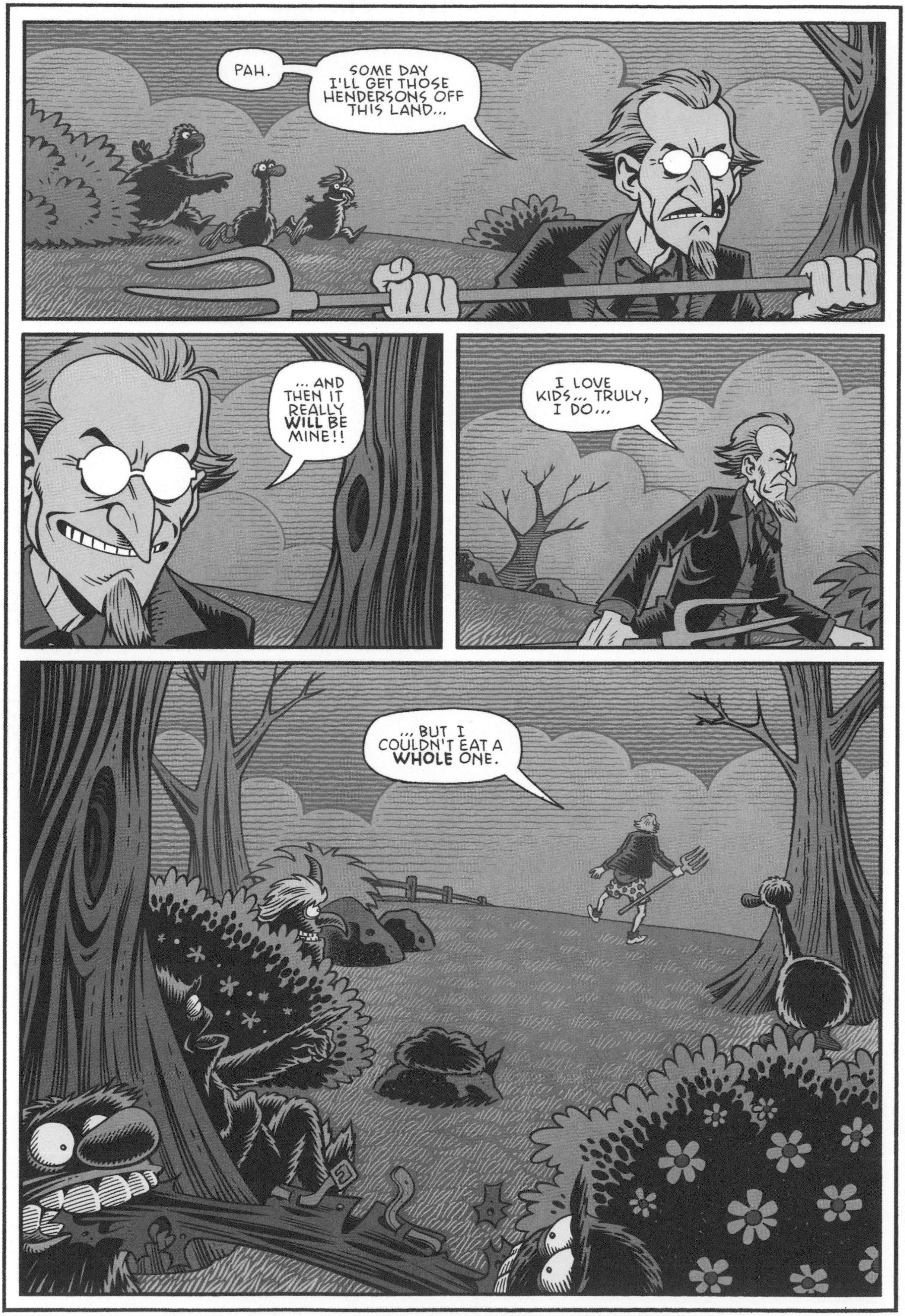
PAH.
SOME DAY I'LL GET THOSE HENDERSONS OFF THIS LAND...
... AND THEN IT REALLY **WILL** BE MINE!!
I LOVE KIDS... TRULY, I DO...
..., BUT I COULDN'T EAT A **WHOLE** ONE.

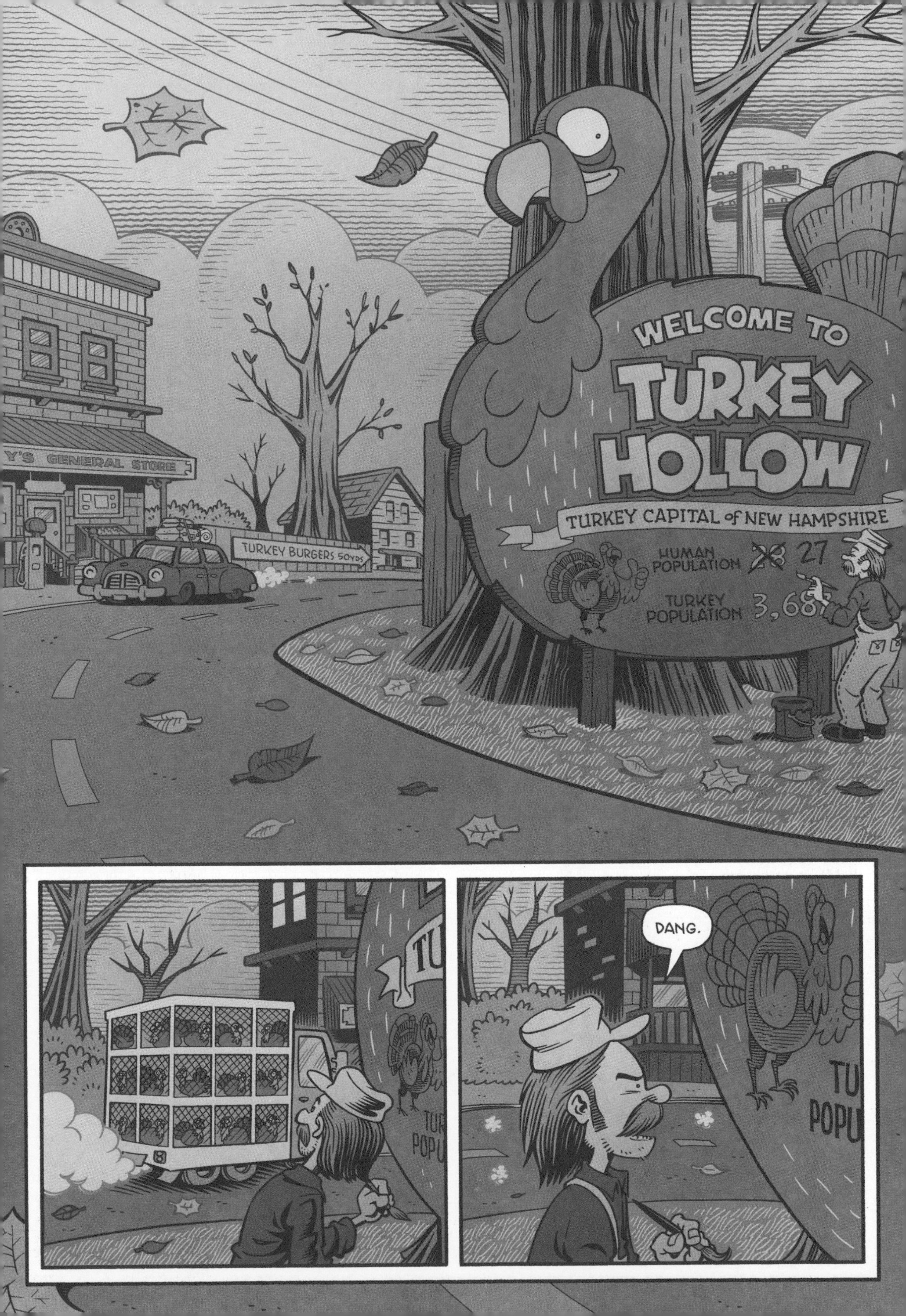
Y'S GENERAL STORE
TURKEY BURGERS 50YDS
WELCOME TO
TURKEY HOLLOW
TURKEY CAPITAL of NEW HAMPSHIRE
HUMAN POPULATION 28 27
TURKEY POPULATION 3,68
DANG.

COWLEY'S GENERAL STORE

BATHROOM THIS WAY

Please wait for attendant when refueling

POST OFFICE

JAIL VISITORS PLEASE REPORT TO COUNTER

STAMPS HERE

LOST DOG

DANCE LESSONS

BABY-SITTER WANTED

HAVE YOU SEEN THIS CHICKEN

FIRE-RING BELL

TOWN H. POLICE S...

AFTERNOON, GROVER! THOSE APPLES LOOK MIGHTY TASTY!

CLYTEMNESTRA HENDERSON! WHY, HELLO THERE!

"I THINK THAT I SHALL NEVER SEE... AN APPLE LOVELY AS A TREE."

THEY'RE FRESH! NOW... WILL YOU BE WANTING MY SERVICES AS **MAYOR, SHERIFF, STOREKEEPER** OR **POSTMASTER** TODAY?

ACTUALLY, MISTER COWLEY, AUNT CLY WAS GOING TO BUY ME A NEW GUITAR PICK.

**GUITAR PICK!** WHAT ARE YOU DOING WITH THEM, TIMMY... **EATING** THEM?

COME INSIDE AND WE'LL HAVE A LOOK AROUND.

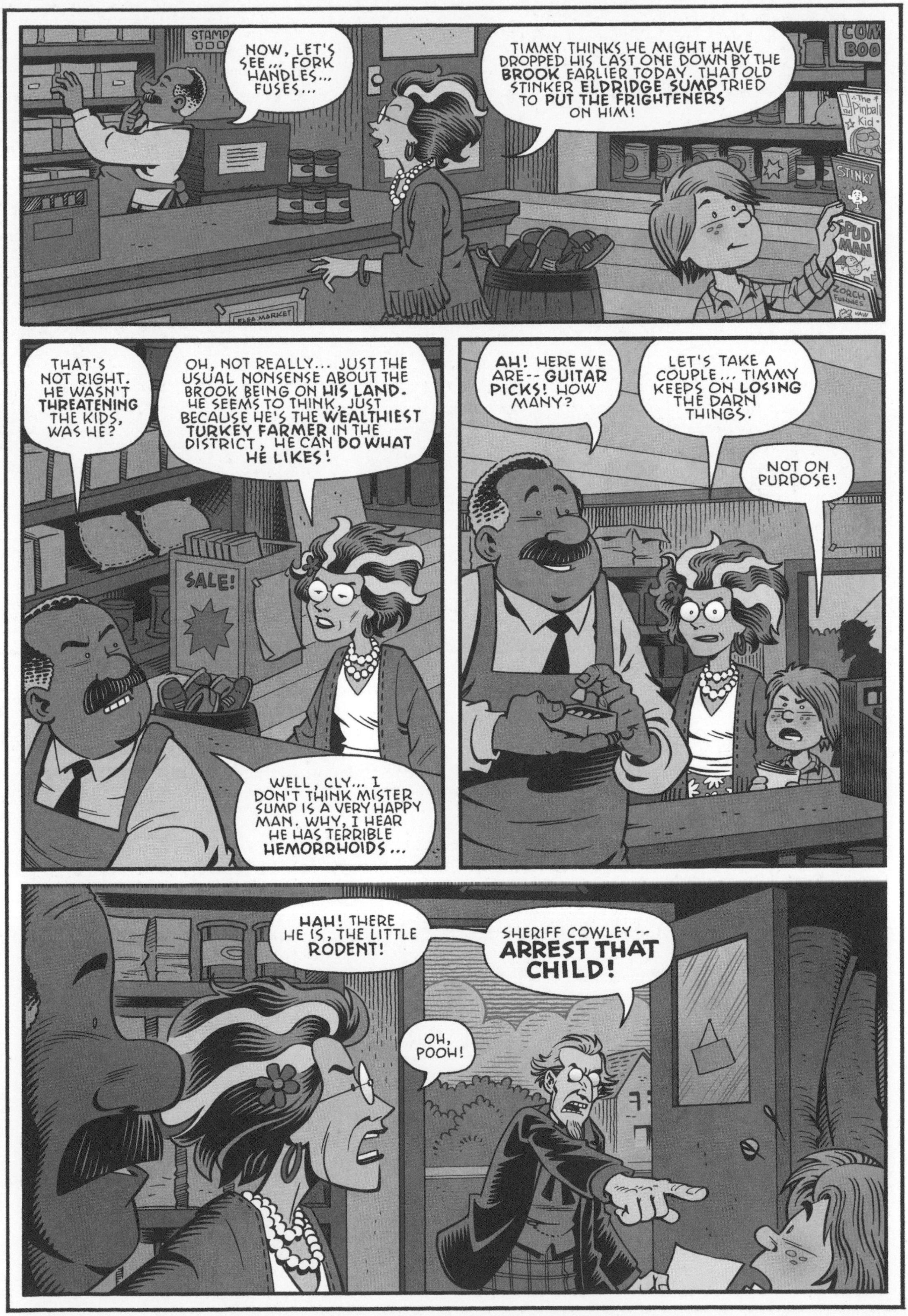

NOW, LET'S SEE... FORK HANDLES... FUSES...
TIMMY THINKS HE MIGHT HAVE DROPPED HIS LAST ONE DOWN BY THE **BROOK** EARLIER TODAY. THAT OLD STINKER **ELDRIDGE SUMP** TRIED TO **PUT THE FRIGHTENERS** ON HIM!
The Pinball Kid
STINKY
SPUD MAN
ZORCH FUNNIES
FLEA MARKET
THAT'S NOT RIGHT. HE WASN'T **THREATENING** THE KIDS, WAS HE?
OH, NOT REALLY... JUST THE USUAL NONSENSE ABOUT THE BROOK BEING ON **HIS LAND**. HE SEEMS TO THINK, JUST BECAUSE HE'S THE **WEALTHIEST TURKEY FARMER** IN THE DISTRICT, HE CAN **DO WHAT HE LIKES!**
SALE!
WELL, CLY... I DON'T THINK MISTER SUMP IS A VERY HAPPY MAN. WHY, I HEAR HE HAS TERRIBLE **HEMORRHOIDS**...
**AH!** HERE WE ARE-- **GUITAR PICKS!** HOW MANY?
LET'S TAKE A COUPLE... TIMMY KEEPS ON **LOSING** THE DARN THINGS.
NOT ON PURPOSE!
**HAH!** THERE HE IS, THE LITTLE **RODENT!**
SHERIFF COWLEY -- **ARREST THAT CHILD!**
OH, POOH!

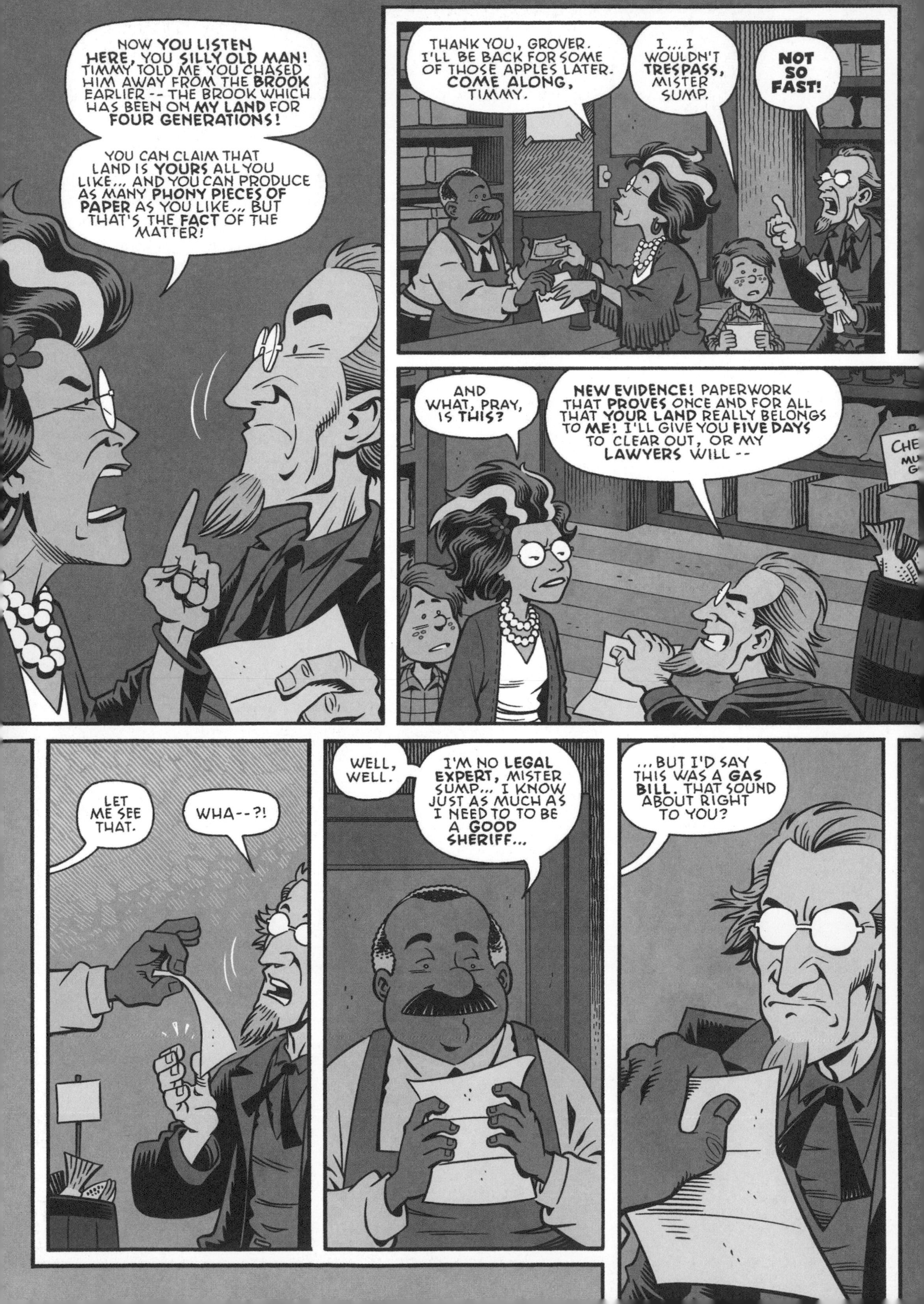
NOW YOU LISTEN HERE, YOU SILLY OLD MAN! TIMMY TOLD ME YOU CHASED HIM AWAY FROM THE BROOK EARLIER -- THE BROOK WHICH HAS BEEN ON MY LAND FOR FOUR GENERATIONS!
YOU CAN CLAIM THAT LAND IS YOURS ALL YOU LIKE... AND YOU CAN PRODUCE AS MANY PHONY PIECES OF PAPER AS YOU LIKE... BUT THAT'S THE FACT OF THE MATTER!
THANK YOU, GROVER. I'LL BE BACK FOR SOME OF THOSE APPLES LATER. COME ALONG, TIMMY.
I... I WOULDN'T TRESPASS, MISTER SUMP.
NOT SO FAST!
AND WHAT, PRAY, IS THIS?
NEW EVIDENCE! PAPERWORK THAT PROVES ONCE AND FOR ALL THAT YOUR LAND REALLY BELONGS TO ME! I'LL GIVE YOU FIVE DAYS TO CLEAR OUT, OR MY LAWYERS WILL --
LET ME SEE THAT.
WHA--?!
WELL, WELL.
I'M NO LEGAL EXPERT, MISTER SUMP... I KNOW JUST AS MUCH AS I NEED TO TO BE A GOOD SHERIFF...
...BUT I'D SAY THIS WAS A GAS BILL. THAT SOUND ABOUT RIGHT TO YOU?

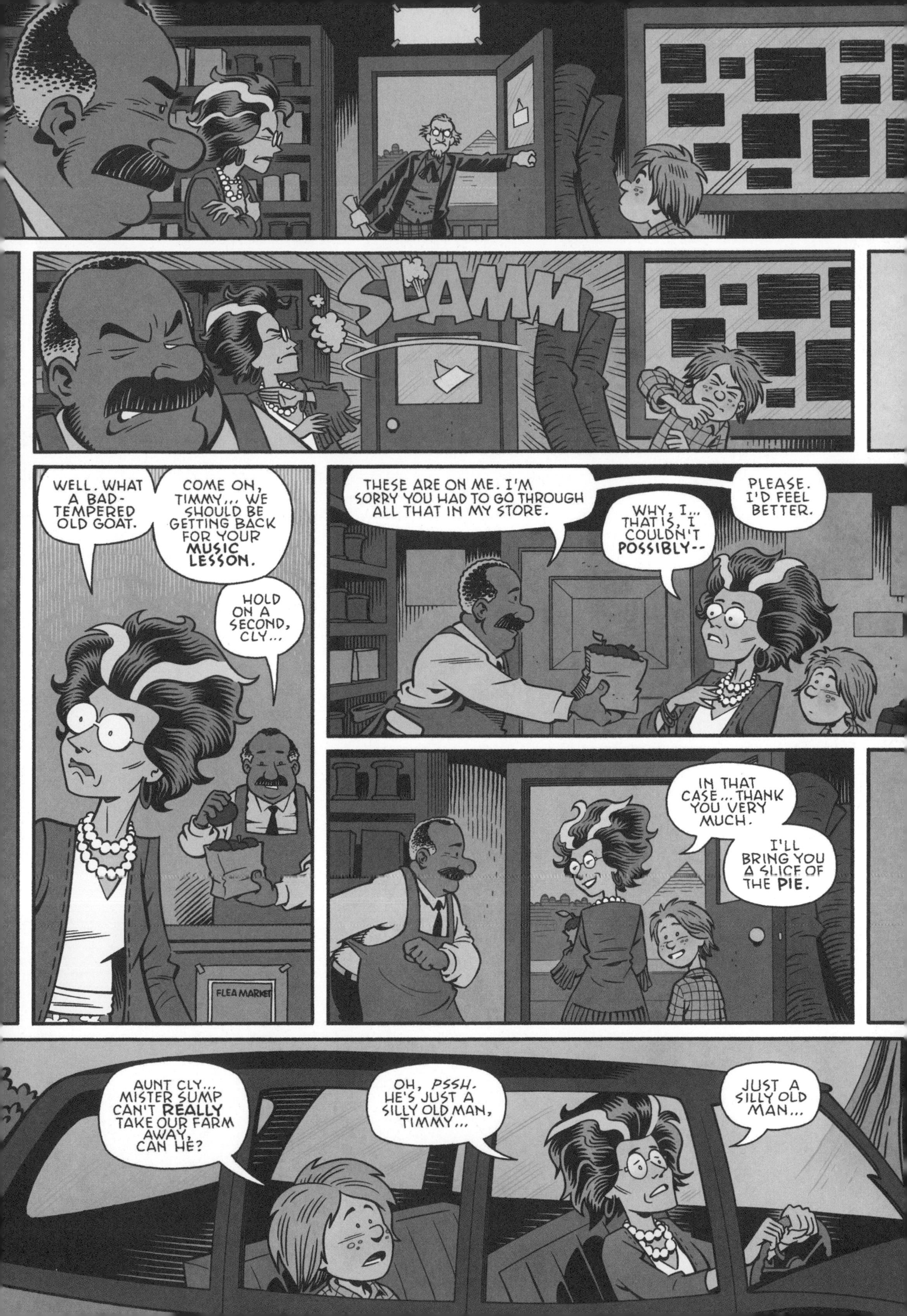
SLAMM
WELL. WHAT A BAD-TEMPERED OLD GOAT.
COME ON, TIMMY... WE SHOULD BE GETTING BACK FOR YOUR **MUSIC LESSON.**
HOLD ON A SECOND, CLY...
FLEA MARKET
THESE ARE ON ME. I'M SORRY YOU HAD TO GO THROUGH ALL THAT IN MY STORE.
WHY, I... THAT IS, I COULDN'T **POSSIBLY**--
PLEASE. I'D FEEL BETTER.
IN THAT CASE... THANK YOU VERY MUCH.
I'LL BRING YOU A SLICE OF THE **PIE.**
AUNT CLY... MISTER SUMP CAN'T **REALLY** TAKE OUR FARM AWAY, CAN HE?
OH, *PSSH.* HE'S JUST A SILLY OLD MAN, TIMMY...
JUST A SILLY OLD MAN...

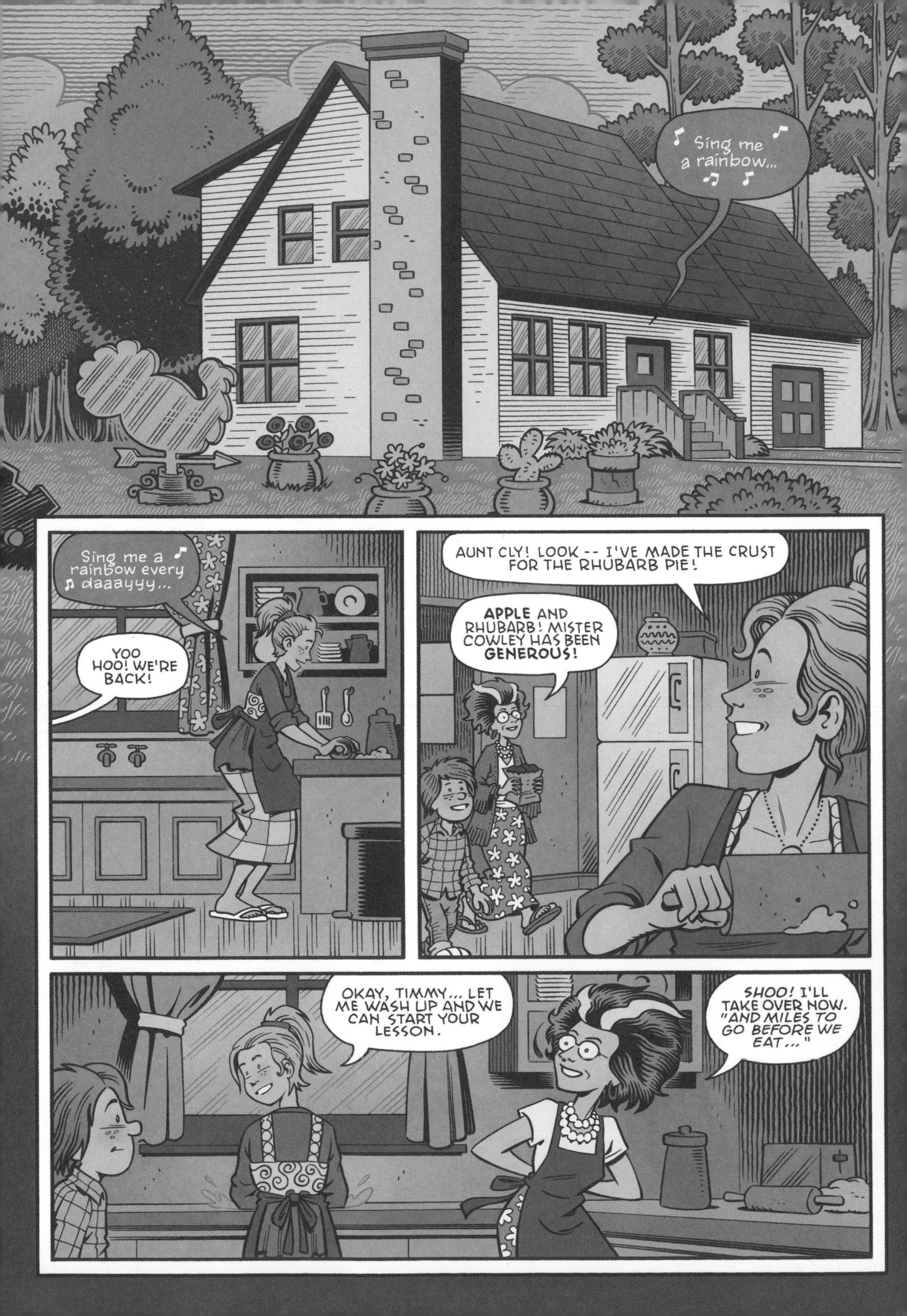
Sing me a rainbow...
Sing me a rainbow every daaayyy...
YOO HOO! WE'RE BACK!
AUNT CLY! LOOK -- I'VE MADE THE CRUST FOR THE RHUBARB PIE!
APPLE AND RHUBARB! MISTER COWLEY HAS BEEN GENEROUS!
OKAY, TIMMY... LET ME WASH UP AND WE CAN START YOUR LESSON.
SHOO! I'LL TAKE OVER NOW. "AND MILES TO GO BEFORE WE EAT..."

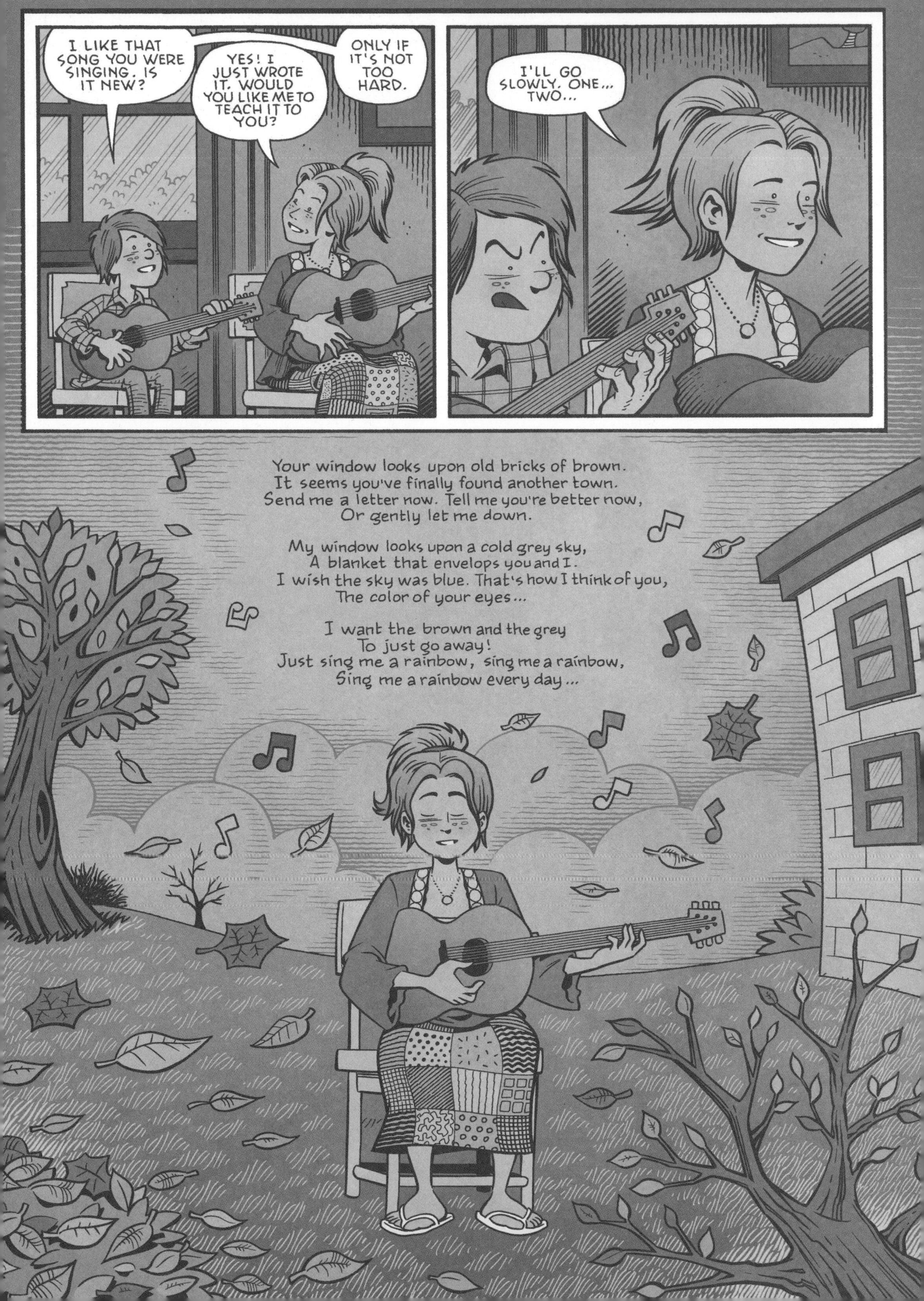
I LIKE THAT SONG YOU WERE SINGING. IS IT NEW?
YES! I JUST WROTE IT. WOULD YOU LIKE ME TO TEACH IT TO YOU?
ONLY IF IT'S NOT TOO HARD.
I'LL GO SLOWLY. ONE... TWO...
Your window looks upon old bricks of brown.
It seems you've finally found another town.
Send me a letter now. Tell me you're better now,
Or gently let me down.
My window looks upon a cold grey sky,
A blanket that envelops you and I.
I wish the sky was blue. That's how I think of you,
The color of your eyes...
I want the brown and the grey
To just go away!
Just sing me a rainbow, sing me a rainbow,
Sing me a rainbow every day...

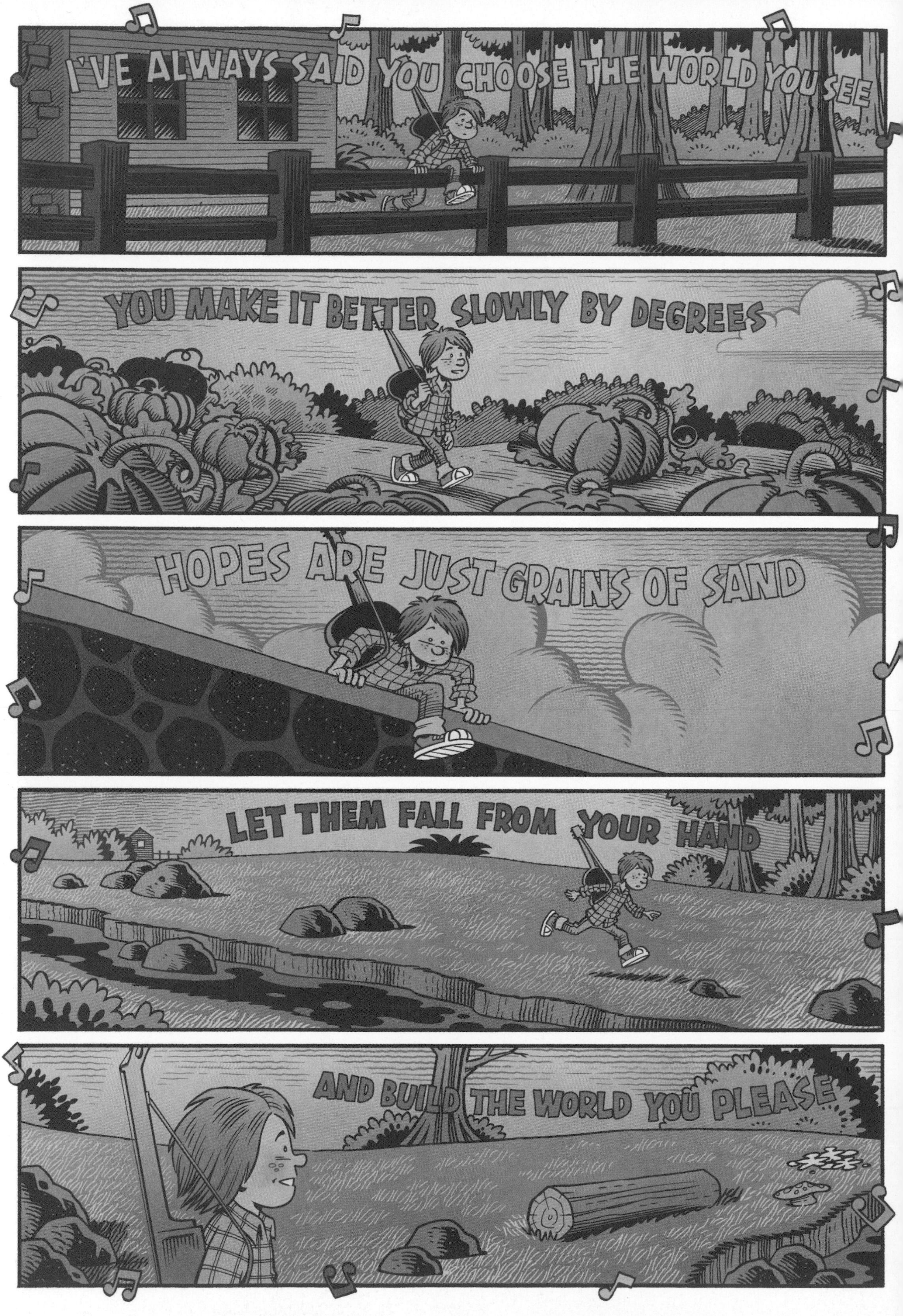
I'VE ALWAYS SAID YOU CHOOSE THE WORLD YOU SEE
YOU MAKE IT BETTER SLOWLY BY DEGREES
HOPES ARE JUST GRAINS OF SAND
LET THEM FALL FROM YOUR HAND
AND BUILD THE WORLD YOU PLEASE

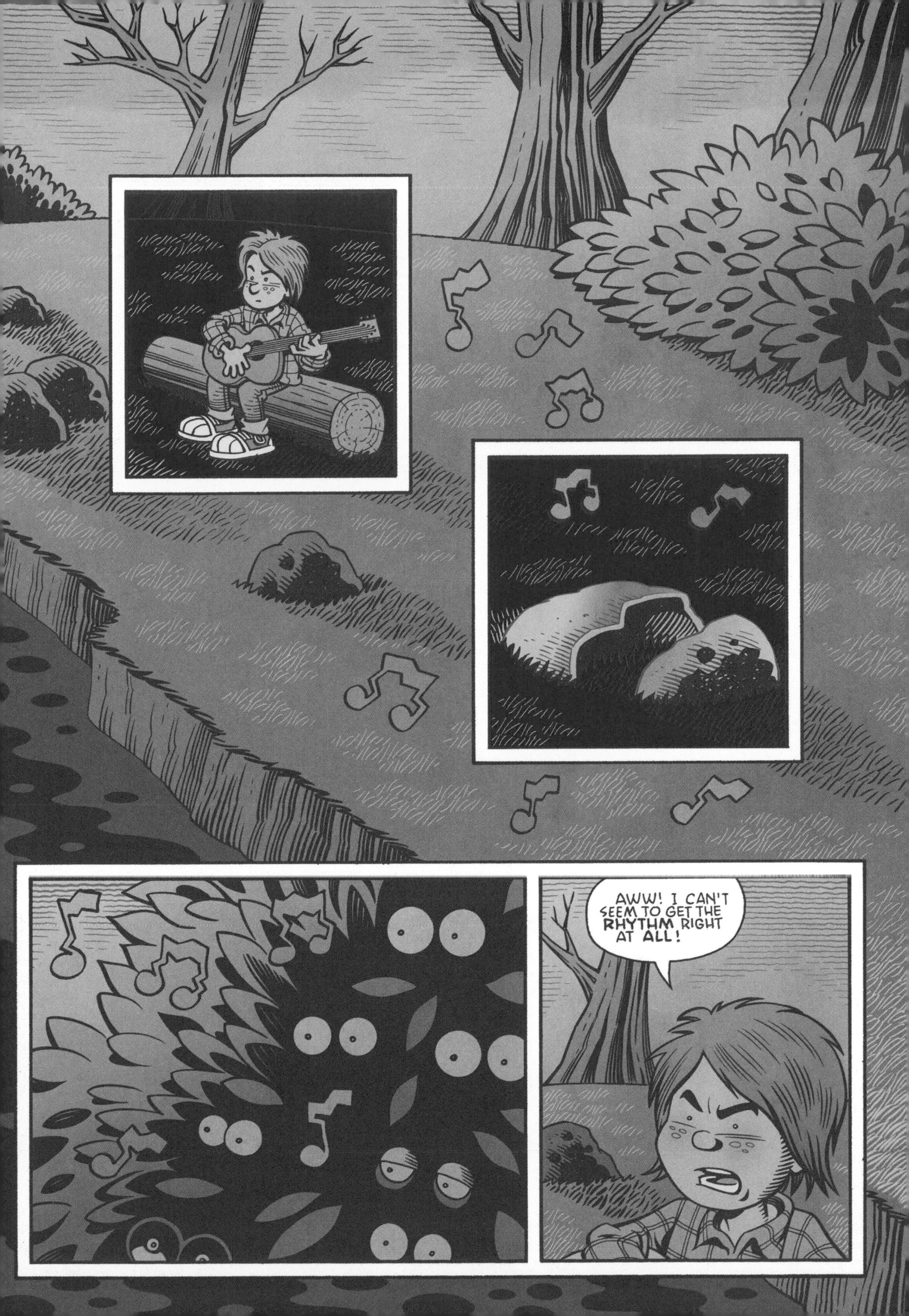
AWW! I CAN'T SEEM TO GET THE RHYTHM RIGHT AT ALL!

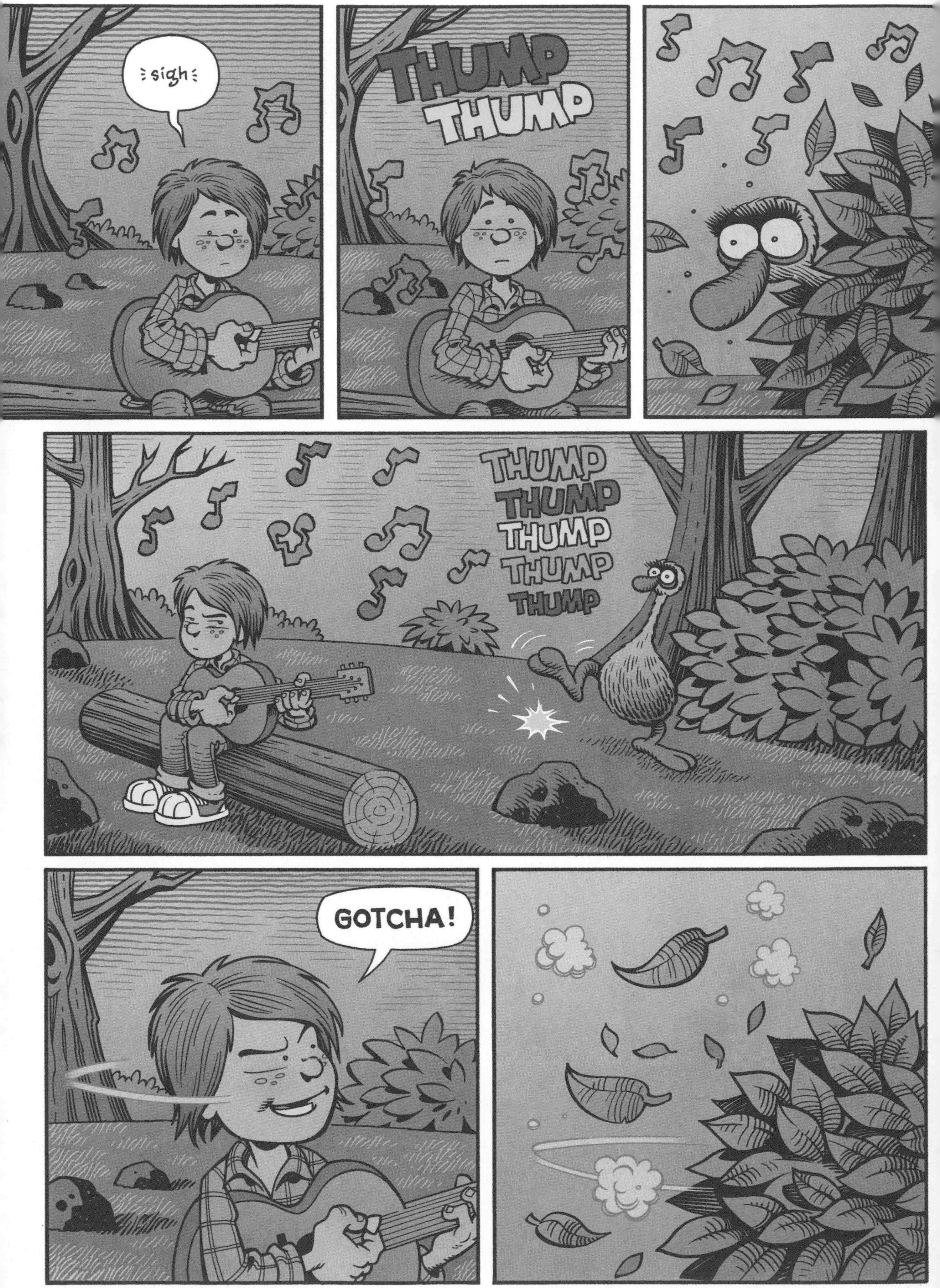

sigh
THUMP
THUMP
THUMP
THUMP
THUMP
THUMP
THUMP
GOTCHA!

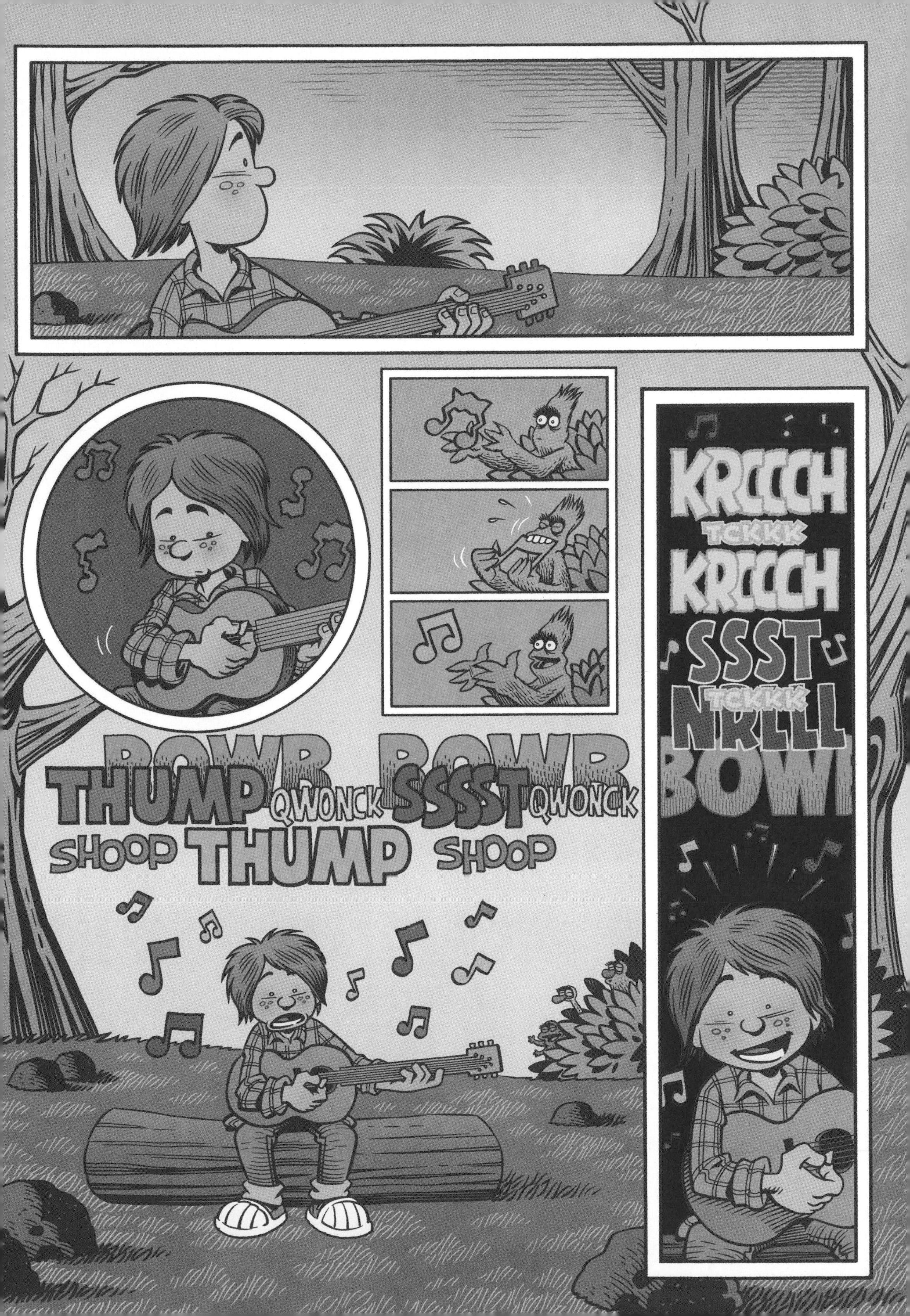
KRCCCH
TCKKK
KRCCCH
SSST
TCKKK
NRLLL
BOWR BOWR
THUMP QWONCK SSSST QWONCK
SHOOP THUMP SHOOP
BOWI

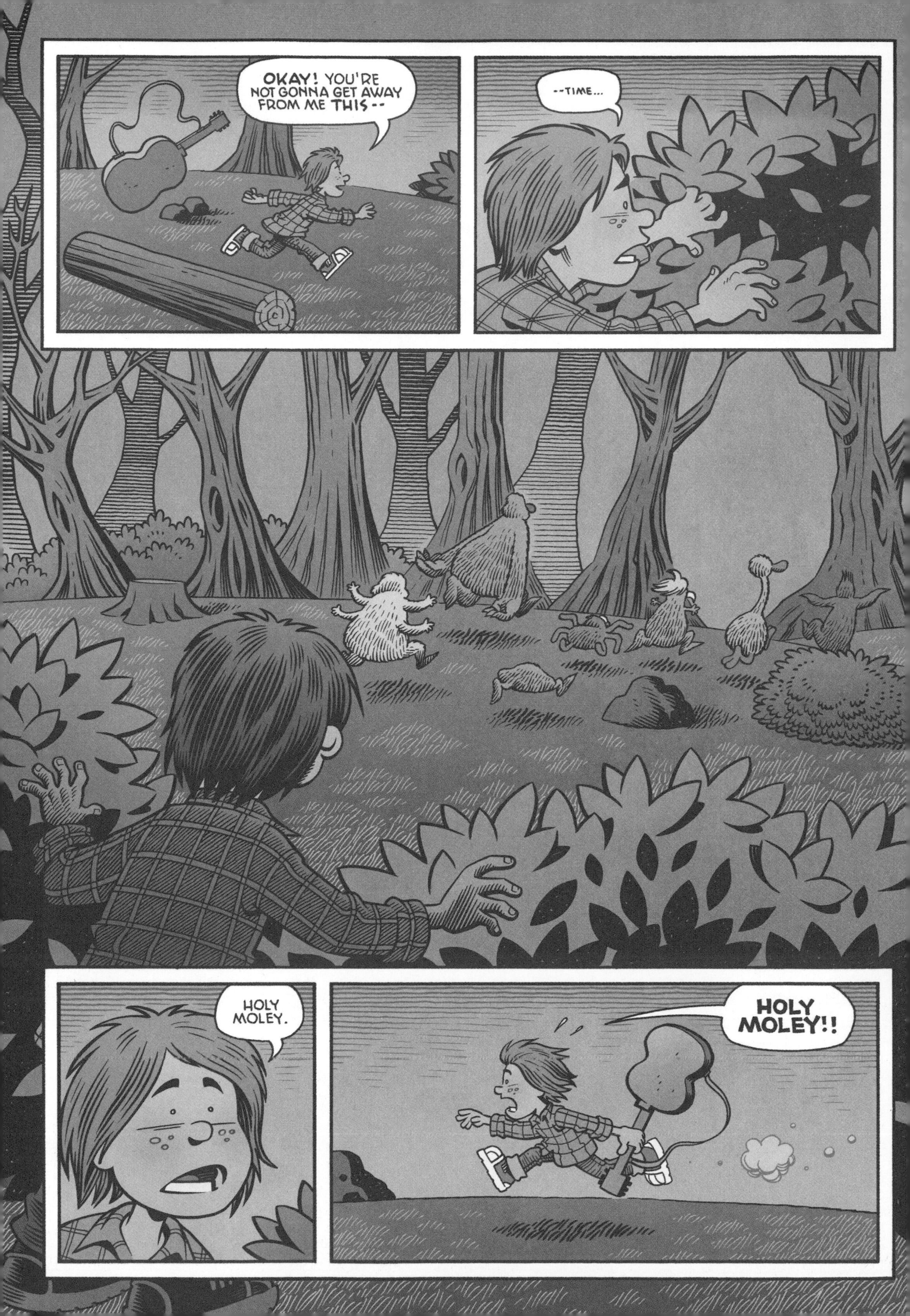
OKAY! YOU'RE NOT GONNA GET AWAY FROM ME THIS--
--TIME...
HOLY MOLEY.
HOLY MOLEY!!

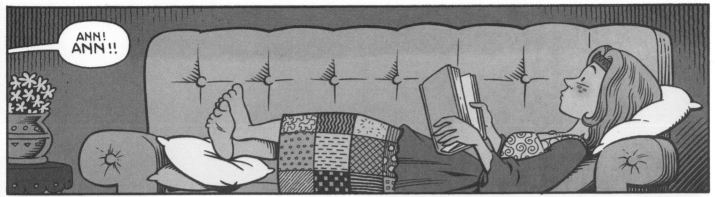

ANN! ANN!!

TIMMY! WHAT IN THE WORLD -- ?

ANN! YOU'RE NOT GOING TO **BELIEVE** THIS... WHAT I **SAW** -- IT WAS... IT WAS...

SPIT IT OUT! **WHAT?!**

...MONSTERS!!

OH, FOR...! FOR A SECOND I THOUGHT YOU WERE **SERIOUS**! GET READY FOR BED, WILL YOU? WE'VE GOT **CHORES** IN THE MORNING.

B-BUT... BUT... I **AM** SERIOUS! AND I HAVEN'T EVEN TOLD YOU THE MOST **AMAZING PART** YET!

I SOUNDED **GREAT**, ANN... I COULD **PLAY.**

I COULD **REALLY PLAY!!**

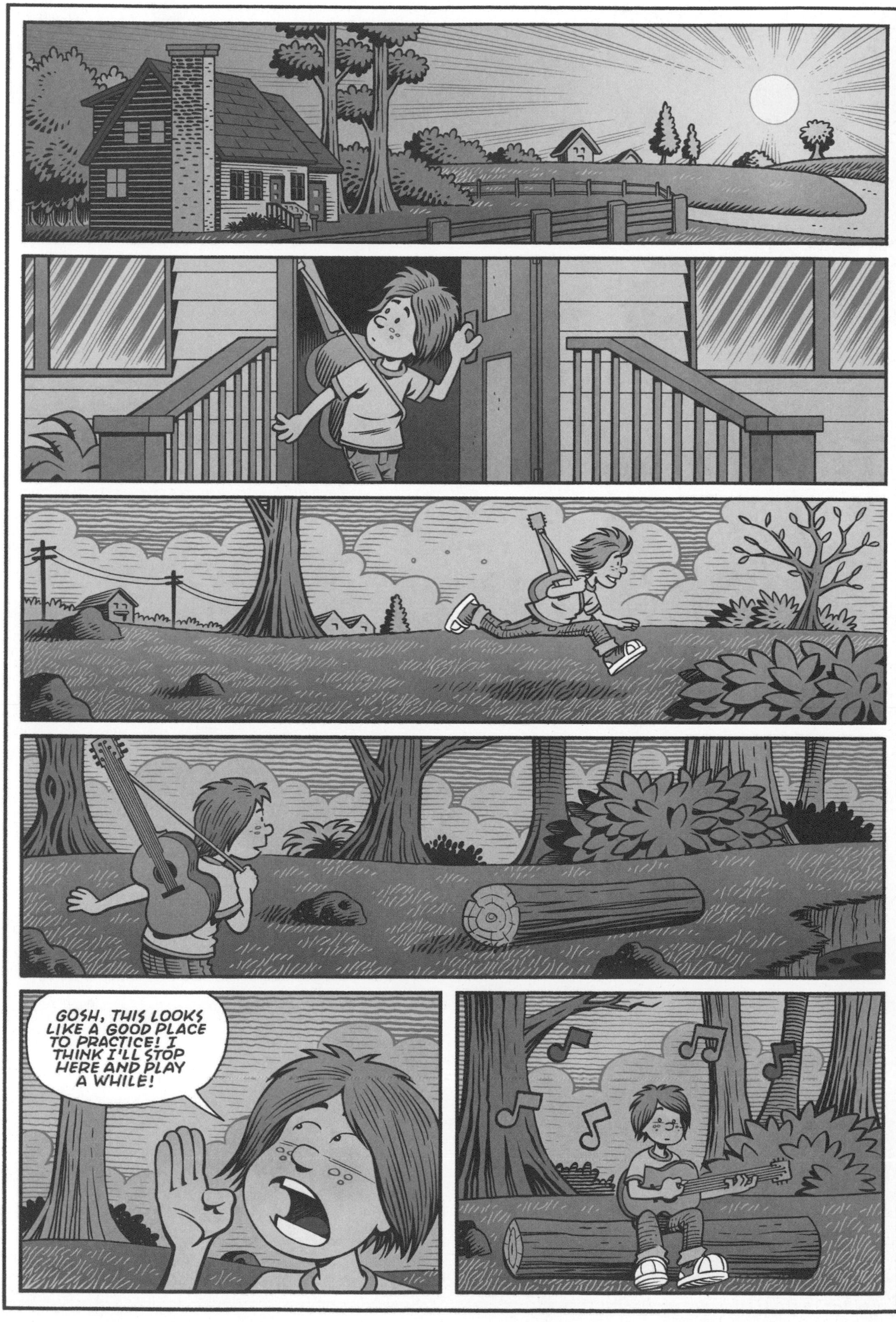
GOSH, THIS LOOKS LIKE A GOOD PLACE TO PRACTICE! I THINK I'LL STOP HERE AND PLAY A WHILE!

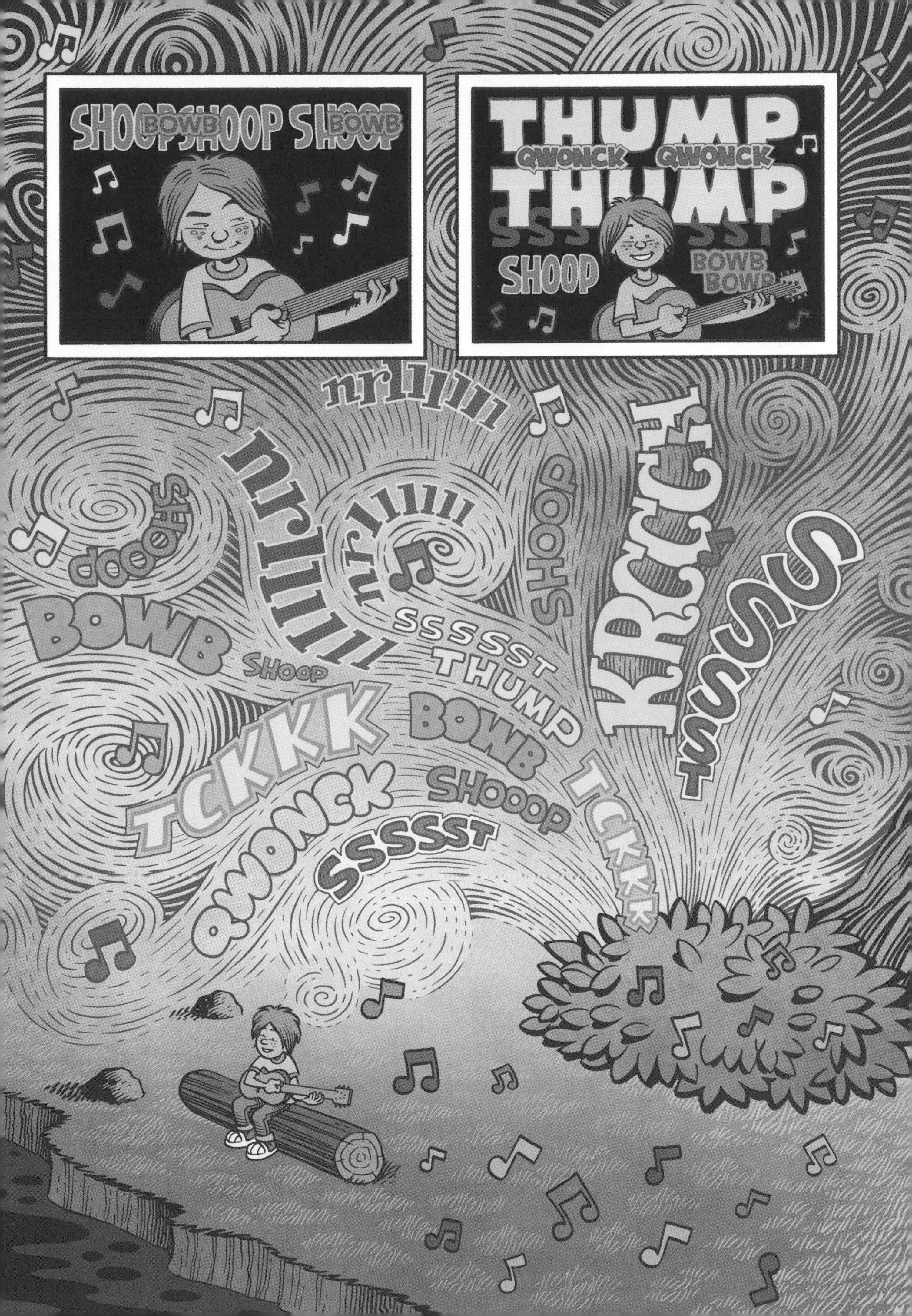

SHOOPSHOOP SHOOP
BOWB
BOWB
THUMP
QWONCK QWONCK
THUMP
SSS
SST
SHOOP
BOWB
BOWB
nrllllll
KRCCCH
SHOOP
nrllllllll
nrlllllll
SHOOP
BOWB
SHOOP
SSSSST
THUMP
BOWB
TCKKK
SSSSST
TCKKK
QWONCK
SHOOOP
SSSSST
TCKKKK

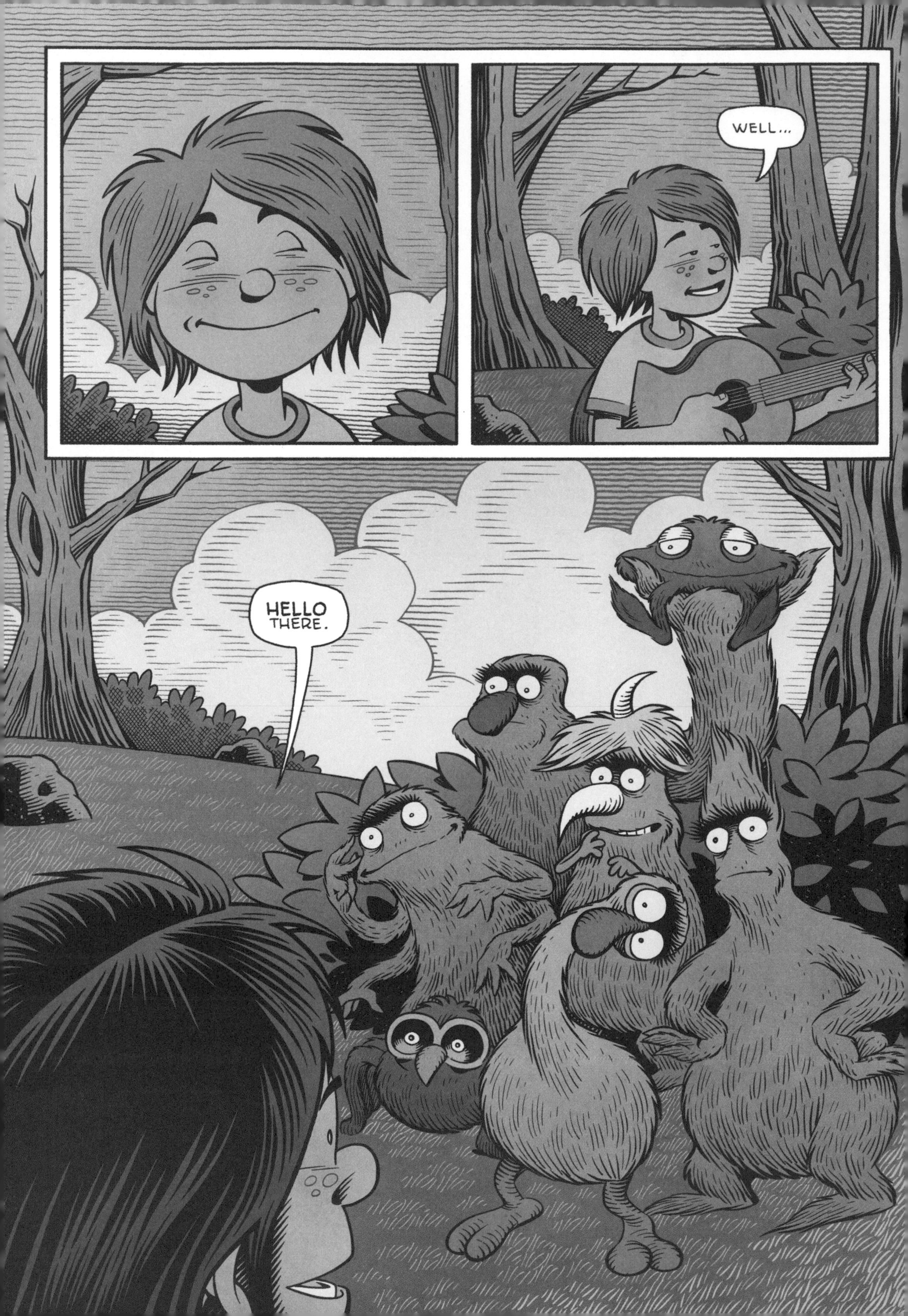
WELL...
HELLO THERE.

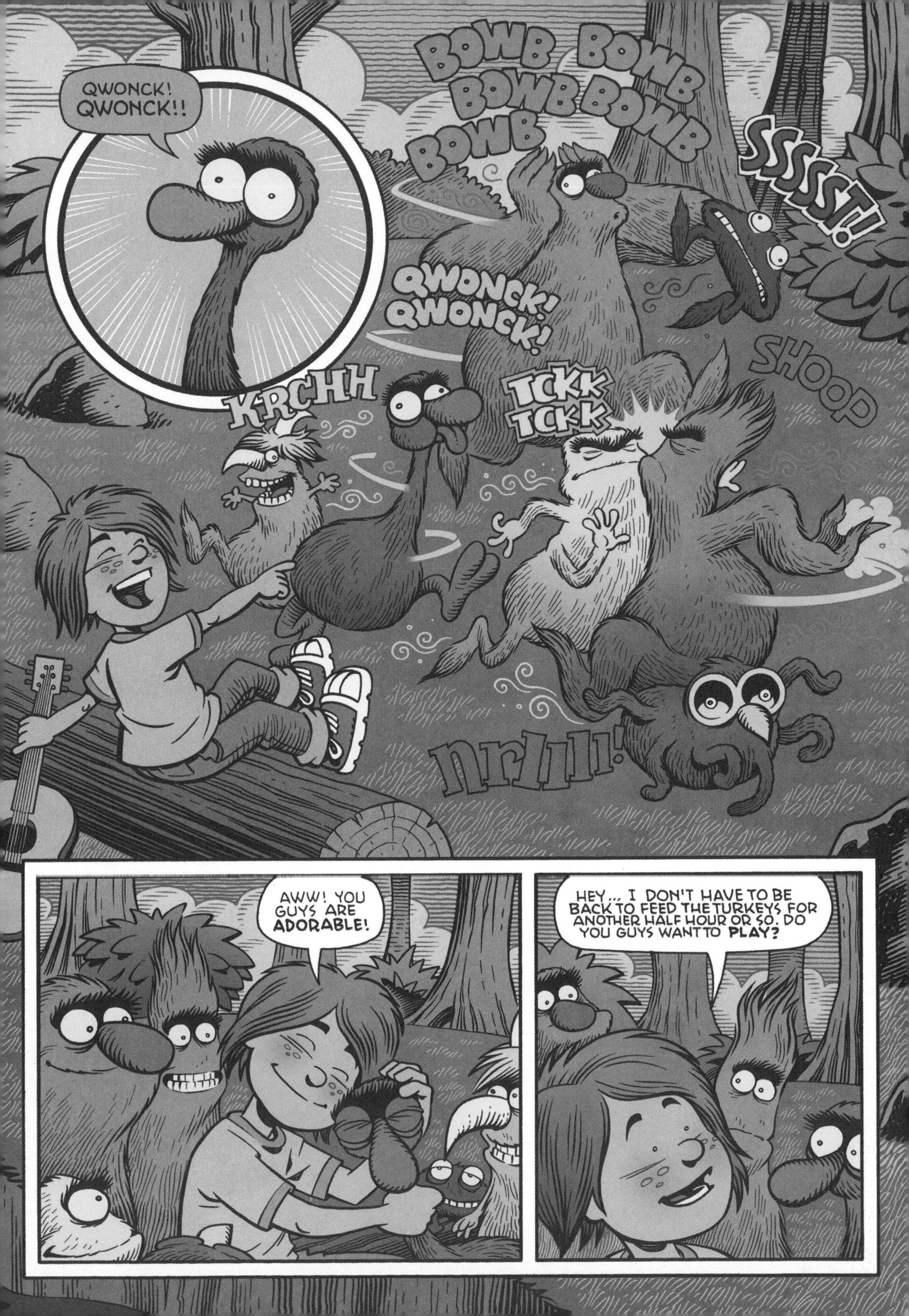
QWONCK! QWONCK!!
BOWB BOWB BOWB BOWB BOWB
SSSSST!!
QWONCK! QWONCK!
SHOOP
KRCHH
TCKK TCKK
nrllll!
AWW! YOU GUYS ARE ADORABLE!
HEY... I DON'T HAVE TO BE BACK TO FEED THE TURKEYS FOR ANOTHER HALF HOUR OR SO. DO YOU GUYS WANT TO PLAY?

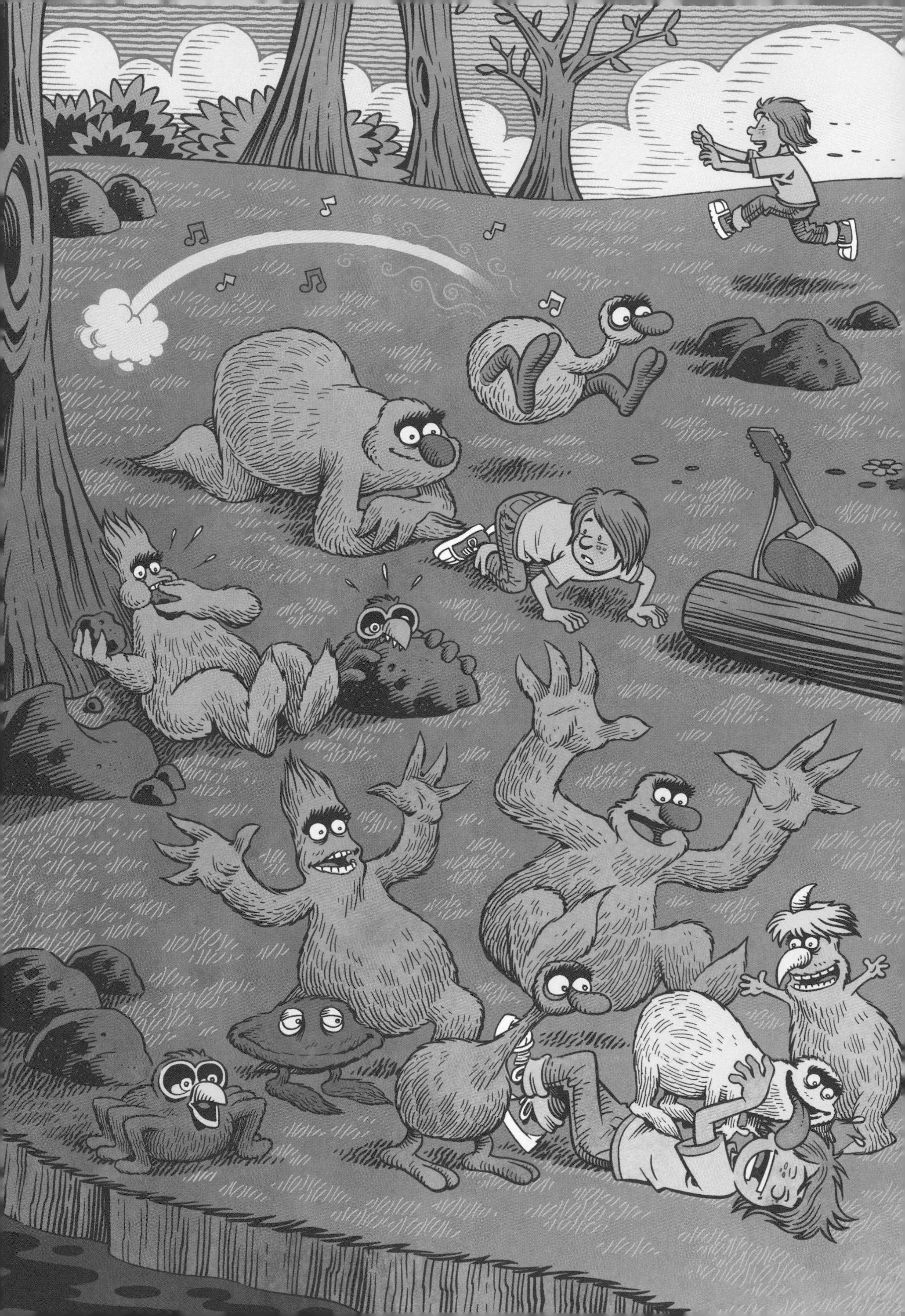

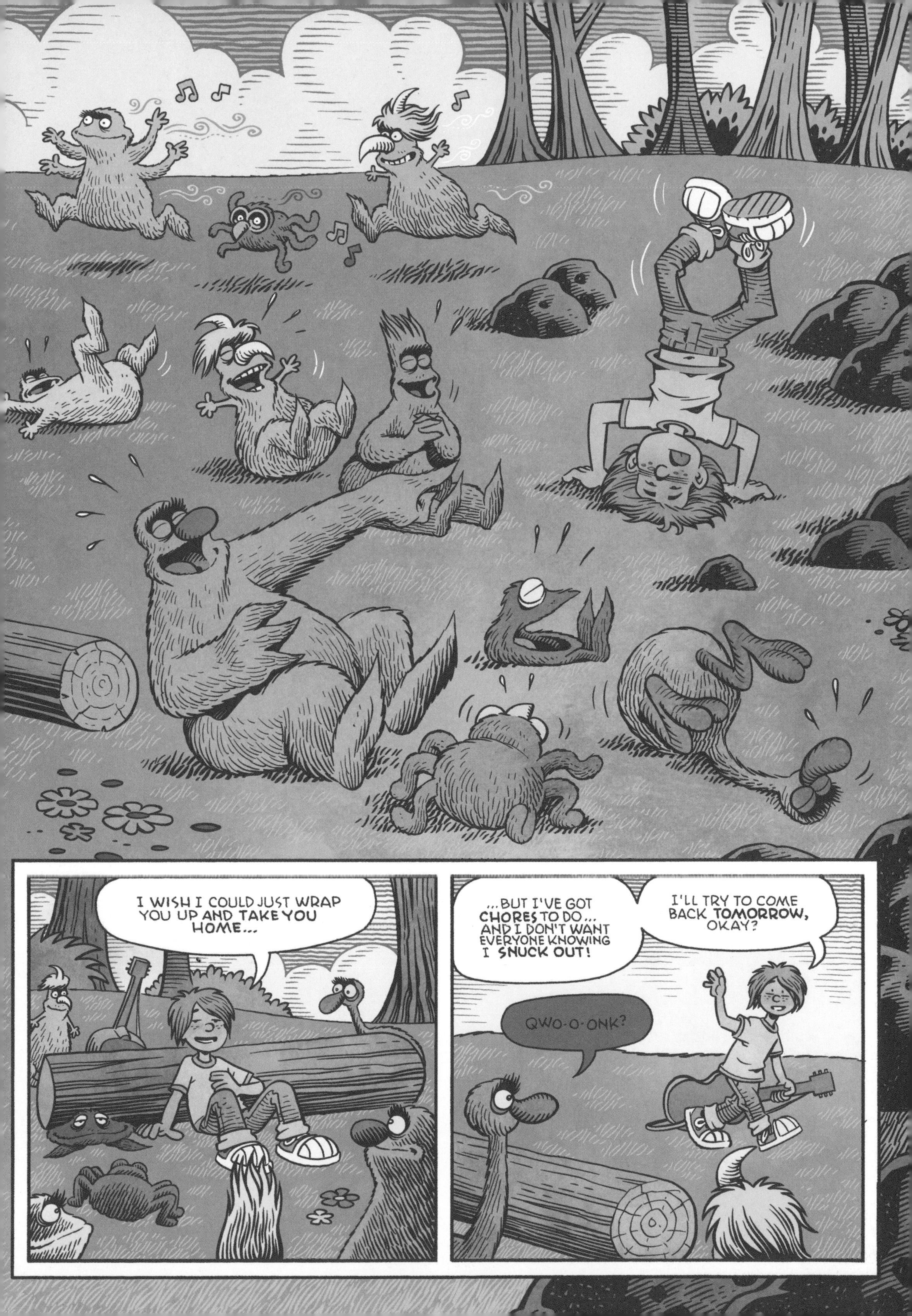

I WISH I COULD JUST WRAP YOU UP AND TAKE YOU HOME...
...BUT I'VE GOT CHORES TO DO... AND I DON'T WANT EVERYONE KNOWING I SNUCK OUT!
I'LL TRY TO COME BACK TOMORROW, OKAY?
QWO-O-ONK?

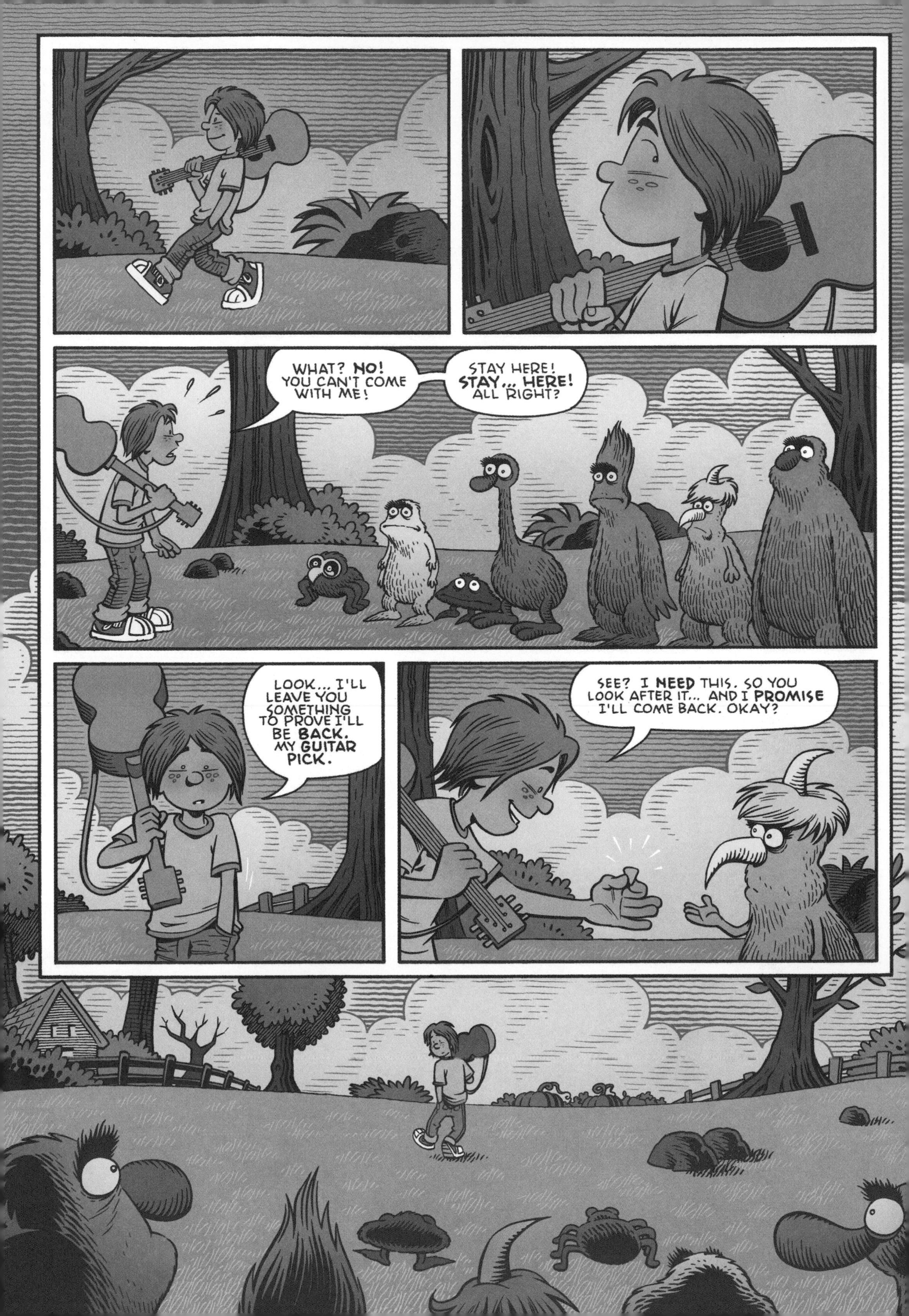
WHAT? NO! YOU CAN'T COME WITH ME!
STAY HERE! STAY... HERE! ALL RIGHT?
LOOK... I'LL LEAVE YOU SOMETHING TO PROVE I'LL BE BACK. MY GUITAR PICK.
SEE? I NEED THIS. SO YOU LOOK AFTER IT... AND I PROMISE I'LL COME BACK. OKAY?

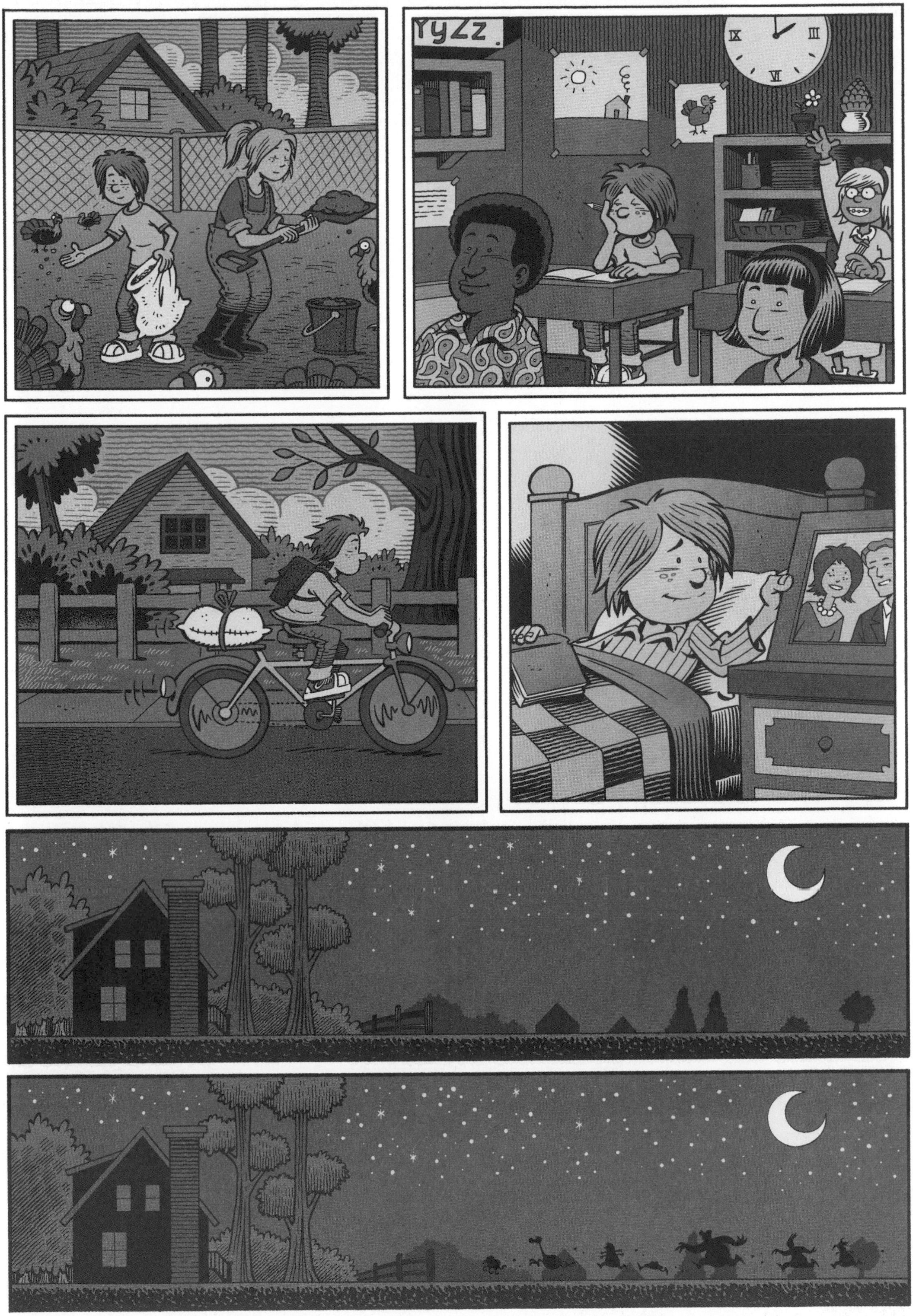
YyZz.

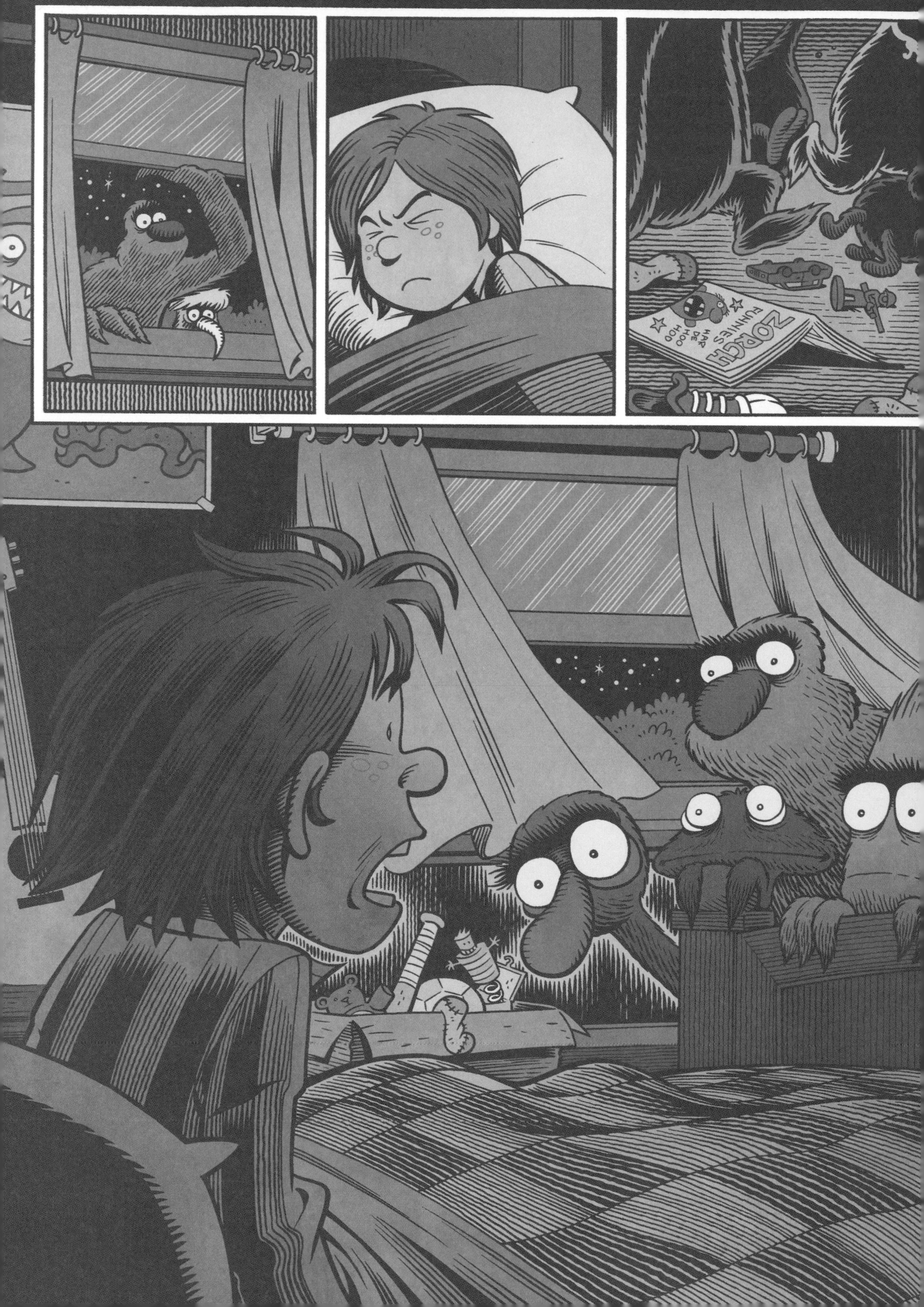
ZORCH FUNNIES
HAR DE HOO HOO

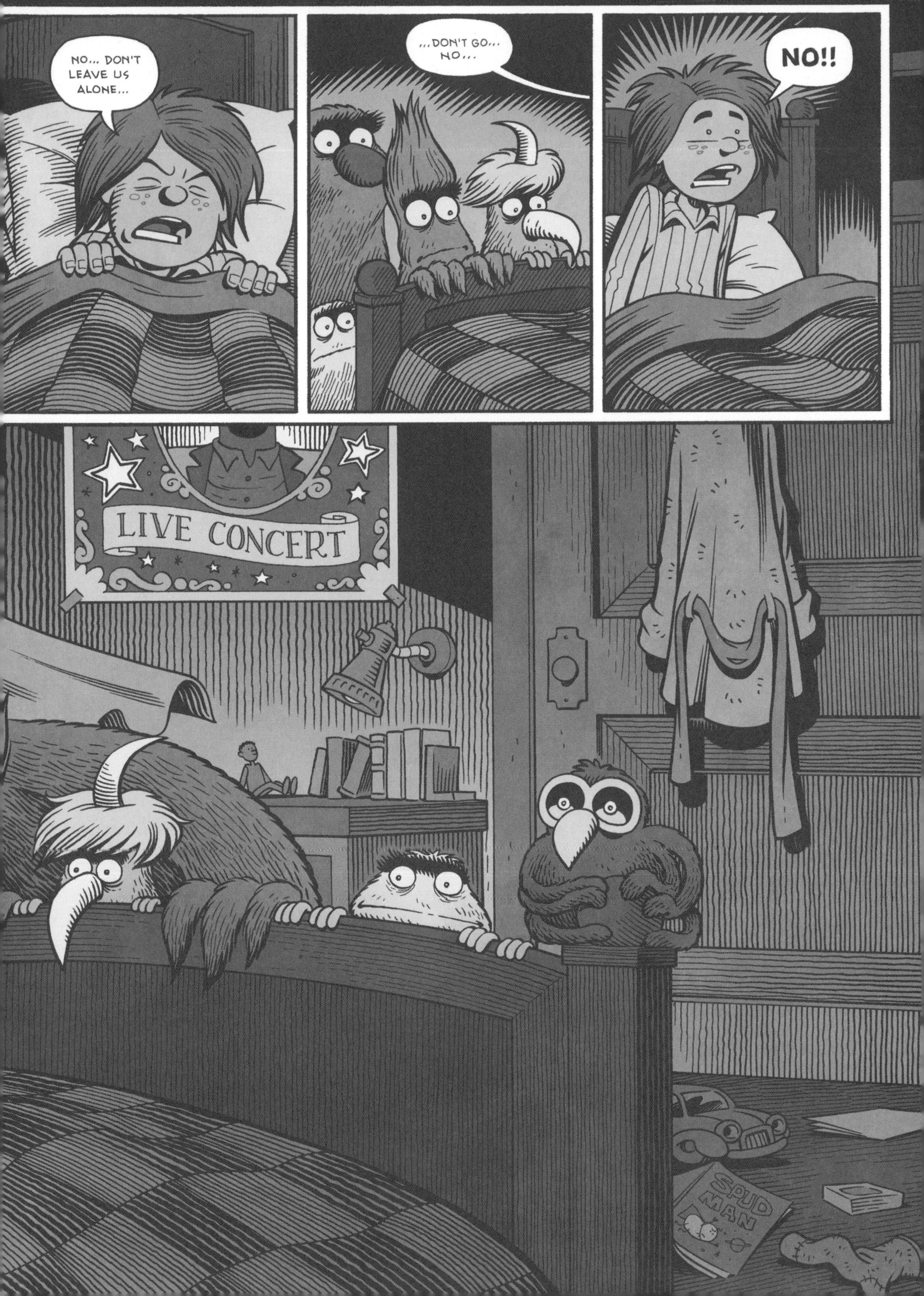

NO... DON'T LEAVE US ALONE...
...DON'T GO... NO...
NO!!
LIVE CONCERT
SPUD MAN

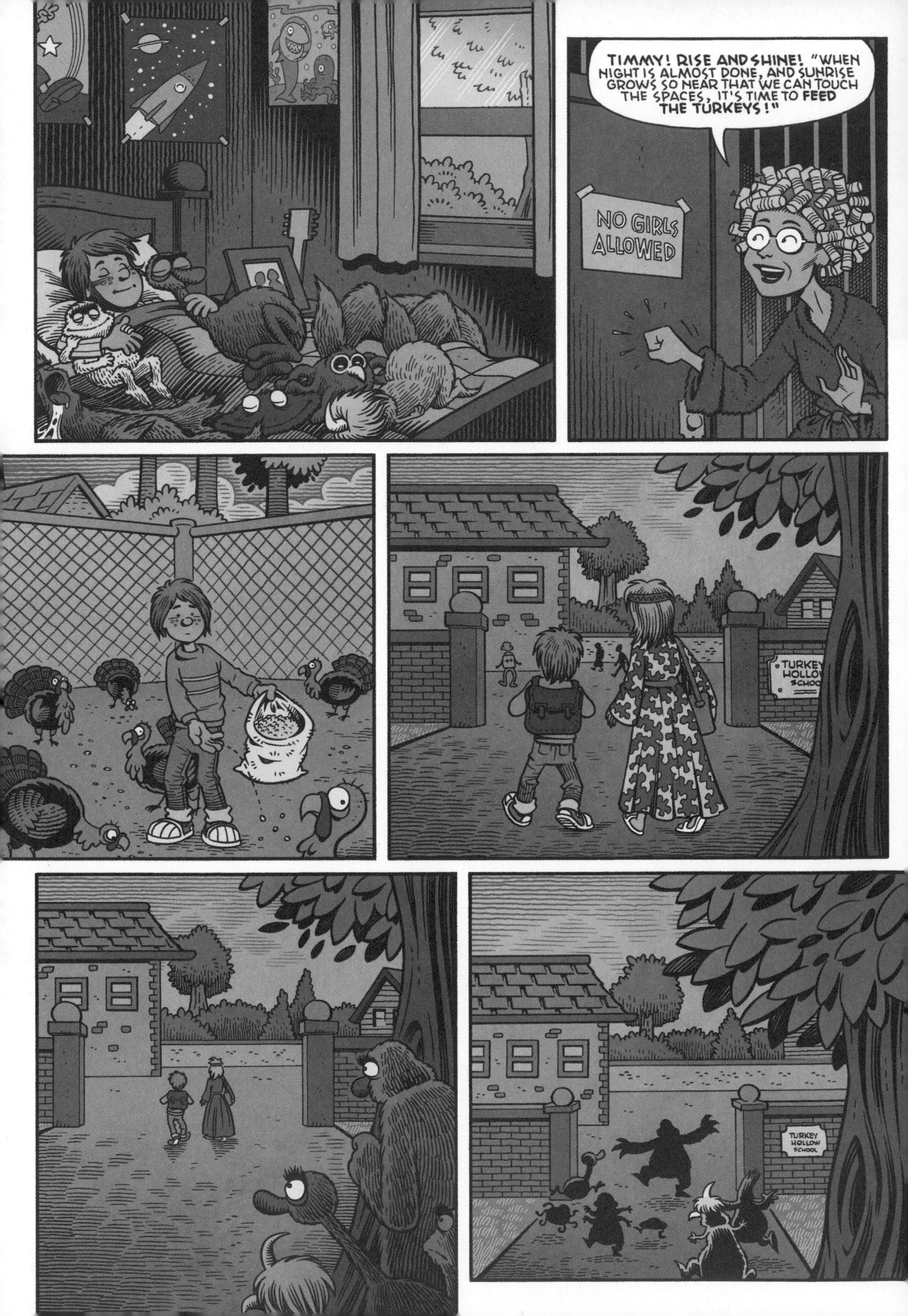

TIMMY! RISE AND SHINE! "WHEN NIGHT IS ALMOST DONE, AND SUNRISE GROWS SO NEAR THAT WE CAN TOUCH THE SPACES, IT'S TIME TO FEED THE TURKEYS!"
NO GIRLS ALLOWED
TURKEY HOLLOW SCHOOL
TURKEY HOLLOW SCHOOL

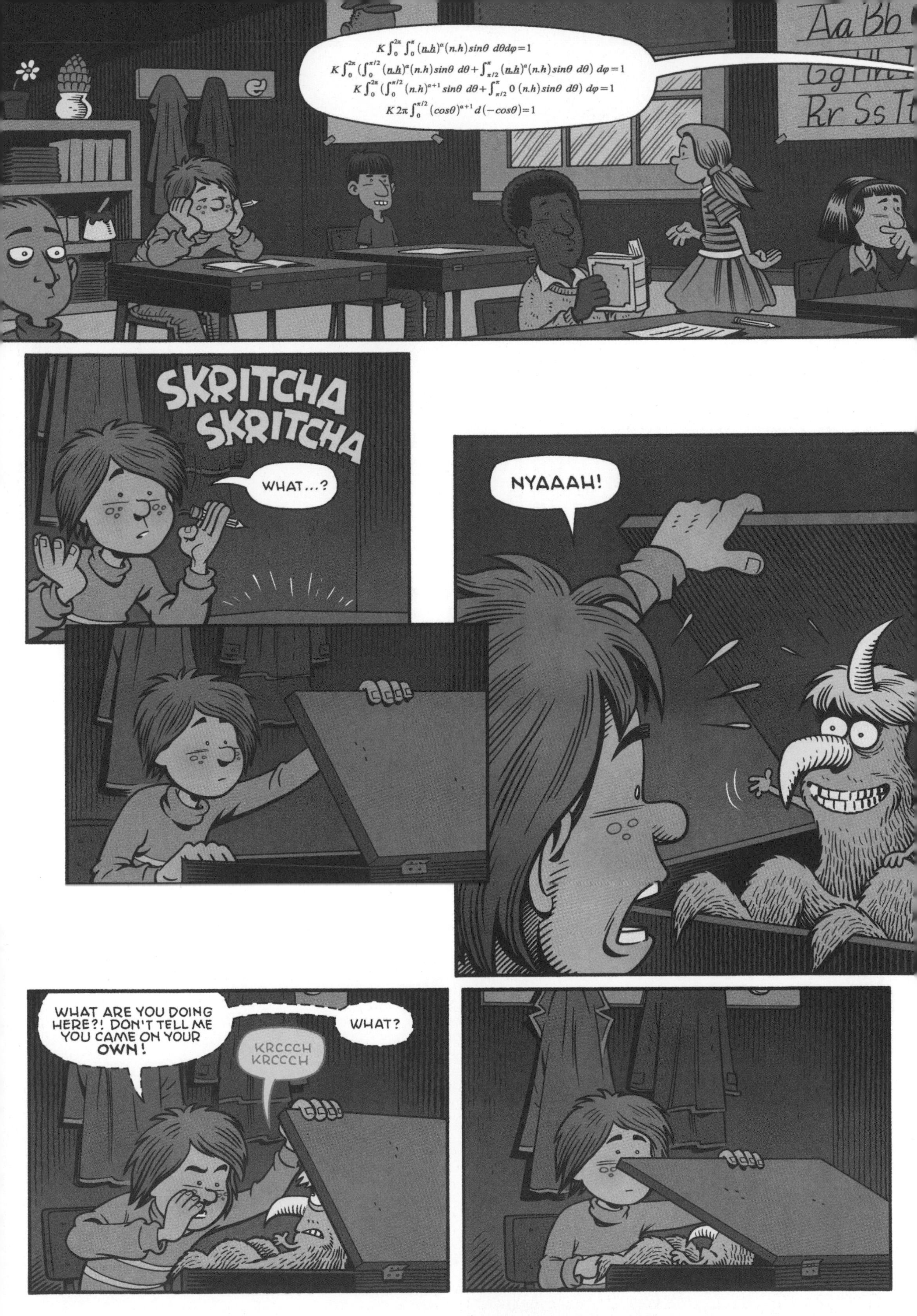

$K\int_0^{2\pi}\int_0^{\pi}(\underline{n.h})^{\alpha}(n.h)sin\theta\ d\theta d\varphi=1$
$K\int_0^{2\pi}(\int_0^{\pi/2}(\underline{n.h})^{\alpha}(n.h)sin\theta\ d\theta+\int_{\pi/2}^{\pi}(\underline{n.h})^{\alpha}(n.h)sin\theta\ d\theta)\ d\varphi=1$
$K\int_0^{2\pi}(\int_0^{\pi/2}(n.h)^{\alpha+1}sin\theta\ d\theta+\int_{\pi/2}^{\pi}0\,(n.h)sin\theta\ d\theta)\ d\varphi=1$
$K\,2\pi\int_0^{\pi/2}(cos\theta)^{\alpha+1}d(-cos\theta)=1$
Aa Bb
Gg Hh
Rr Ss Tt
SKRITCHA SKRITCHA
WHAT...?
NYAAAH!
WHAT ARE YOU DOING HERE?! DON'T TELL ME YOU CAME ON YOUR OWN!
WHAT?
KRCCCH KRCCCH

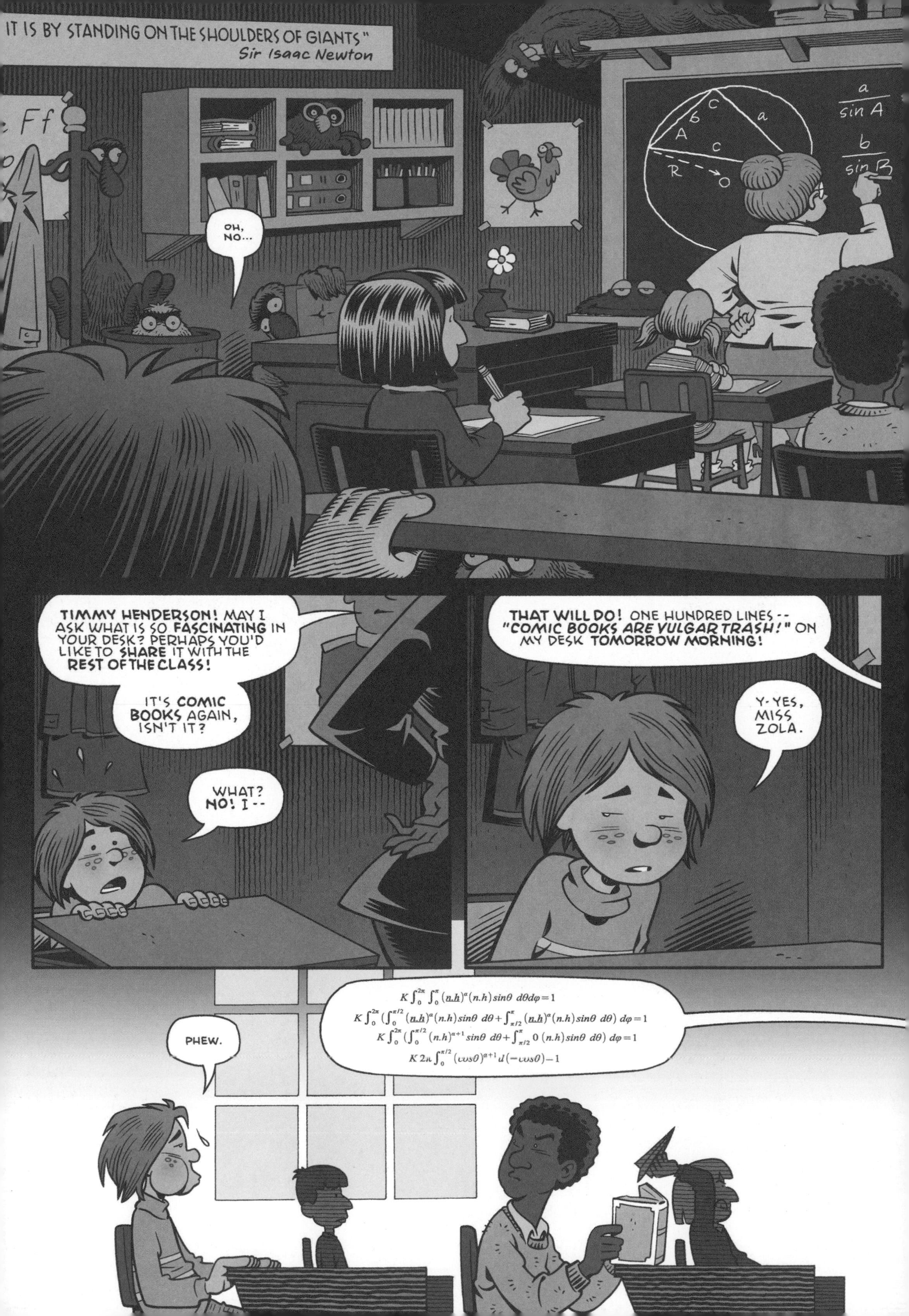

IT IS BY STANDING ON THE SHOULDERS OF GIANTS"
Sir Isaac Newton
a / sin A
b / sin B
OH, NO...
TIMMY HENDERSON! MAY I ASK WHAT IS SO FASCINATING IN YOUR DESK? PERHAPS YOU'D LIKE TO SHARE IT WITH THE REST OF THE CLASS!
IT'S COMIC BOOKS AGAIN, ISN'T IT?
WHAT? NO! I --
THAT WILL DO! ONE HUNDRED LINES -- "COMIC BOOKS ARE VULGAR TRASH!" ON MY DESK TOMORROW MORNING!
Y-YES, MISS ZOLA.
$K\int_0^{2\pi}\int_0^{\pi}(\underline{n.h})^{\alpha}(n.h)\sin\theta\ d\theta d\varphi=1$
$K\int_0^{2\pi}(\int_0^{\pi/2}(\underline{n.h})^{\alpha}(n.h)\sin\theta\ d\theta+\int_{\pi/2}^{\pi}(\underline{n.h})^{\alpha}(n.h)\sin\theta\ d\theta)\ d\varphi=1$
$K\int_0^{2\pi}(\int_0^{\pi/2}(n.h)^{\alpha+1}\sin\theta\ d\theta+\int_{\pi/2}^{\pi}0\ (n.h)\sin\theta\ d\theta)\ d\varphi=1$
$K\,2\pi\int_0^{\pi/2}(\cos\theta)^{\alpha+1}d(-\cos\theta)-1$
PHEW.

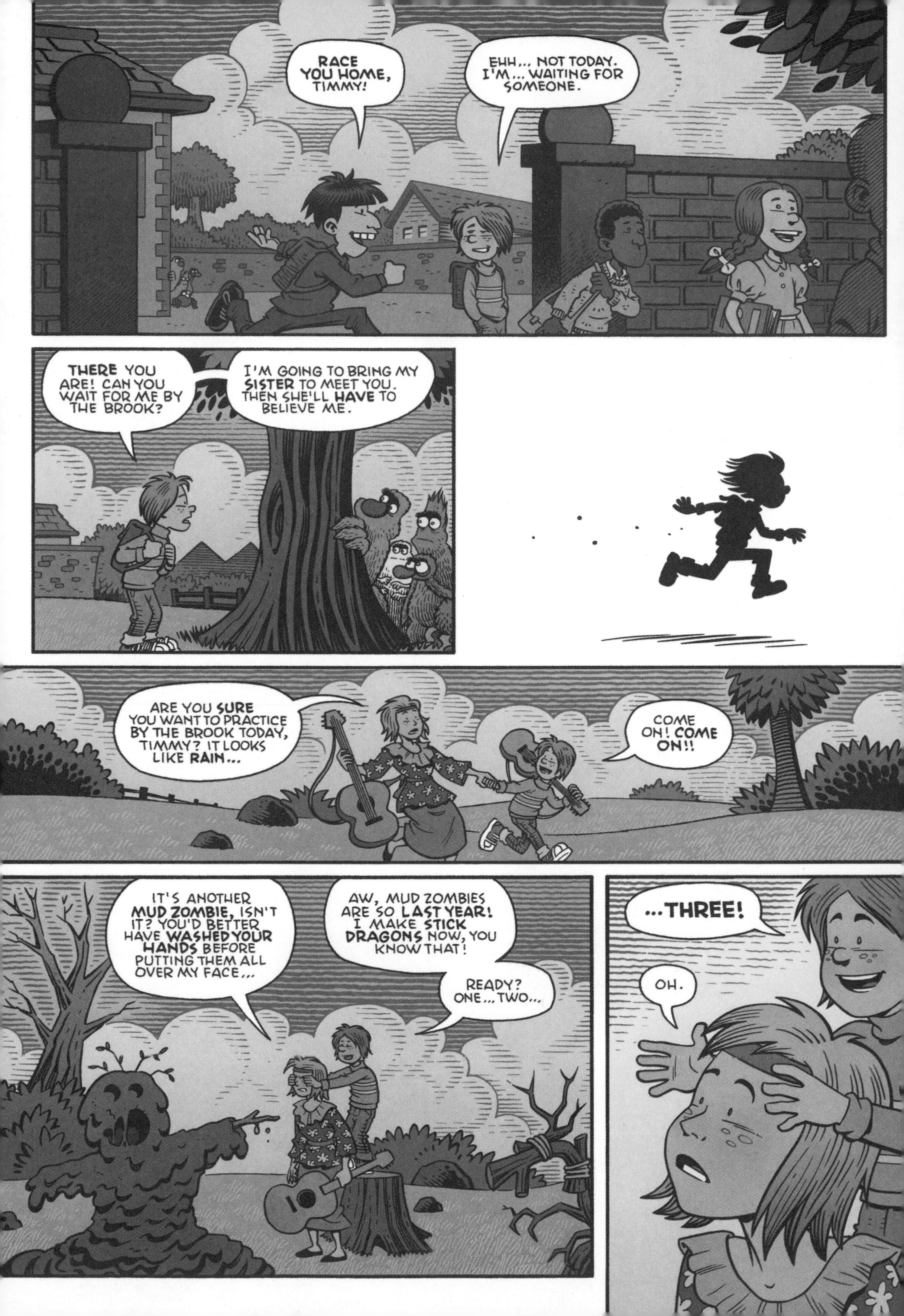
RACE YOU HOME, TIMMY!
EHH... NOT TODAY. I'M... WAITING FOR SOMEONE.
THERE YOU ARE! CAN YOU WAIT FOR ME BY THE BROOK?
I'M GOING TO BRING MY SISTER TO MEET YOU. THEN SHE'LL HAVE TO BELIEVE ME.
ARE YOU SURE YOU WANT TO PRACTICE BY THE BROOK TODAY, TIMMY? IT LOOKS LIKE RAIN...
COME ON! COME ON!!
IT'S ANOTHER MUD ZOMBIE, ISN'T IT? YOU'D BETTER HAVE WASHED YOUR HANDS BEFORE PUTTING THEM ALL OVER MY FACE...
AW, MUD ZOMBIES ARE SO LAST YEAR! I MAKE STICK DRAGONS NOW, YOU KNOW THAT!
READY? ONE... TWO...
...THREE!
OH.

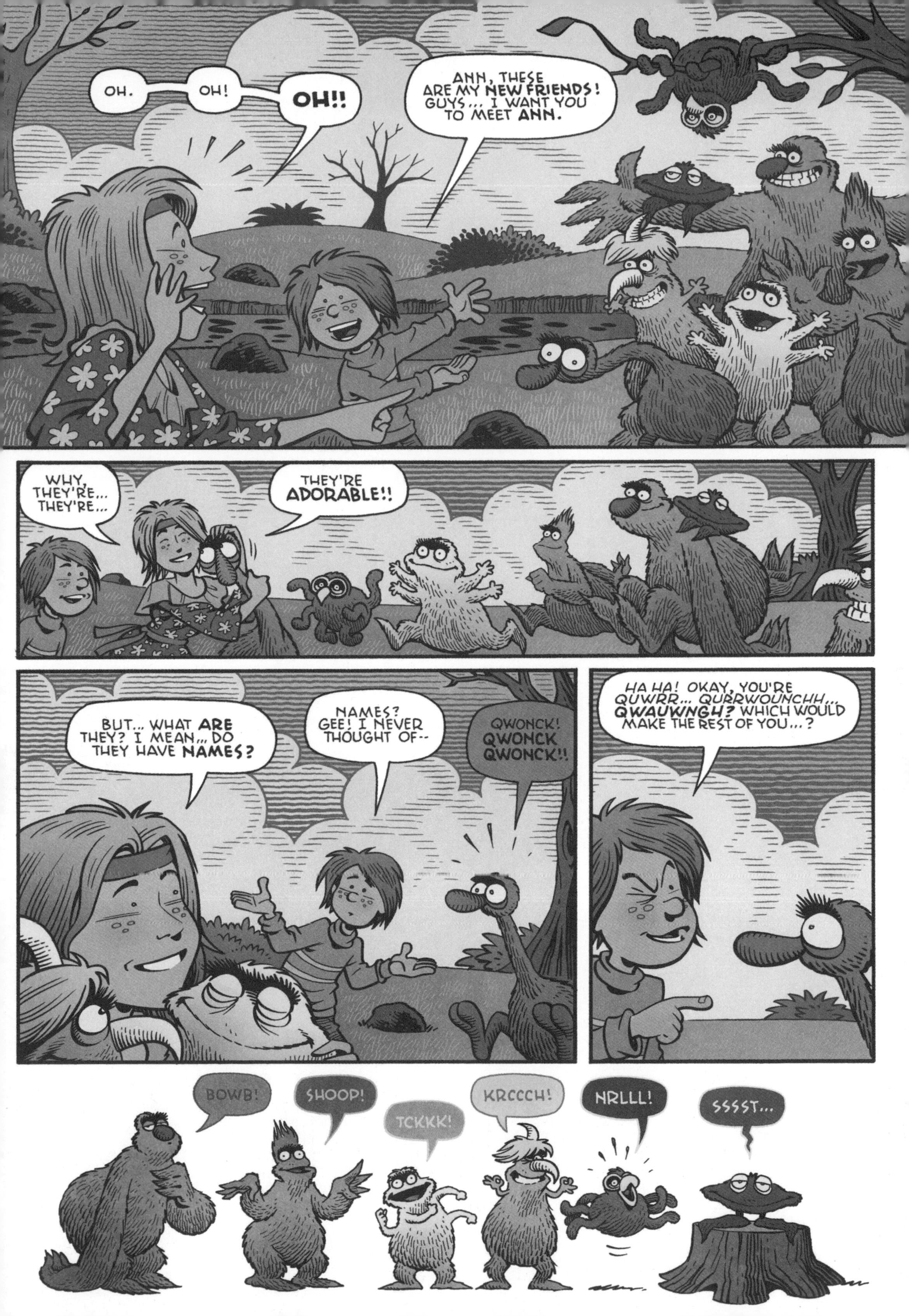
OH.
OH!
OH!!
ANN, THESE ARE MY NEW FRIENDS! GUYS... I WANT YOU TO MEET ANN.
WHY, THEY'RE... THEY'RE...
THEY'RE ADORABLE!!
BUT... WHAT ARE THEY? I MEAN... DO THEY HAVE NAMES?
NAMES? GEE! I NEVER THOUGHT OF--
QWONCK! QWONCK QWONCK!!
HA HA! OKAY, YOU'RE QUWRR... QURRWOUNCHH... QWAUWNGH? WHICH WOULD MAKE THE REST OF YOU...?
BOWB!
SHOOP!
TCKKK!
KRCCCH!
NRLLL!
SSSST...

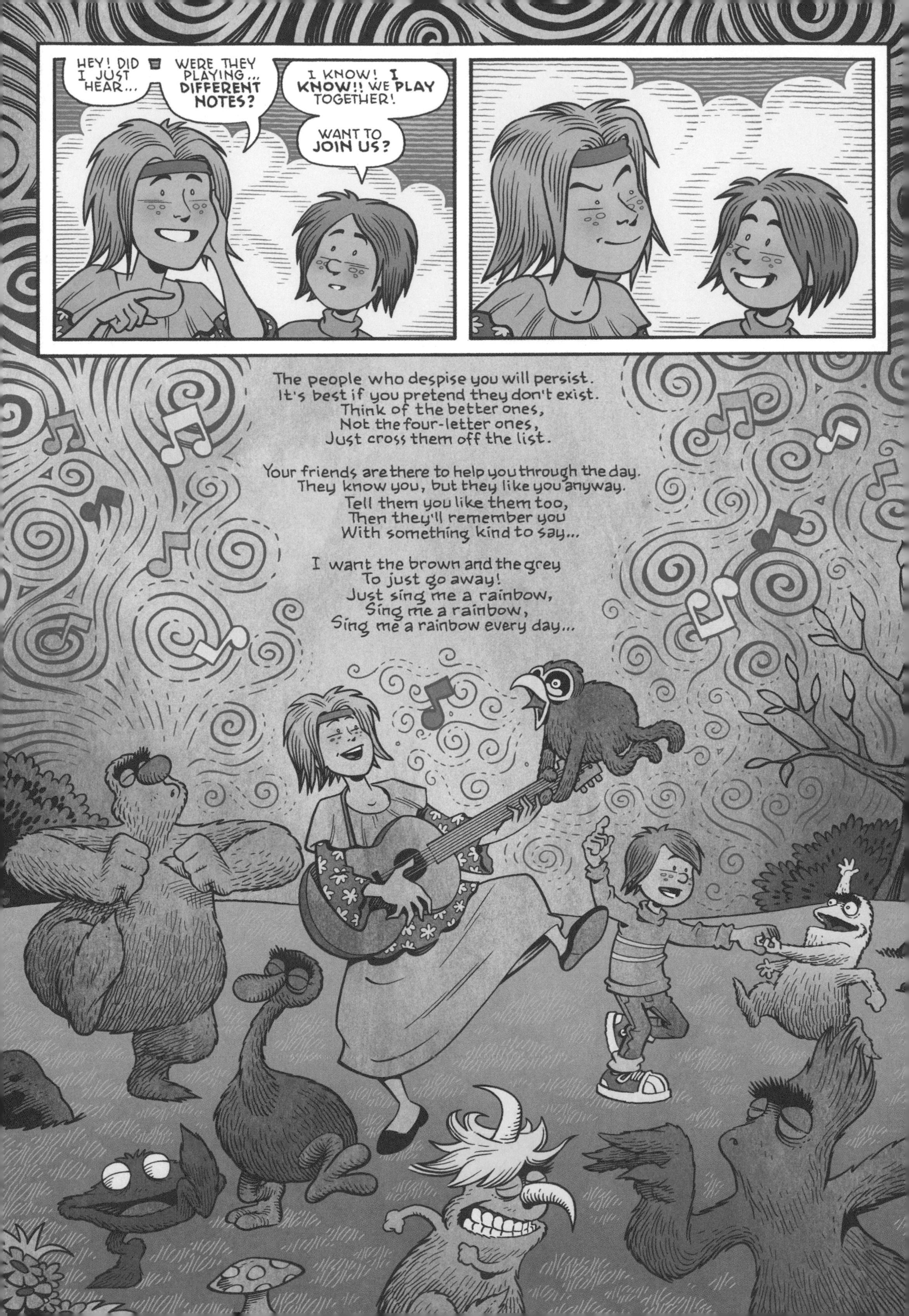

HEY! DID I JUST HEAR...
WERE THEY PLAYING... DIFFERENT NOTES?
I KNOW! I KNOW!! WE PLAY TOGETHER!
WANT TO JOIN US?
The people who despise you will persist.
It's best if you pretend they don't exist.
Think of the better ones,
Not the four-letter ones,
Just cross them off the list.
Your friends are there to help you through the day.
They know you, but they like you anyway.
Tell them you like them too,
Then they'll remember you
With something kind to say...
I want the brown and the grey
To just go away!
Just sing me a rainbow,
Sing me a rainbow,
Sing me a rainbow every day...

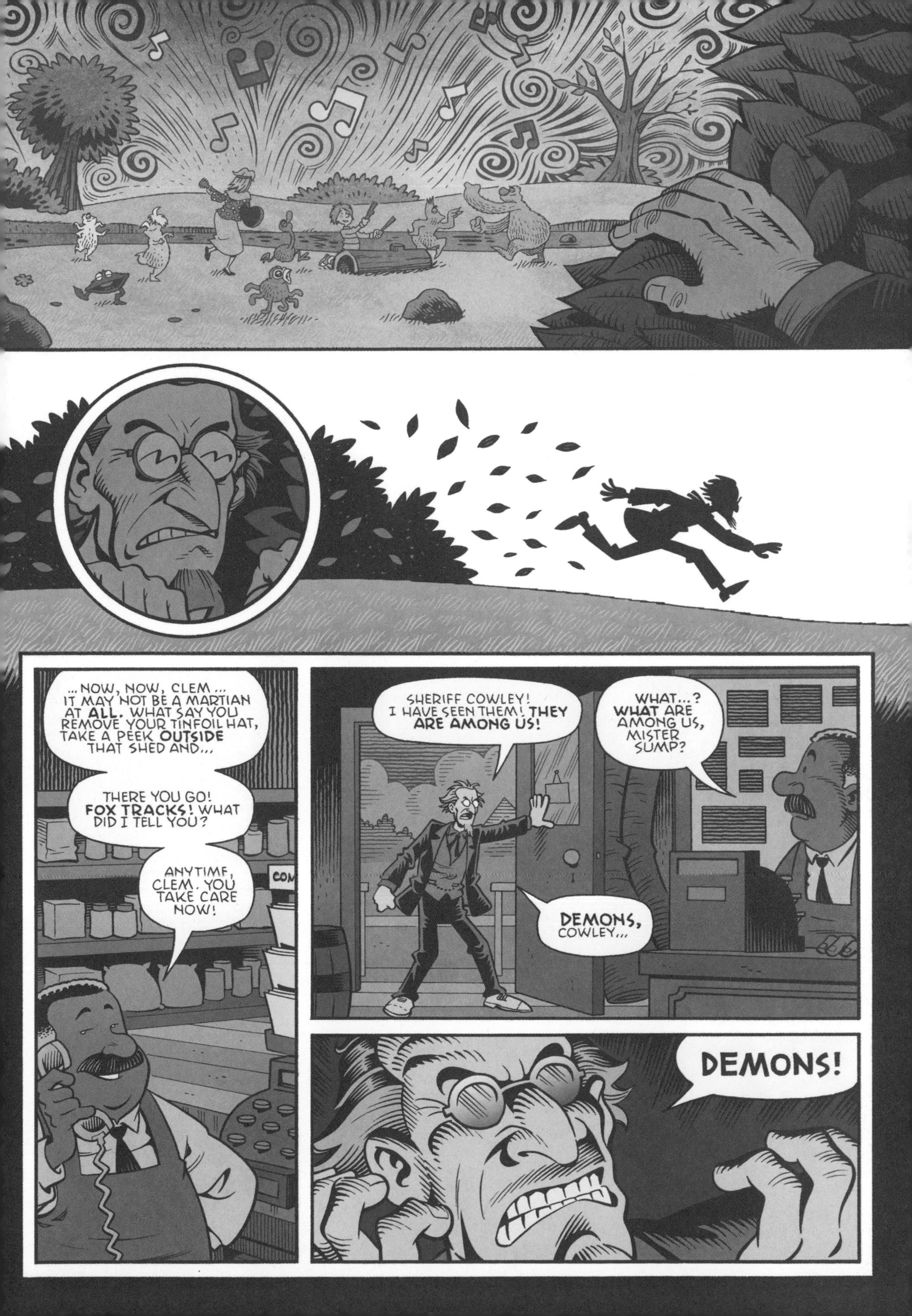

...NOW, NOW, CLEM ... IT MAY NOT BE A MARTIAN AT **ALL**. WHAT SAY YOU REMOVE YOUR TINFOIL HAT, TAKE A PEEK **OUTSIDE** THAT SHED AND...
THERE YOU GO! **FOX TRACKS!** WHAT DID I TELL YOU?
ANYTIME, CLEM. YOU TAKE CARE NOW!
SHERIFF COWLEY! I HAVE SEEN THEM! **THEY ARE AMONG US!**
WHAT...? **WHAT** ARE AMONG US, MISTER SUMP?
**DEMONS,** COWLEY...
**DEMONS!**

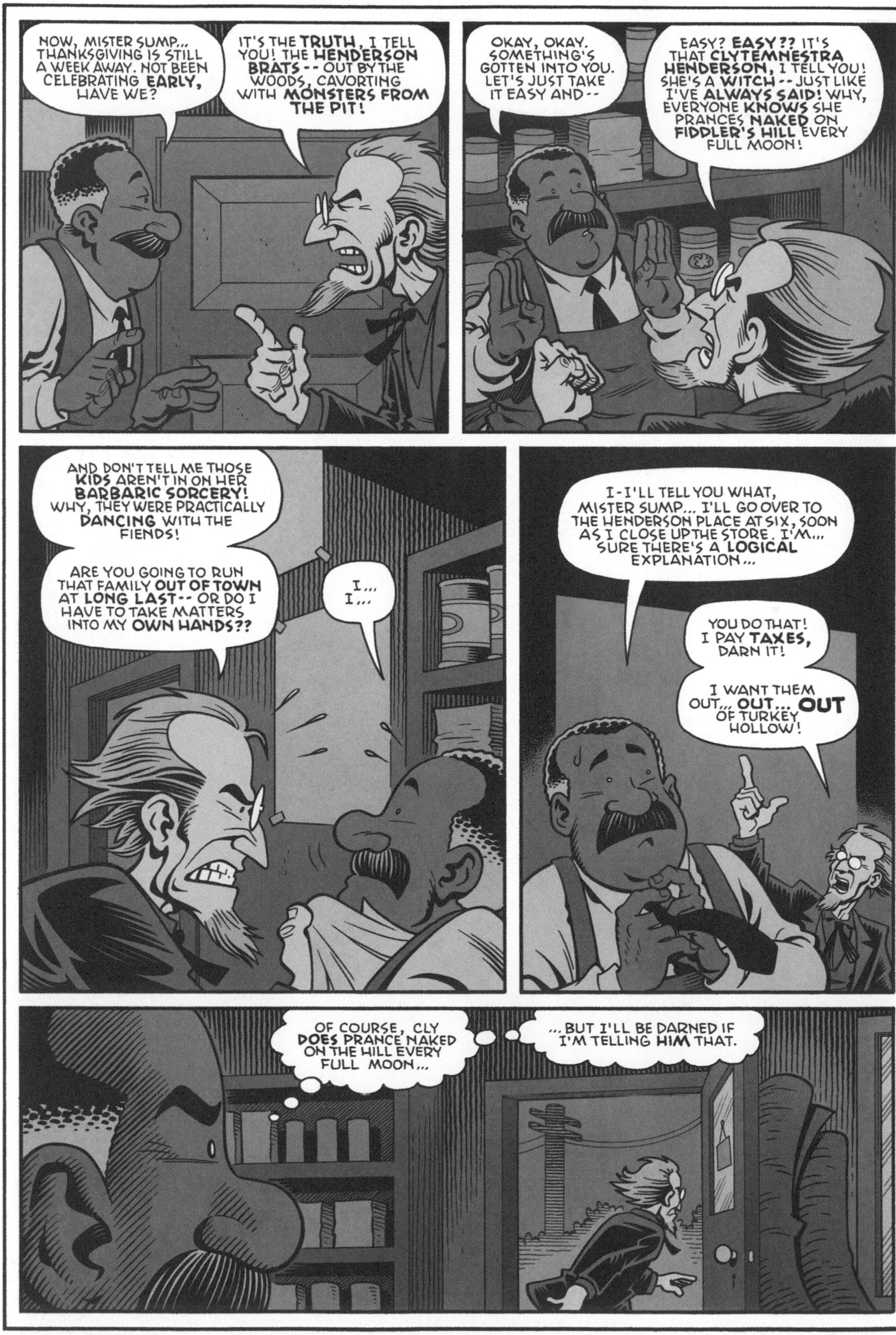

NOW, MISTER SUMP... THANKSGIVING IS STILL A WEEK AWAY. NOT BEEN CELEBRATING **EARLY**, HAVE WE?
IT'S THE **TRUTH**, I TELL YOU! THE **HENDERSON BRATS** -- OUT BY THE WOODS, CAVORTING WITH **MONSTERS FROM THE PIT!**
OKAY, OKAY. SOMETHING'S GOTTEN INTO YOU. LET'S JUST TAKE IT EASY AND --
EASY? **EASY??** IT'S THAT **CLYTEMNESTRA HENDERSON**, I TELL YOU! SHE'S A **WITCH** -- JUST LIKE I'VE **ALWAYS SAID!** WHY, EVERYONE **KNOWS** SHE PRANCES **NAKED** ON **FIDDLER'S HILL** EVERY FULL MOON!
AND DON'T TELL ME THOSE **KIDS** AREN'T IN ON HER **BARBARIC SORCERY!** WHY, THEY WERE PRACTICALLY **DANCING** WITH THE FIENDS!
ARE YOU GOING TO RUN THAT FAMILY **OUT OF TOWN** AT **LONG LAST** -- OR DO I HAVE TO TAKE MATTERS INTO MY **OWN HANDS??**
I... I...
I-I'LL TELL YOU WHAT, MISTER SUMP... I'LL GO OVER TO THE HENDERSON PLACE AT SIX, SOON AS I CLOSE UP THE STORE. I'M... SURE THERE'S A **LOGICAL** EXPLANATION...
YOU DO THAT! I PAY **TAXES**, DARN IT!
I WANT THEM OUT... **OUT**... **OUT** OF TURKEY HOLLOW!
OF COURSE, CLY **DOES** PRANCE NAKED ON THE HILL EVERY FULL MOON...
...BUT I'LL BE DARNED IF I'M TELLING **HIM** THAT.

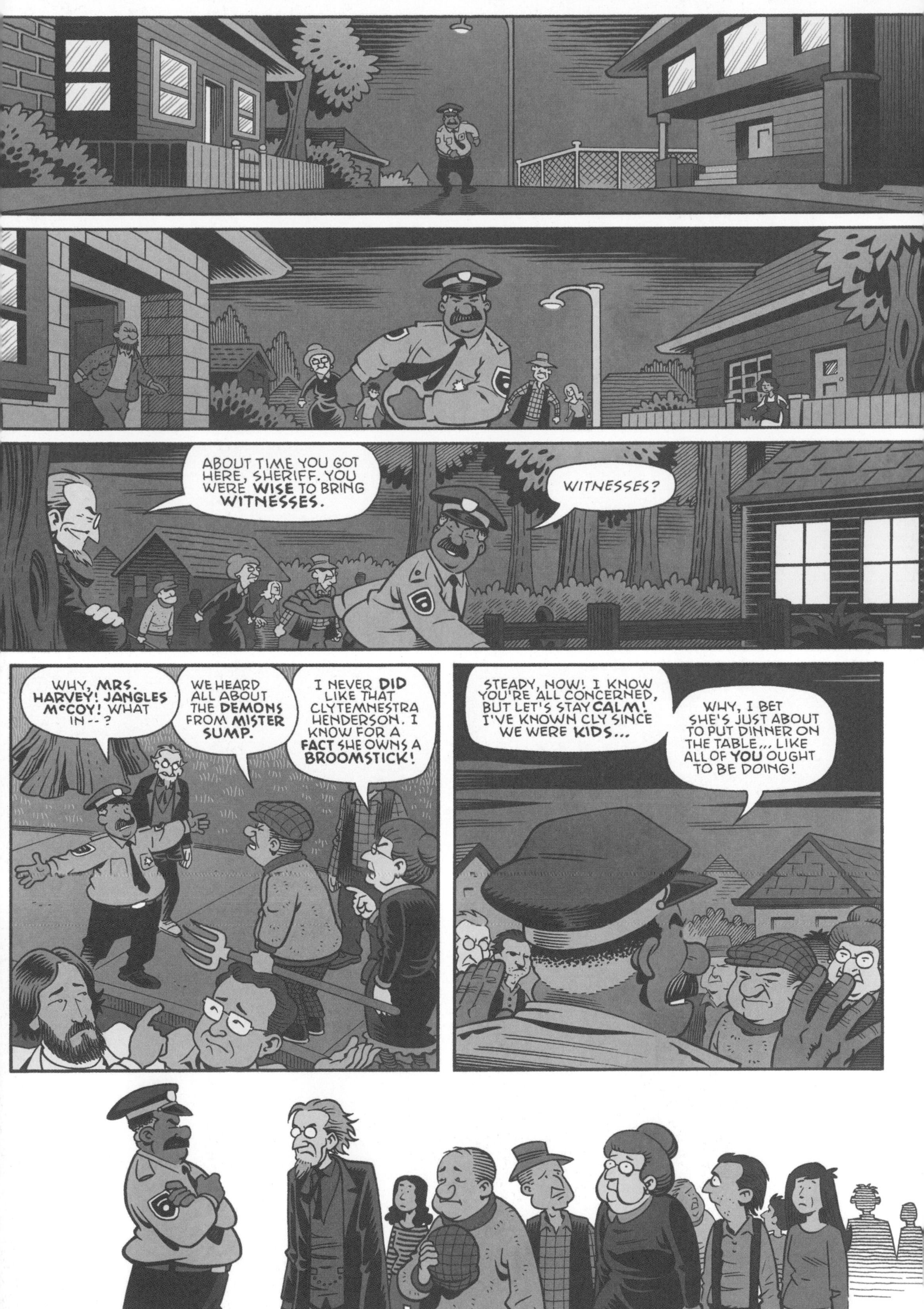
ABOUT TIME YOU GOT HERE, SHERIFF. YOU WERE WISE TO BRING WITNESSES.
WITNESSES?
WHY, MRS. HARVEY! JANGLES McCOY! WHAT IN--?
WE HEARD ALL ABOUT THE DEMONS FROM MISTER SUMP.
I NEVER DID LIKE THAT CLYTEMNESTRA HENDERSON. I KNOW FOR A FACT SHE OWNS A BROOMSTICK!
STEADY, NOW! I KNOW YOU'RE ALL CONCERNED, BUT LET'S STAY CALM! I'VE KNOWN CLY SINCE WE WERE KIDS...
WHY, I BET SHE'S JUST ABOUT TO PUT DINNER ON THE TABLE... LIKE ALL OF YOU OUGHT TO BE DOING!

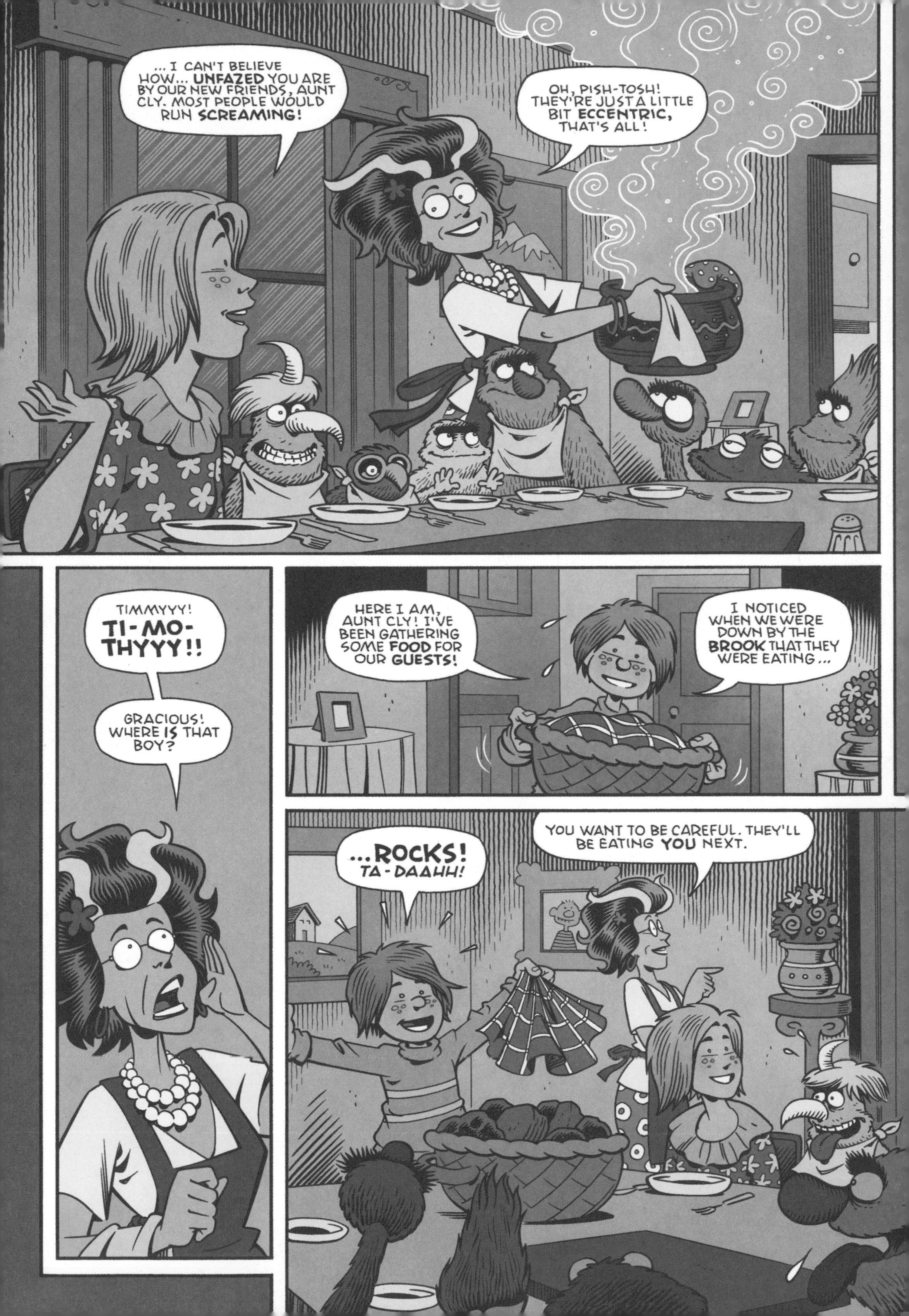

...I CAN'T BELIEVE HOW... **UNFAZED** YOU ARE BY OUR NEW FRIENDS, AUNT CLY. MOST PEOPLE WOULD RUN **SCREAMING**!
OH, PISH-TOSH! THEY'RE JUST A LITTLE BIT **ECCENTRIC**, THAT'S ALL!
TIMMYYY! **TI-MO-THYYY!!**
GRACIOUS! WHERE **IS** THAT BOY?
HERE I AM, AUNT CLY! I'VE BEEN GATHERING SOME **FOOD** FOR OUR **GUESTS**!
I NOTICED WHEN WE WERE DOWN BY THE **BROOK** THAT THEY WERE EATING...
**...ROCKS!** TA-DAAHH!
YOU WANT TO BE CAREFUL. THEY'LL BE EATING **YOU** NEXT.

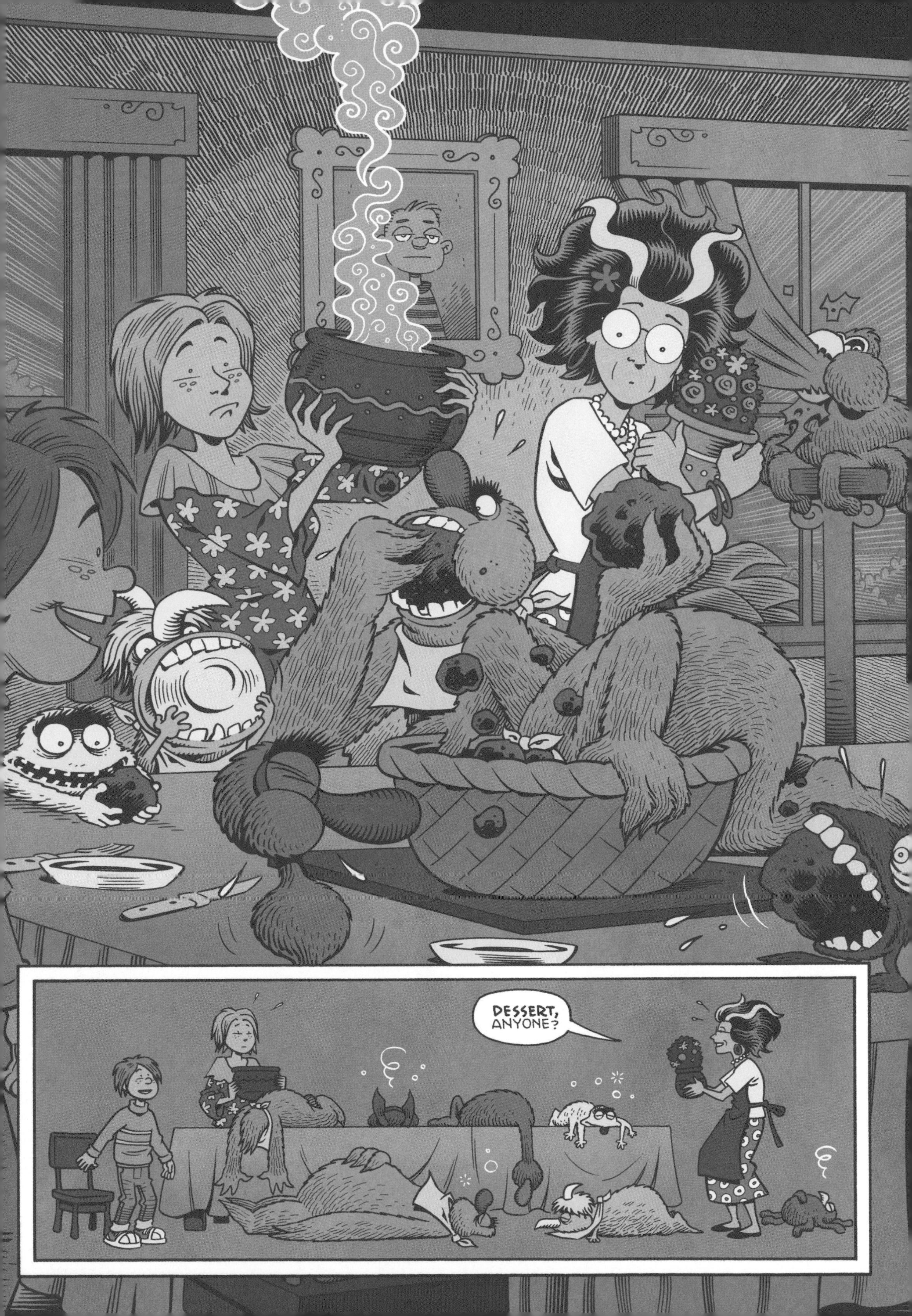
DESSERT, ANYONE?

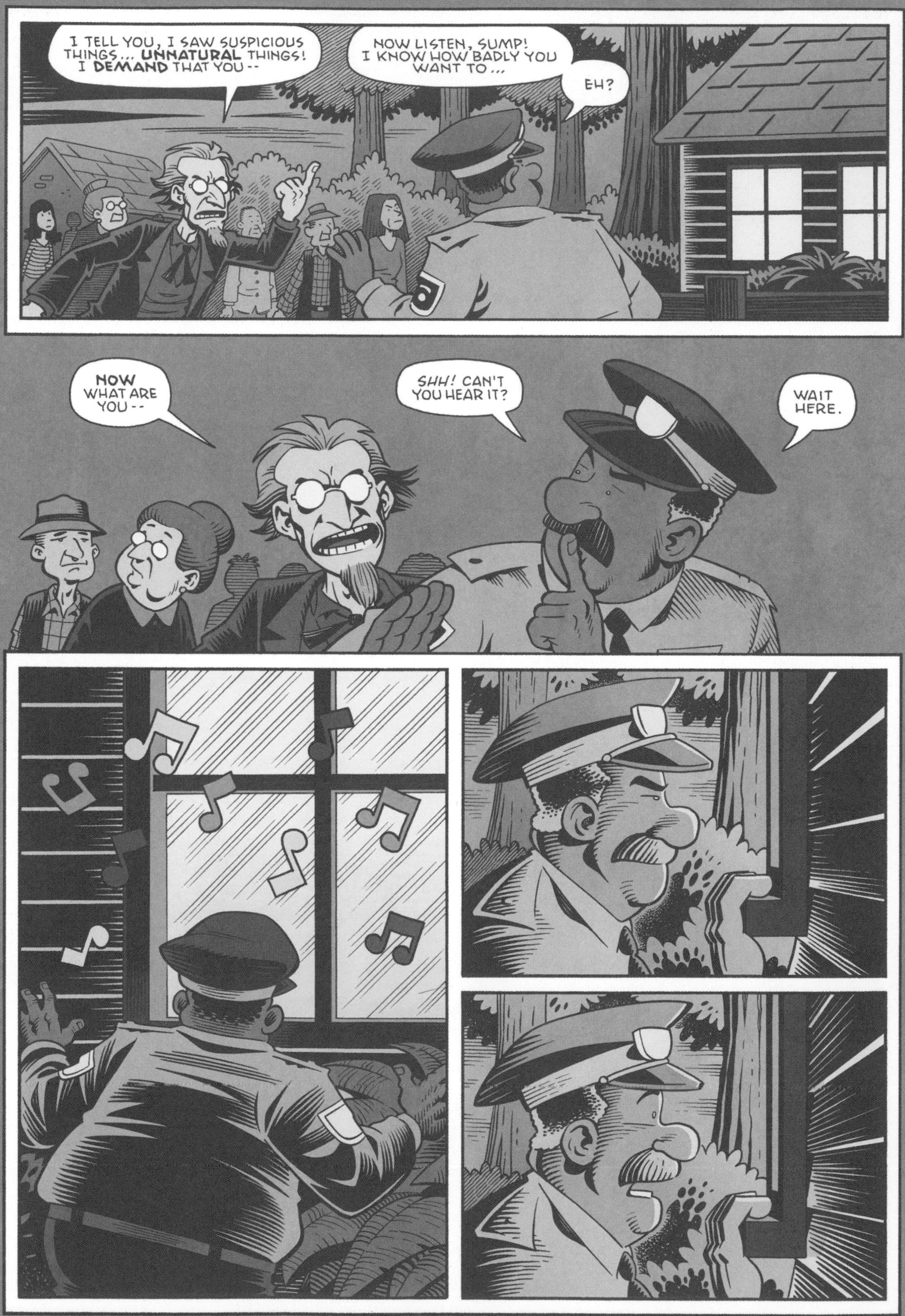
I TELL YOU, I SAW SUSPICIOUS THINGS... **UNNATURAL** THINGS! I **DEMAND** THAT YOU --
NOW LISTEN, SUMP! I KNOW HOW BADLY YOU WANT TO ...
EH?
**NOW** WHAT ARE YOU --
SHH! CAN'T YOU HEAR IT?
WAIT HERE.

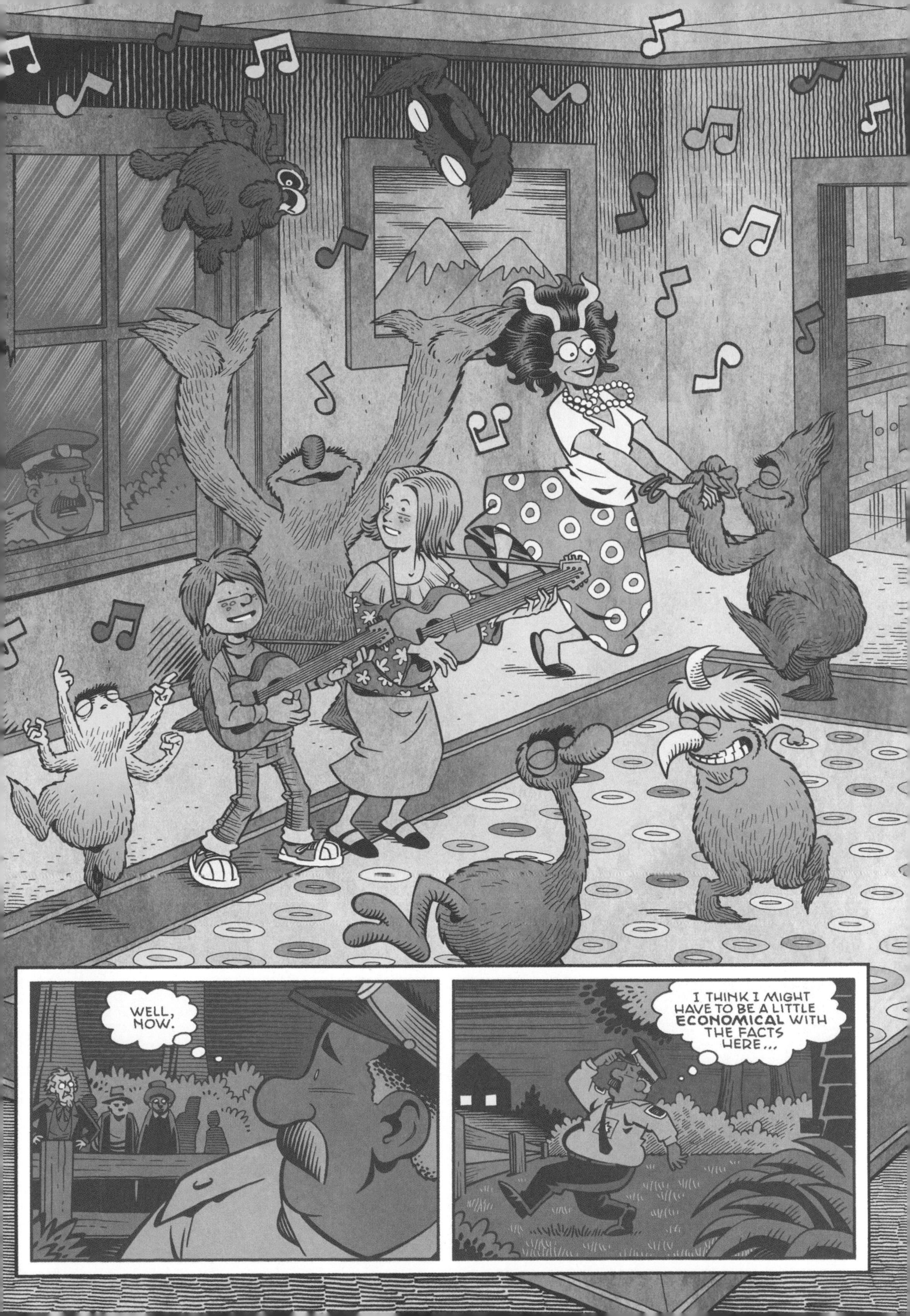
WELL, NOW.
I THINK I MIGHT HAVE TO BE A LITTLE ECONOMICAL WITH THE FACTS HERE...

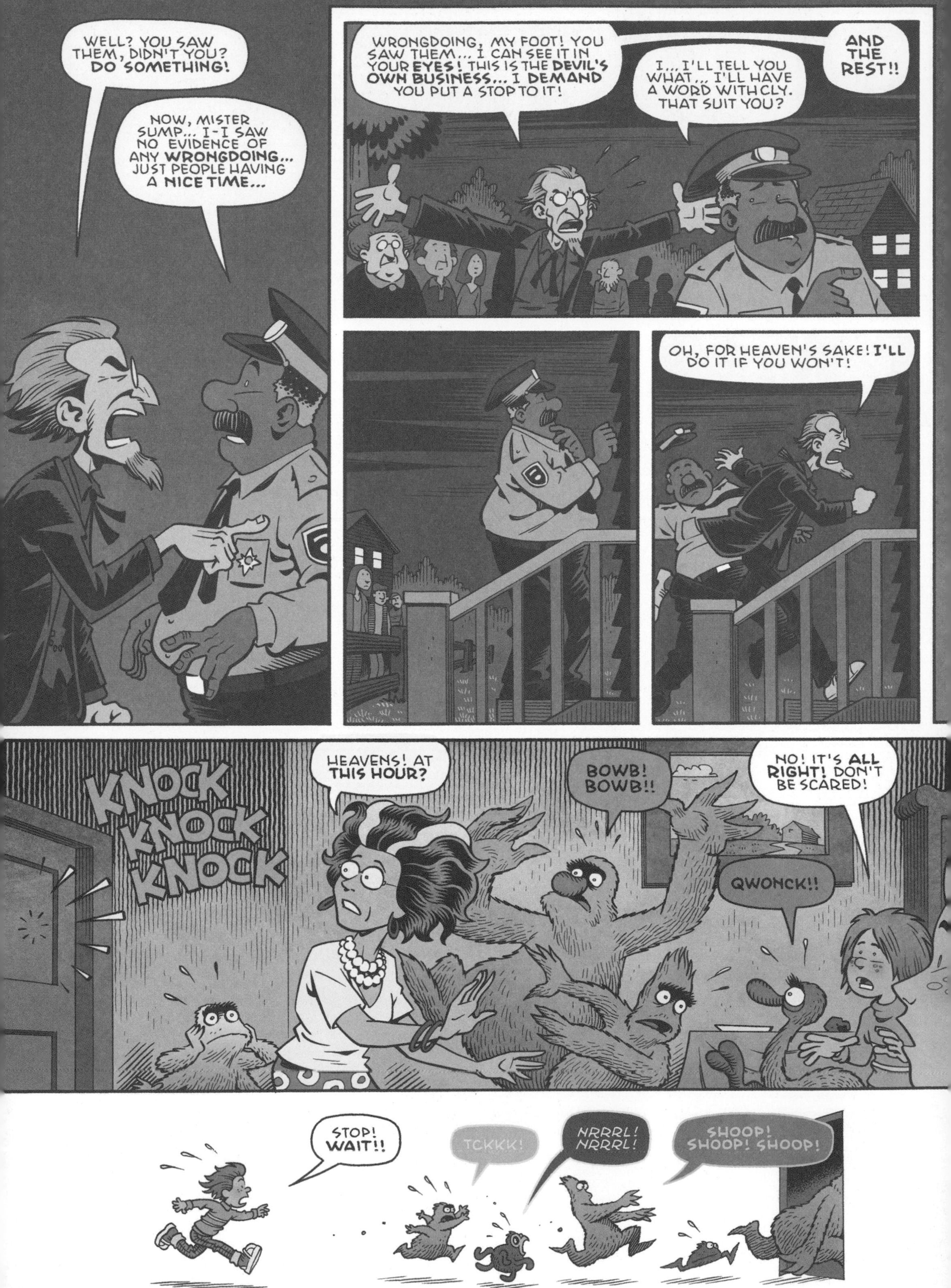
WELL? YOU SAW THEM, DIDN'T YOU? DO SOMETHING!
NOW, MISTER SUMP... I-I SAW NO EVIDENCE OF ANY WRONGDOING... JUST PEOPLE HAVING A NICE TIME...
WRONGDOING, MY FOOT! YOU SAW THEM... I CAN SEE IT IN YOUR EYES! THIS IS THE DEVIL'S OWN BUSINESS... I DEMAND YOU PUT A STOP TO IT!
I... I'LL TELL YOU WHAT... I'LL HAVE A WORD WITH CLY. THAT SUIT YOU?
AND THE REST!!
OH, FOR HEAVEN'S SAKE! I'LL DO IT IF YOU WON'T!
KNOCK KNOCK KNOCK
HEAVENS! AT THIS HOUR?
BOWB! BOWB!!
NO! IT'S ALL RIGHT! DON'T BE SCARED!
QWONCK!!
STOP! WAIT!!
TCKKK!
NRRRL! NRRRL!
SHOOP! SHOOP! SHOOP!

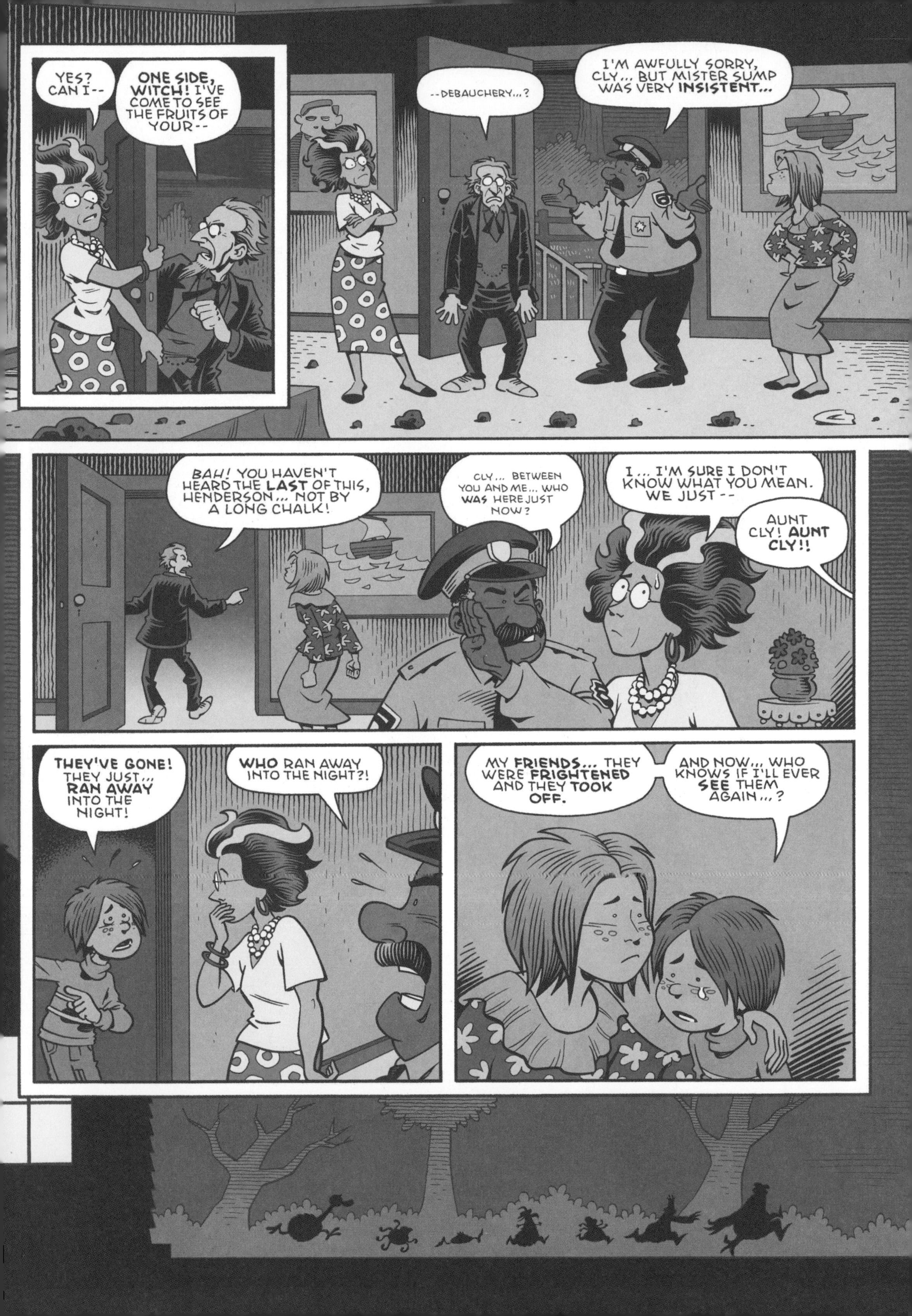

YES? CAN I--
ONE SIDE, WITCH! I'VE COME TO SEE THE FRUITS OF YOUR--
--DEBAUCHERY...?
I'M AWFULLY SORRY, CLY... BUT MISTER SUMP WAS VERY INSISTENT...
BAH! YOU HAVEN'T HEARD THE LAST OF THIS, HENDERSON... NOT BY A LONG CHALK!
CLY... BETWEEN YOU AND ME... WHO WAS HERE JUST NOW?
I... I'M SURE I DON'T KNOW WHAT YOU MEAN. WE JUST--
AUNT CLY! AUNT CLY!!
THEY'VE GONE! THEY JUST... RAN AWAY INTO THE NIGHT!
WHO RAN AWAY INTO THE NIGHT?!
MY FRIENDS... THEY WERE FRIGHTENED AND THEY TOOK OFF.
AND NOW... WHO KNOWS IF I'LL EVER SEE THEM AGAIN...?

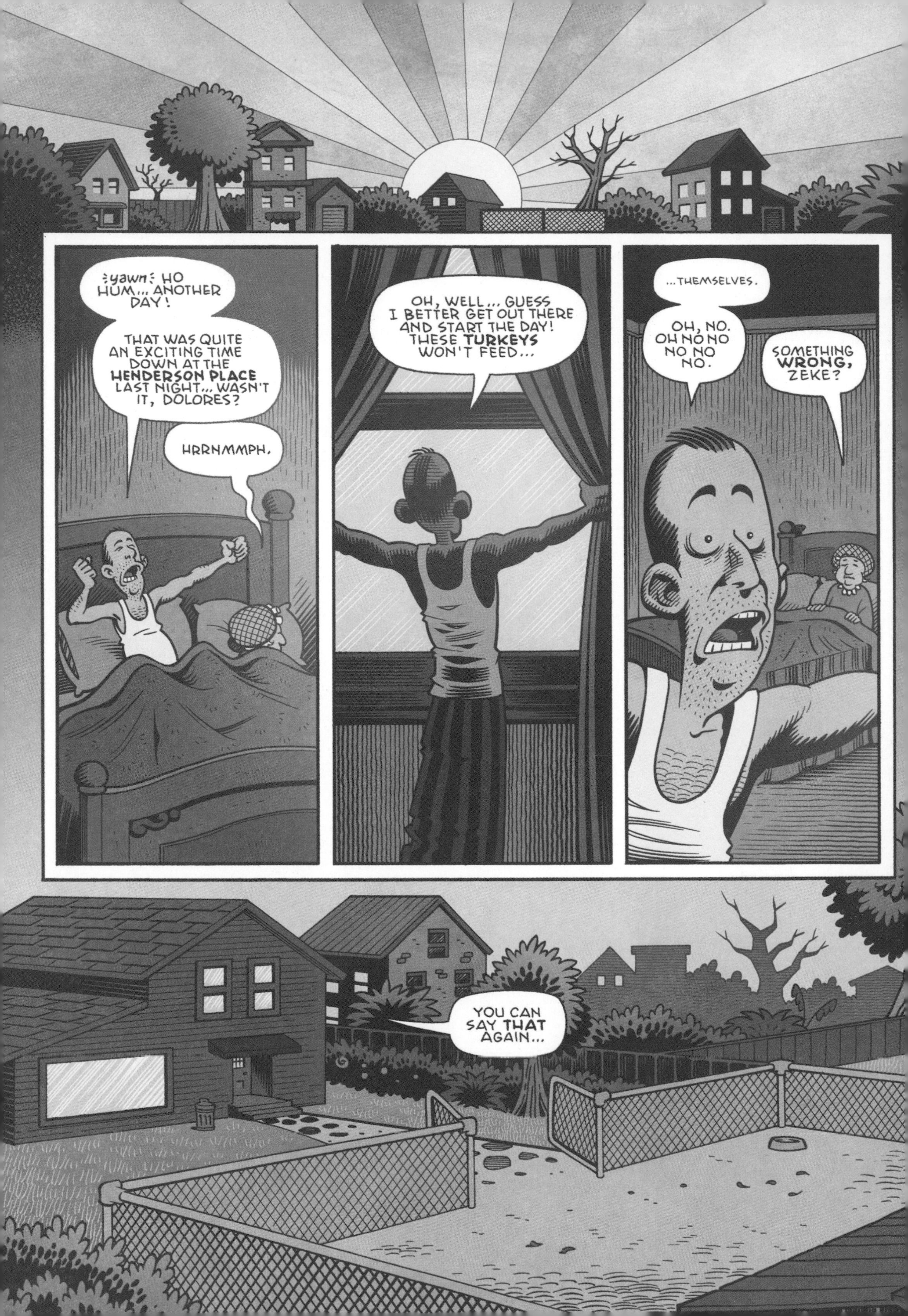

:yawn: HO HUM... ANOTHER DAY!
THAT WAS QUITE AN EXCITING TIME DOWN AT THE **HENDERSON PLACE** LAST NIGHT... WASN'T IT, DOLORES?
HRRNMMPH.
OH, WELL... GUESS I BETTER GET OUT THERE AND START THE DAY! THESE **TURKEYS** WON'T FEED...
...THEMSELVES.
OH, NO. OH NO NO NO NO NO.
SOMETHING **WRONG,** ZEKE?
YOU CAN SAY **THAT** AGAIN...

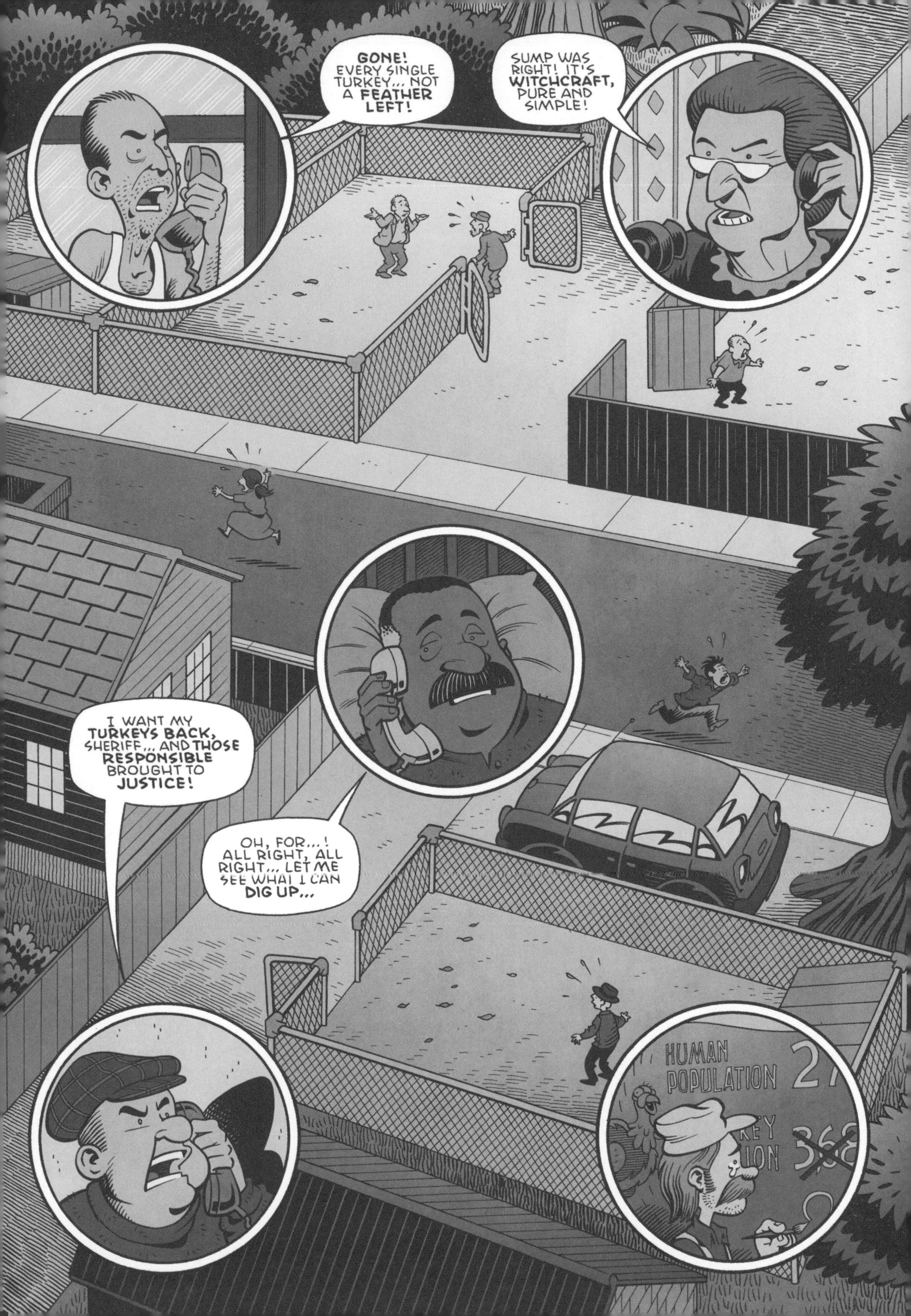
GONE! EVERY SINGLE TURKEY... NOT A FEATHER LEFT!
SUMP WAS RIGHT! IT'S WITCHCRAFT, PURE AND SIMPLE!
I WANT MY TURKEYS BACK, SHERIFF... AND THOSE RESPONSIBLE BROUGHT TO JUSTICE!
OH, FOR...! ALL RIGHT, ALL RIGHT... LET ME SEE WHAT I CAN DIG UP...
HUMAN POPULATION

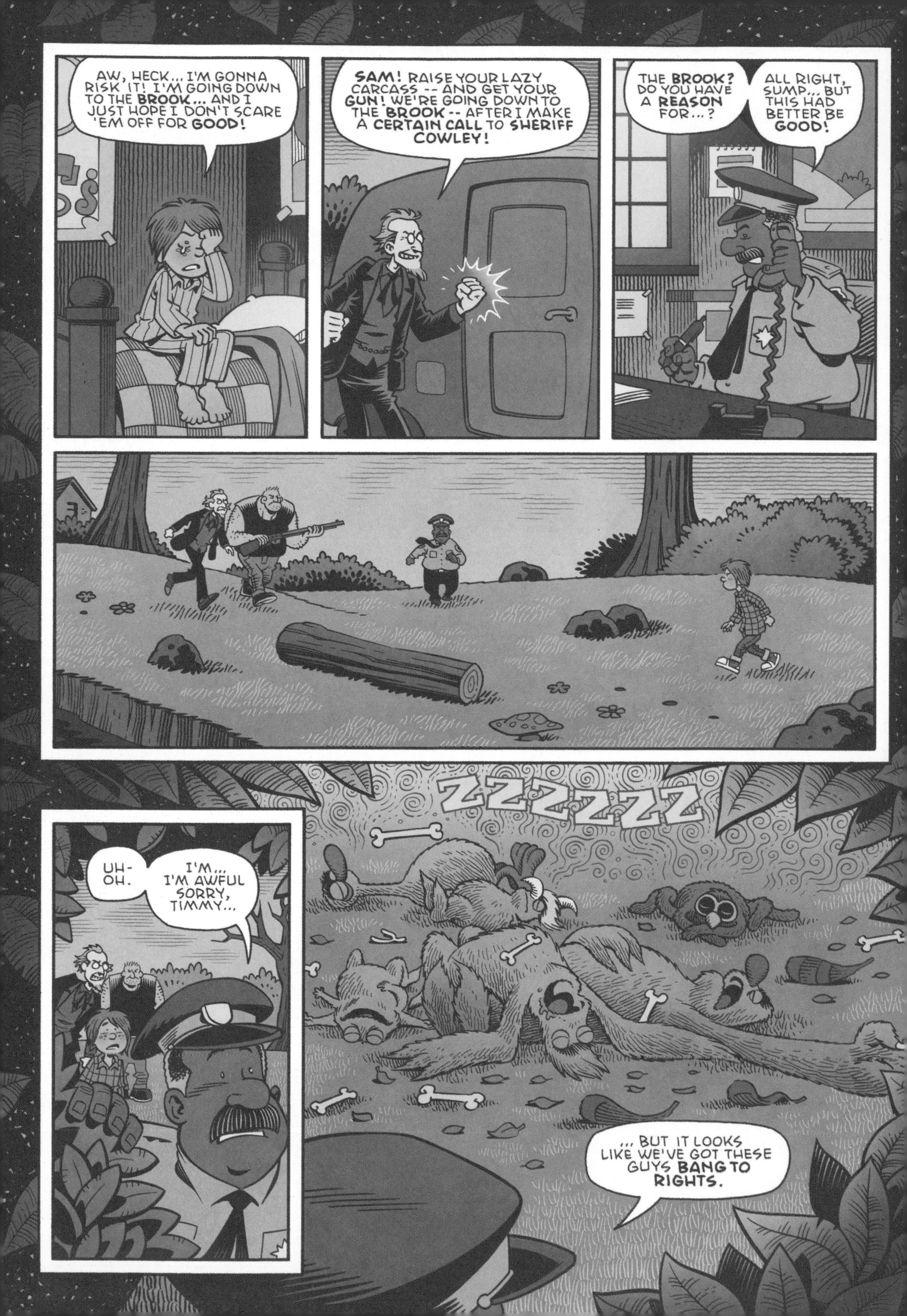
AW, HECK... I'M GONNA RISK IT! I'M GOING DOWN TO THE BROOK... AND I JUST HOPE I DON'T SCARE 'EM OFF FOR GOOD!
SAM! RAISE YOUR LAZY CARCASS -- AND GET YOUR GUN! WE'RE GOING DOWN TO THE BROOK -- AFTER I MAKE A CERTAIN CALL TO SHERIFF COWLEY!
THE BROOK? DO YOU HAVE A REASON FOR...?
ALL RIGHT, SUMP... BUT THIS HAD BETTER BE GOOD!
ZZZZZZ
UH-OH.
I'M... I'M AWFUL SORRY, TIMMY...
... BUT IT LOOKS LIKE WE'VE GOT THESE GUYS BANG TO RIGHTS.

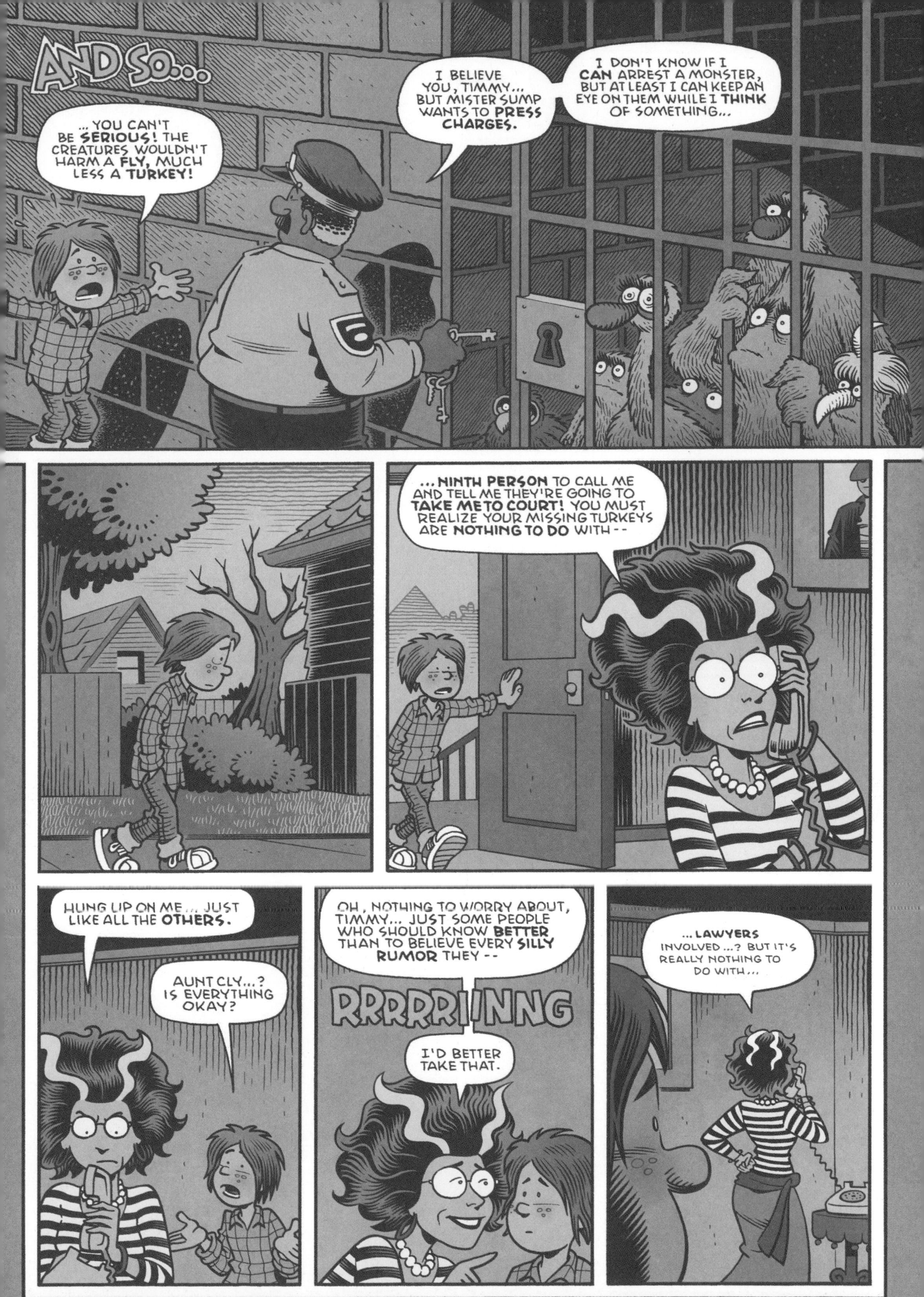
AND SO...
... YOU CAN'T BE SERIOUS! THE CREATURES WOULDN'T HARM A FLY, MUCH LESS A TURKEY!
I BELIEVE YOU, TIMMY... BUT MISTER SUMP WANTS TO PRESS CHARGES.
I DON'T KNOW IF I CAN ARREST A MONSTER, BUT AT LEAST I CAN KEEP AN EYE ON THEM WHILE I THINK OF SOMETHING...
... NINTH PERSON TO CALL ME AND TELL ME THEY'RE GOING TO TAKE ME TO COURT! YOU MUST REALIZE YOUR MISSING TURKEYS ARE NOTHING TO DO WITH --
HUNG UP ON ME... JUST LIKE ALL THE OTHERS.
AUNT CLY...? IS EVERYTHING OKAY?
OH, NOTHING TO WORRY ABOUT, TIMMY... JUST SOME PEOPLE WHO SHOULD KNOW BETTER THAN TO BELIEVE EVERY SILLY RUMOR THEY --
RRRRRIINNG
I'D BETTER TAKE THAT.
... LAWYERS INVOLVED ...? BUT IT'S REALLY NOTHING TO DO WITH...

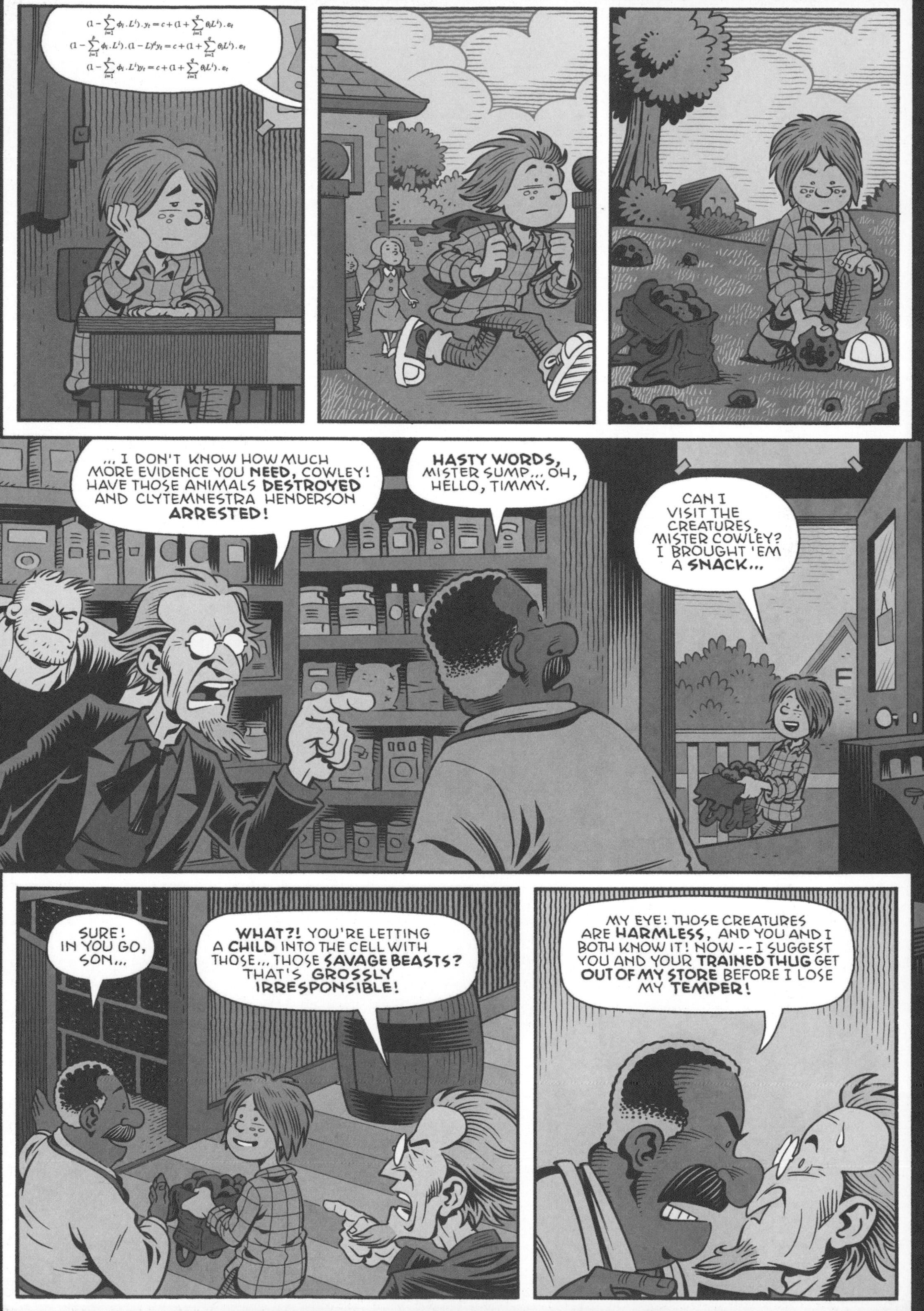
$(1-\sum_{i=1}^{p}\phi_i . L^i) . y_t = c + (1+\sum_{i=1}^{q}\theta_i L^i) . \varepsilon_t$
$(1-\sum_{i=1}^{p}\phi_i . L^i) . (1-L)^d y_t = c + (1+\sum_{i=1}^{q}\theta_i L^i) . \varepsilon_t$
$(1-\sum_{i=1}^{p}\phi_i . L^i) y_t = c + (1+\sum_{i=1}^{q}\theta_i L^i) . \varepsilon_t$
... I DON'T KNOW HOW MUCH MORE EVIDENCE YOU **NEED**, COWLEY! HAVE THOSE ANIMALS **DESTROYED** AND CLYTEMNESTRA HENDERSON **ARRESTED!**
**HASTY WORDS,** MISTER SUMP... OH, HELLO, TIMMY.
CAN I VISIT THE CREATURES, MISTER COWLEY? I BROUGHT 'EM A **SNACK...**
SURE! IN YOU GO, SON...
**WHAT?!** YOU'RE LETTING A **CHILD** INTO THE CELL WITH THOSE... THOSE **SAVAGE BEASTS?** THAT'S **GROSSLY IRRESPONSIBLE!**
MY EYE! THOSE CREATURES ARE **HARMLESS**, AND YOU AND I BOTH KNOW IT! NOW -- I SUGGEST YOU AND YOUR **TRAINED THUG** GET **OUT OF MY STORE** BEFORE I LOSE MY **TEMPER!**

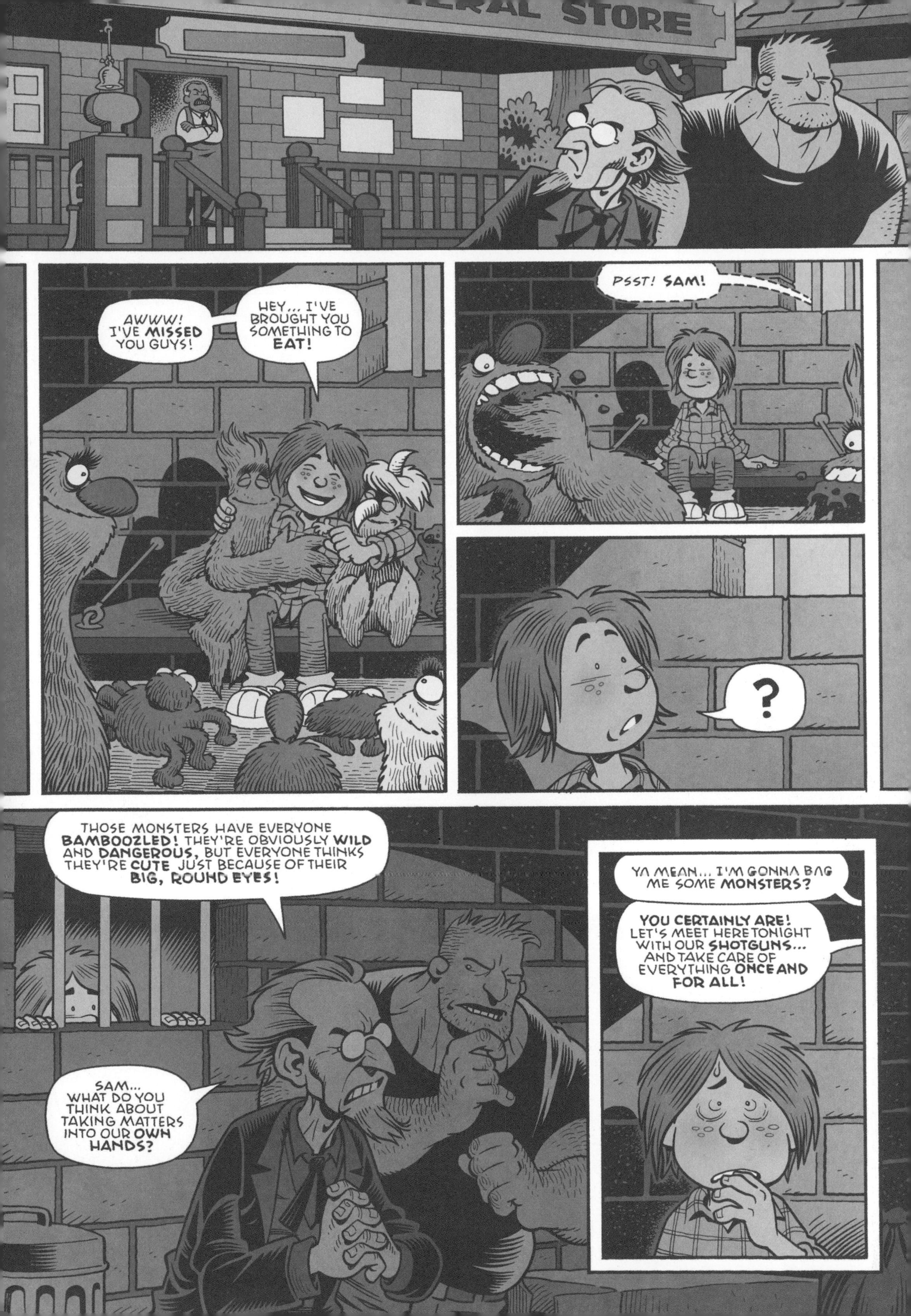
STORE
AWWW! I'VE MISSED YOU GUYS!
HEY... I'VE BROUGHT YOU SOMETHING TO EAT!
PSST! SAM!
?
THOSE MONSTERS HAVE EVERYONE BAMBOOZLED! THEY'RE OBVIOUSLY WILD AND DANGEROUS, BUT EVERYONE THINKS THEY'RE CUTE JUST BECAUSE OF THEIR BIG, ROUND EYES!
SAM... WHAT DO YOU THINK ABOUT TAKING MATTERS INTO OUR OWN HANDS?
YA MEAN... I'M GONNA BAG ME SOME MONSTERS?
YOU CERTAINLY ARE! LET'S MEET HERE TONIGHT WITH OUR SHOTGUNS... AND TAKE CARE OF EVERYTHING ONCE AND FOR ALL!

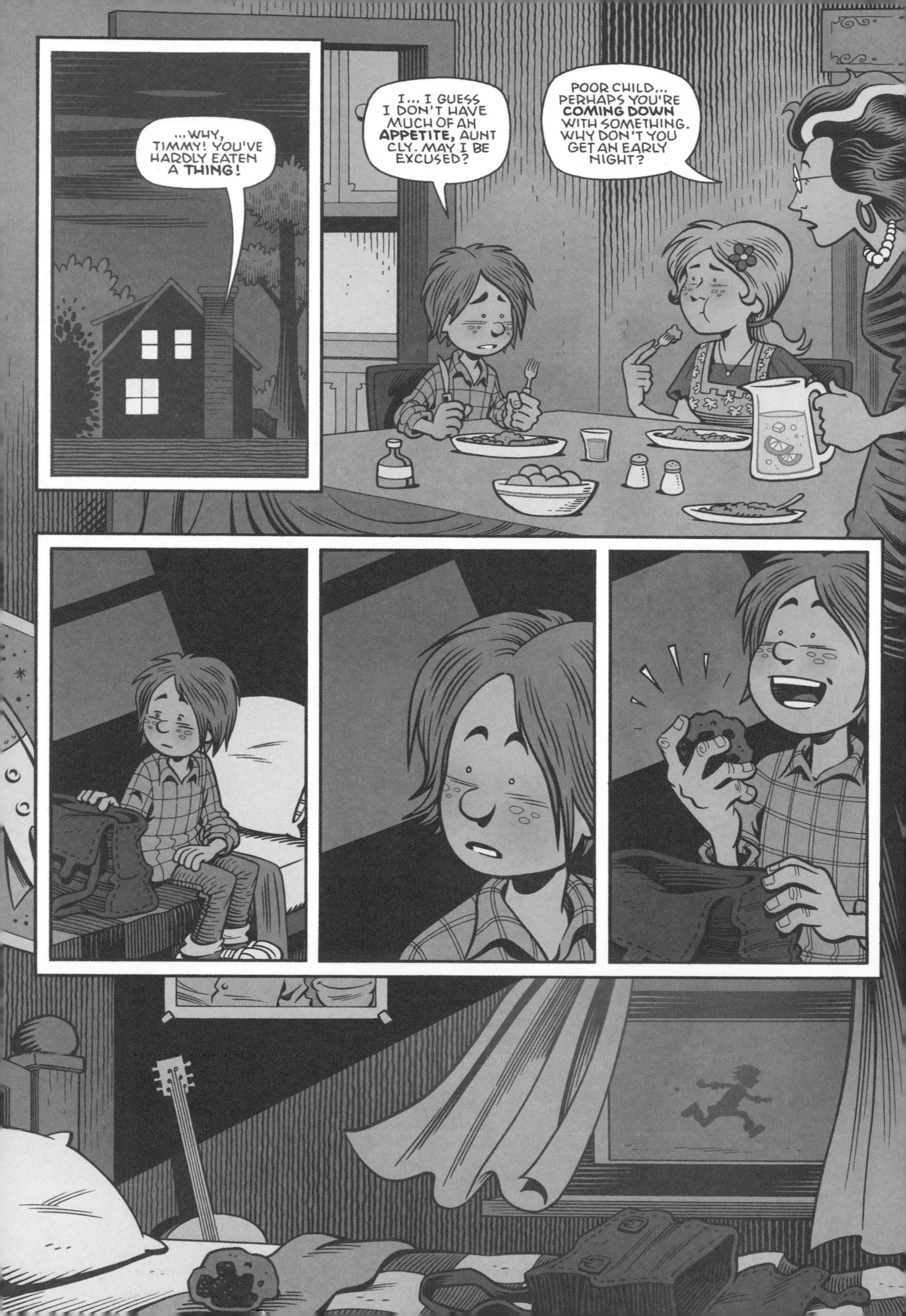

...WHY, TIMMY! YOU'VE HARDLY EATEN A **THING**!
I... I GUESS I DON'T HAVE MUCH OF AN **APPETITE,** AUNT CLY. MAY I BE EXCUSED?
POOR CHILD... PERHAPS YOU'RE **COMING DOWN** WITH SOMETHING. WHY DON'T YOU GET AN EARLY NIGHT?

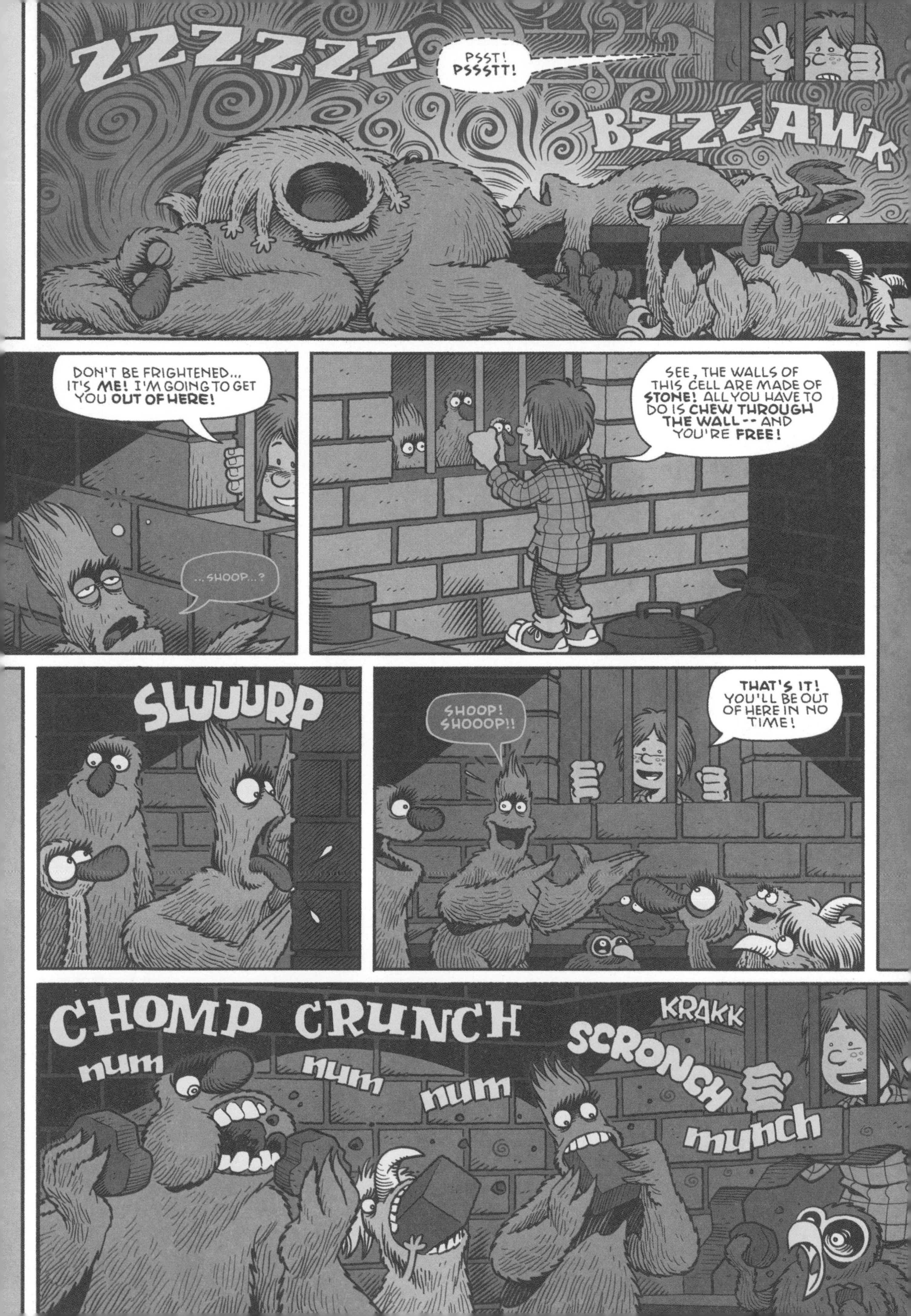
ZZZZZZ
PSST! PSSSTT!
BZZZAWK
DON'T BE FRIGHTENED... IT'S ME! I'M GOING TO GET YOU OUT OF HERE!
...SHOOP...?
SEE, THE WALLS OF THIS CELL ARE MADE OF STONE! ALL YOU HAVE TO DO IS CHEW THROUGH THE WALL-- AND YOU'RE FREE!
SLUUURP
SHOOP! SHOOOP!!
THAT'S IT! YOU'LL BE OUT OF HERE IN NO TIME!
CHOMP CRUNCH
KRAKK
SCRONCH
num num num
munch

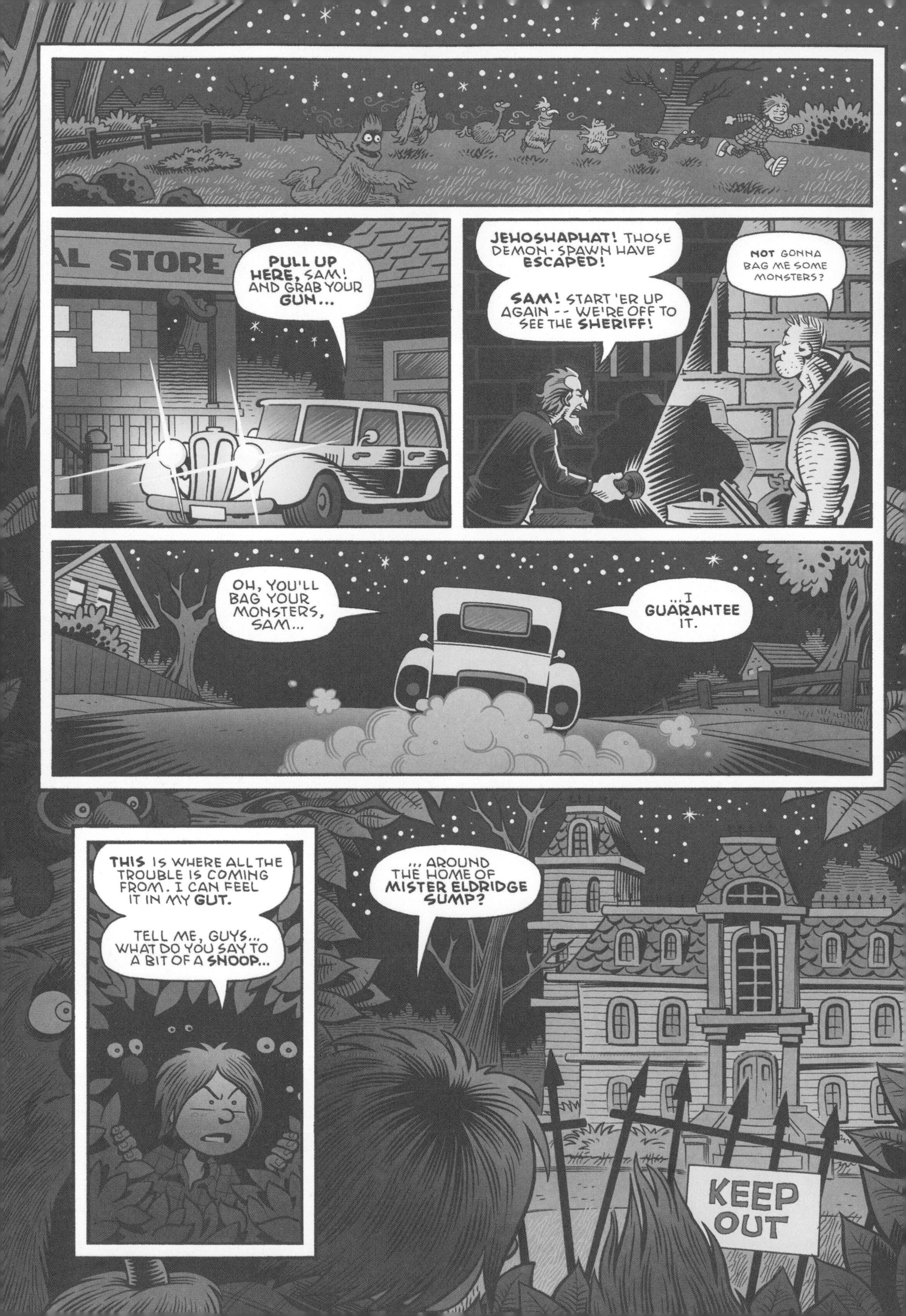
AL STORE
PULL UP HERE, SAM! AND GRAB YOUR GUN...
JEHOSHAPHAT! THOSE DEMON-SPAWN HAVE ESCAPED!
SAM! START 'ER UP AGAIN -- WE'RE OFF TO SEE THE SHERIFF!
NOT GONNA BAG ME SOME MONSTERS?
OH, YOU'LL BAG YOUR MONSTERS, SAM...
...I GUARANTEE IT.
THIS IS WHERE ALL THE TROUBLE IS COMING FROM. I CAN FEEL IT IN MY GUT.
TELL ME, GUYS... WHAT DO YOU SAY TO A BIT OF A SNOOP...
...AROUND THE HOME OF MISTER ELDRIDGE SUMP?
KEEP OUT

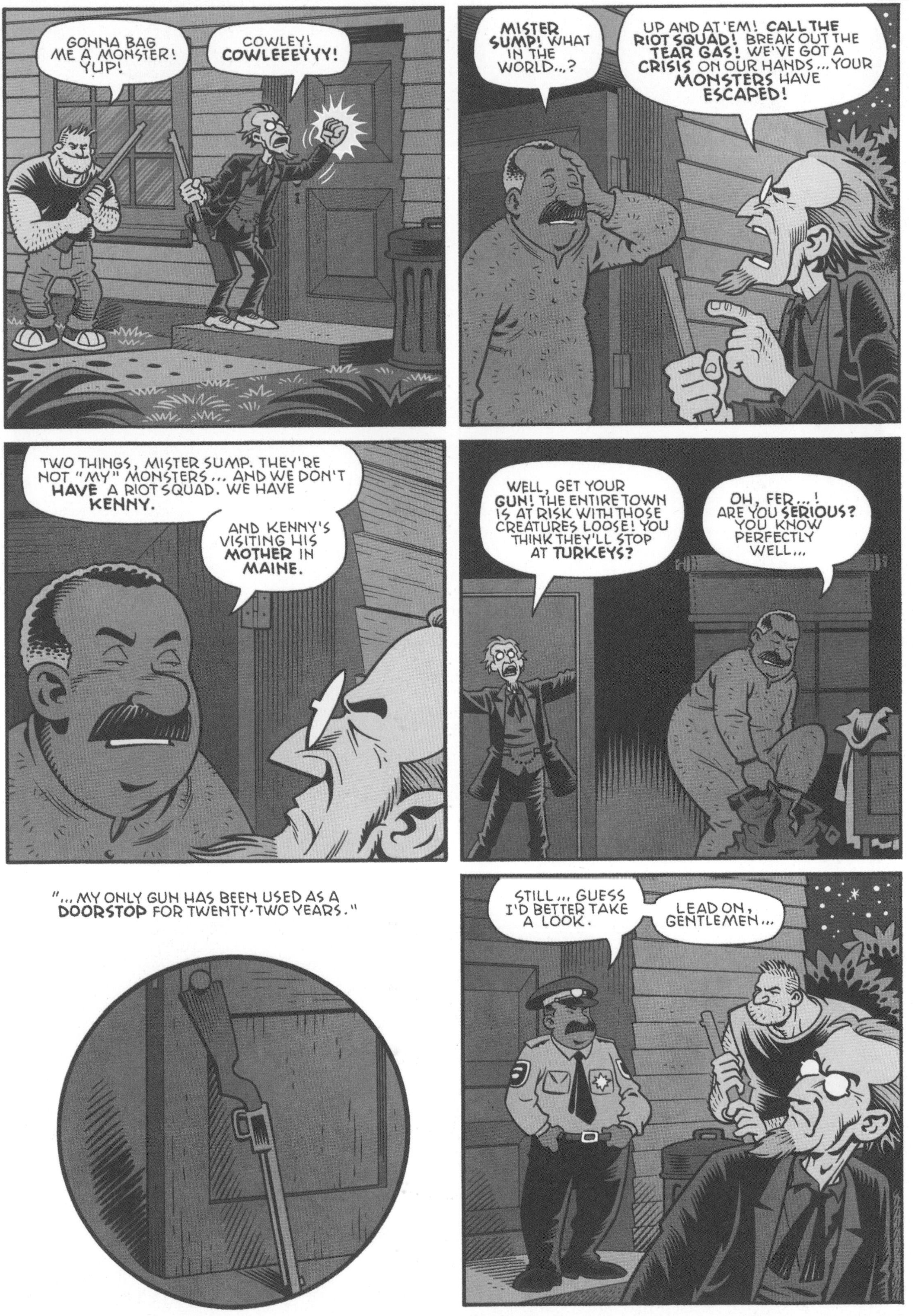
GONNA BAG ME A MONSTER! YUP!
COWLEY! COWLEEEYYY!
MISTER SUMP! WHAT IN THE WORLD...?
UP AND AT 'EM! CALL THE RIOT SQUAD! BREAK OUT THE TEAR GAS! WE'VE GOT A CRISIS ON OUR HANDS... YOUR MONSTERS HAVE ESCAPED!
TWO THINGS, MISTER SUMP. THEY'RE NOT "MY" MONSTERS... AND WE DON'T HAVE A RIOT SQUAD. WE HAVE KENNY.
AND KENNY'S VISITING HIS MOTHER IN MAINE.
WELL, GET YOUR GUN! THE ENTIRE TOWN IS AT RISK WITH THOSE CREATURES LOOSE! YOU THINK THEY'LL STOP AT TURKEYS?
OH, FER...! ARE YOU SERIOUS? YOU KNOW PERFECTLY WELL...
"...MY ONLY GUN HAS BEEN USED AS A DOORSTOP FOR TWENTY-TWO YEARS."
STILL... GUESS I'D BETTER TAKE A LOOK.
LEAD ON, GENTLEMEN...

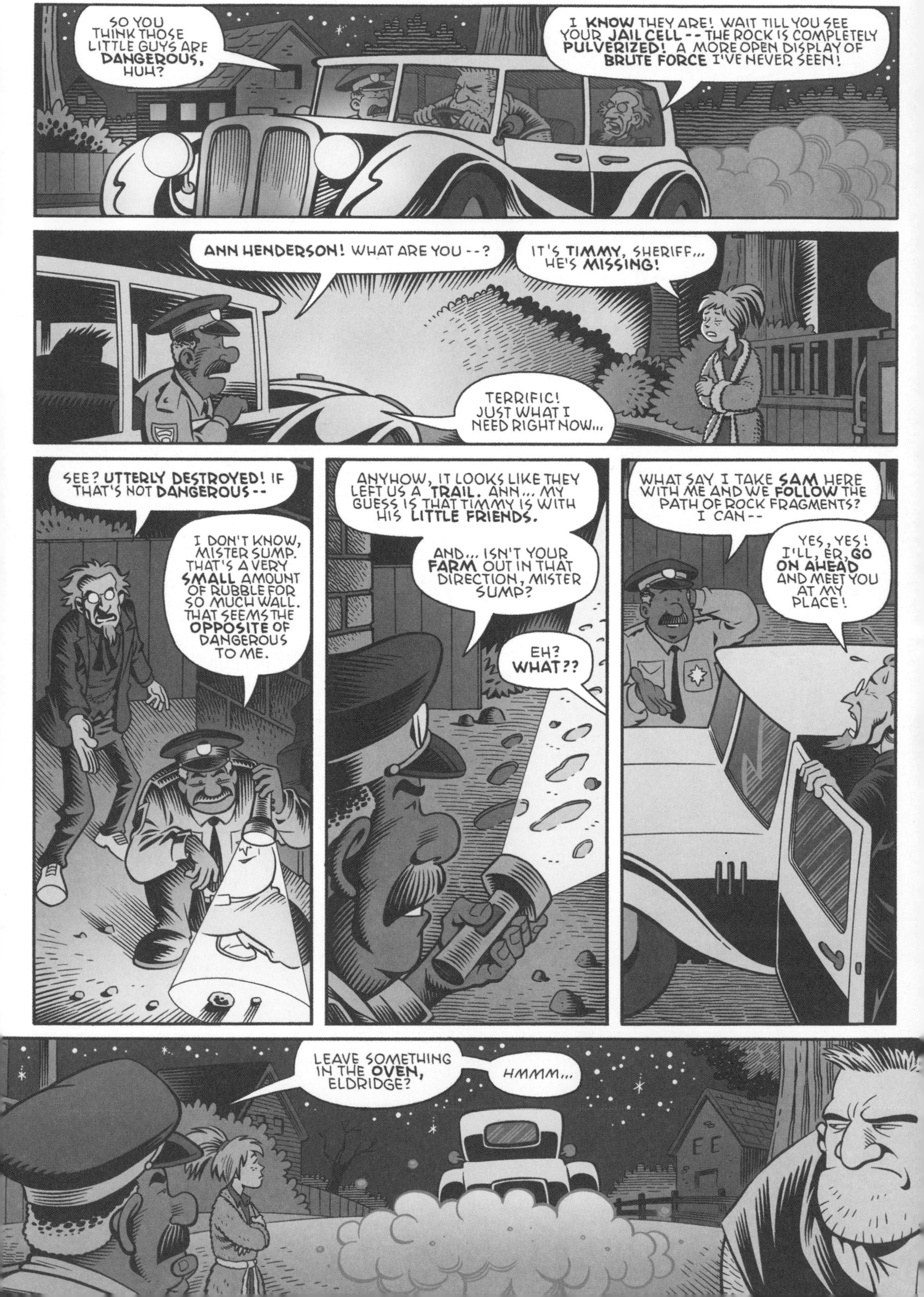

SO YOU THINK THOSE LITTLE GUYS ARE **DANGEROUS,** HUH?
I **KNOW** THEY ARE! WAIT TILL YOU SEE YOUR **JAIL CELL** -- THE ROCK IS COMPLETELY **PULVERIZED!** A MORE OPEN DISPLAY OF **BRUTE FORCE** I'VE NEVER SEEN!
**ANN HENDERSON!** WHAT ARE YOU --?
IT'S **TIMMY,** SHERIFF... HE'S **MISSING!**
TERRIFIC! JUST WHAT I NEED RIGHT NOW...
SEE? **UTTERLY DESTROYED!** IF THAT'S NOT **DANGEROUS** --
I DON'T KNOW, MISTER SUMP. THAT'S A VERY **SMALL** AMOUNT OF RUBBLE FOR SO MUCH WALL. THAT SEEMS THE **OPPOSITE** OF DANGEROUS TO ME.
ANYHOW, IT LOOKS LIKE THEY LEFT US A **TRAIL.** ANN... MY GUESS IS THAT TIMMY IS WITH HIS **LITTLE FRIENDS.**
AND... ISN'T YOUR **FARM** OUT IN THAT DIRECTION, MISTER SUMP?
EH? **WHAT??**
WHAT SAY I TAKE **SAM** HERE WITH ME AND WE **FOLLOW** THE PATH OF ROCK FRAGMENTS? I CAN --
YES, YES! I'LL, ER, **GO ON AHEAD** AND MEET YOU AT MY PLACE!
LEAVE SOMETHING IN THE **OVEN,** ELDRIDGE?
*HMMM...*

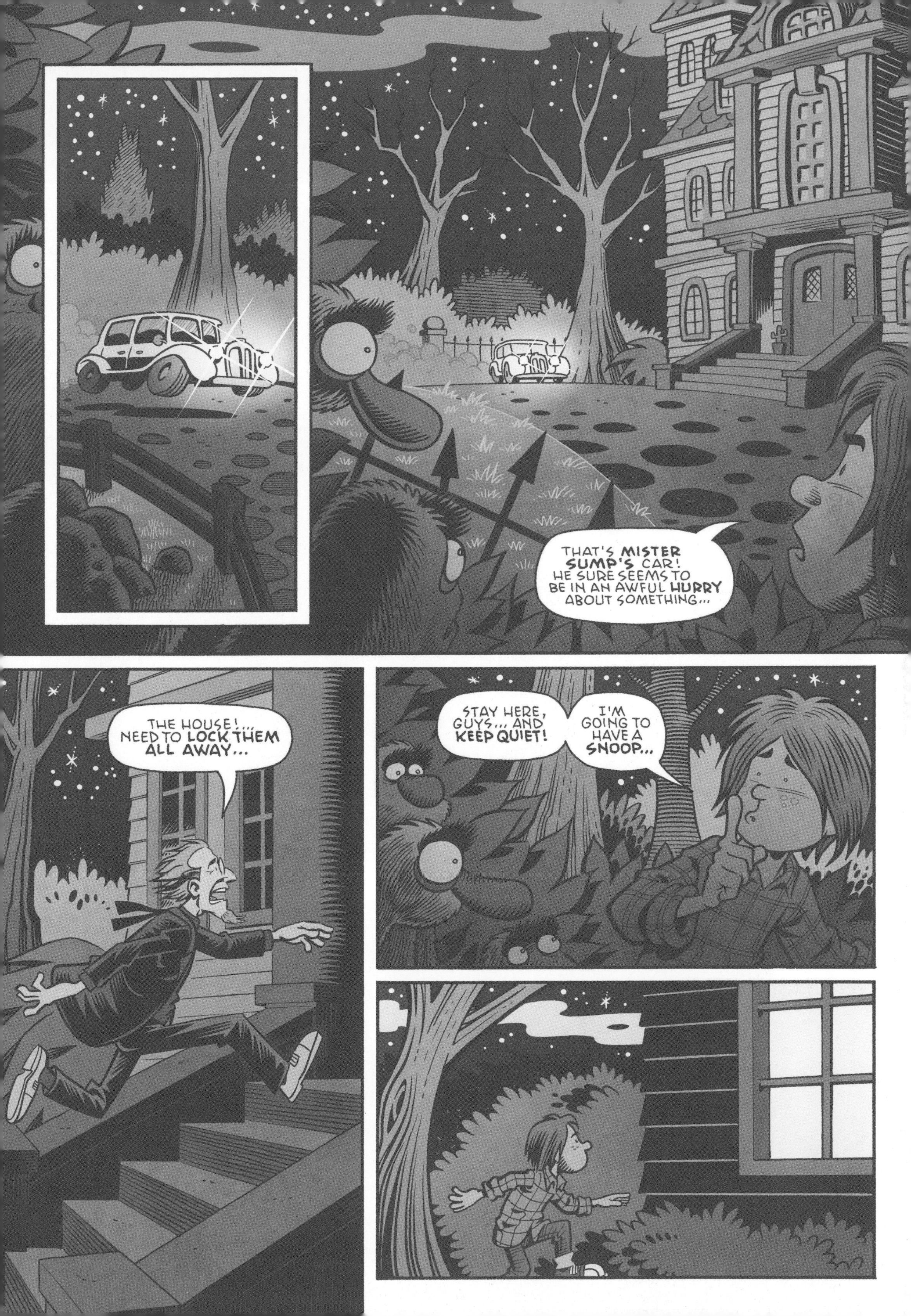
THAT'S MISTER SUMP'S CAR! HE SURE SEEMS TO BE IN AN AWFUL HURRY ABOUT SOMETHING...
THE HOUSE!... NEED TO LOCK THEM ALL AWAY...
STAY HERE, GUYS... AND KEEP QUIET!
I'M GOING TO HAVE A SNOOP...

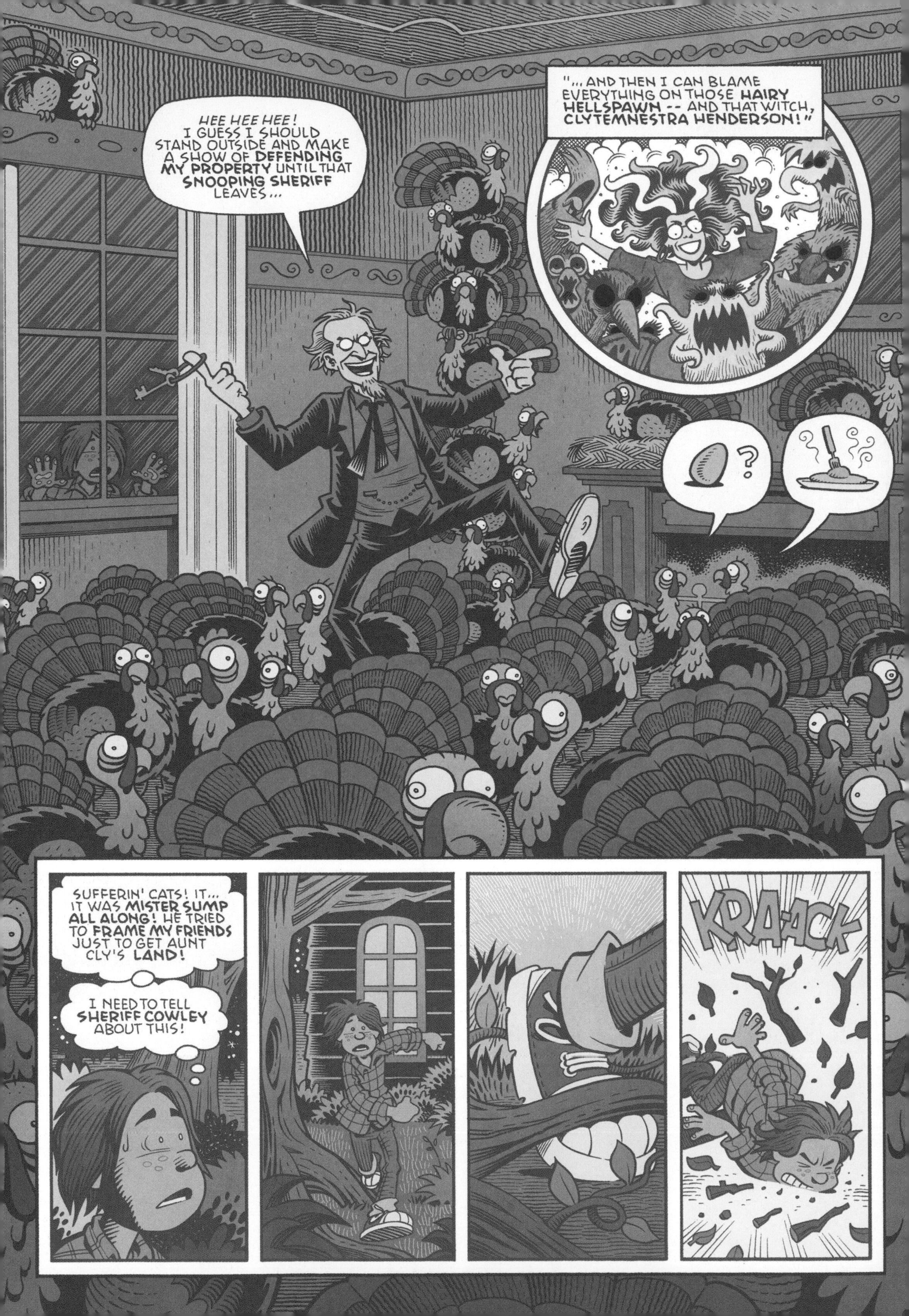

HEE HEE HEE! I GUESS I SHOULD STAND OUTSIDE AND MAKE A SHOW OF DEFENDING MY PROPERTY UNTIL THAT SNOOPING SHERIFF LEAVES...
"...AND THEN I CAN BLAME EVERYTHING ON THOSE HAIRY HELLSPAWN -- AND THAT WITCH, CLYTEMNESTRA HENDERSON!"
?
SUFFERIN' CATS! IT... IT WAS MISTER SUMP ALL ALONG! HE TRIED TO FRAME MY FRIENDS JUST TO GET AUNT CLY'S LAND!
I NEED TO TELL SHERIFF COWLEY ABOUT THIS!
KRA-ACK

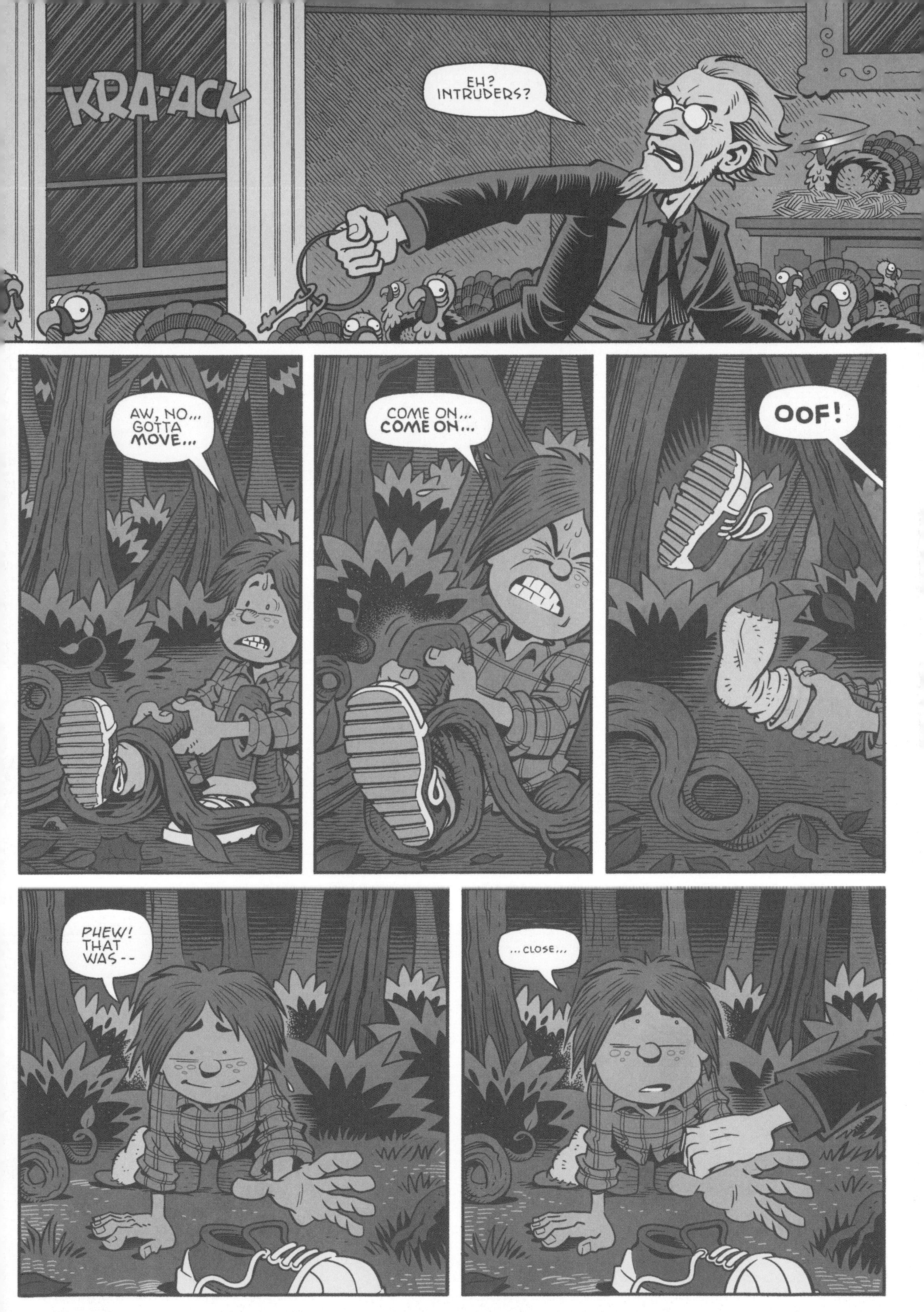
KRA-ACK
EH? INTRUDERS?
AW, NO... GOTTA MOVE...
COME ON... COME ON...
OOF!
PHEW! THAT WAS--
...CLOSE...

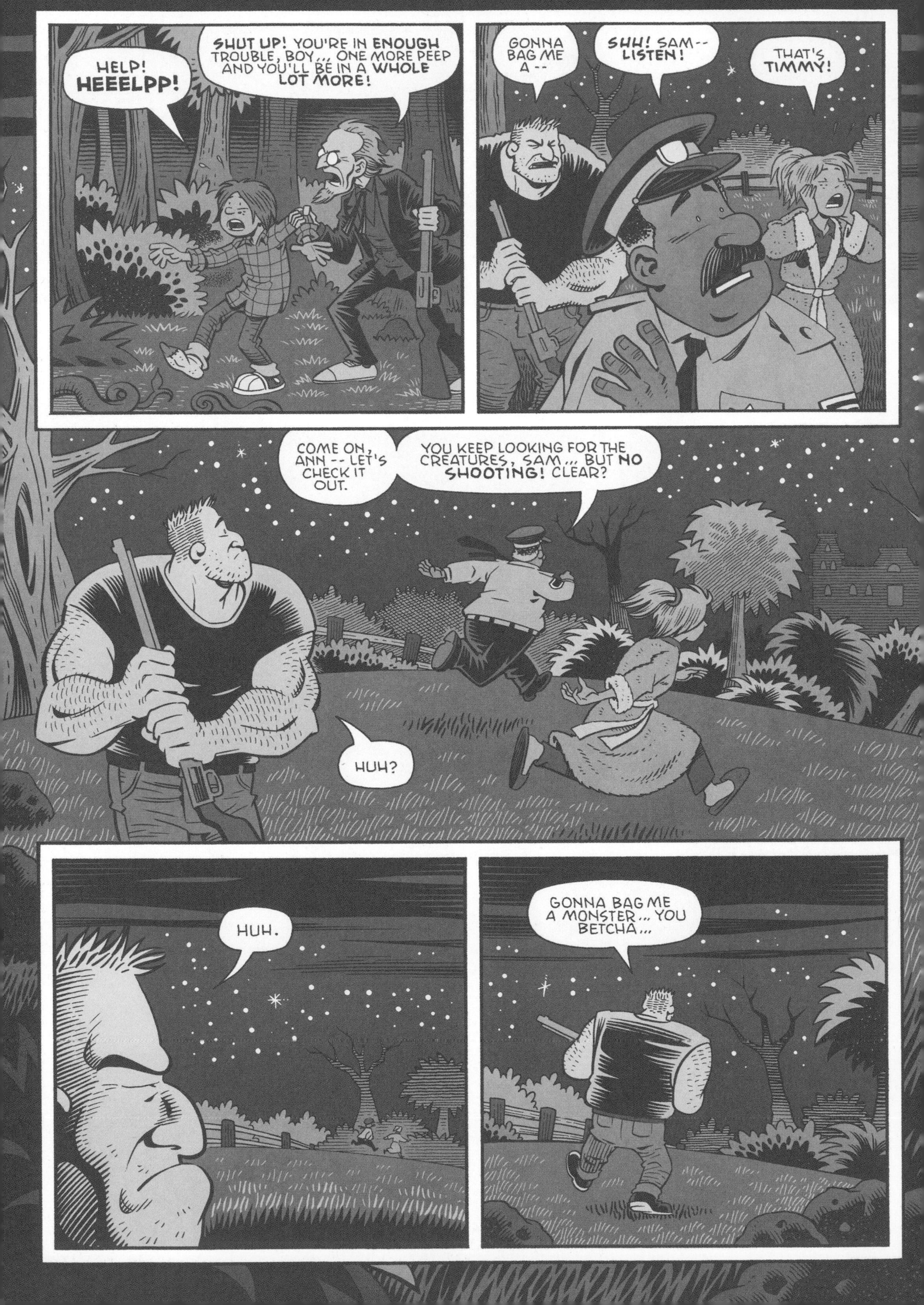
HELP! HEEELPP!
SHUT UP! YOU'RE IN ENOUGH TROUBLE, BOY... ONE MORE PEEP AND YOU'LL BE IN A WHOLE LOT MORE!
GONNA BAG ME A --
SHH! SAM-- LISTEN!
THAT'S TIMMY!
COME ON, ANN -- LET'S CHECK IT OUT.
YOU KEEP LOOKING FOR THE CREATURES, SAM... BUT NO SHOOTING! CLEAR?
HUH?
HUH.
GONNA BAG ME A MONSTER... YOU BETCHA...

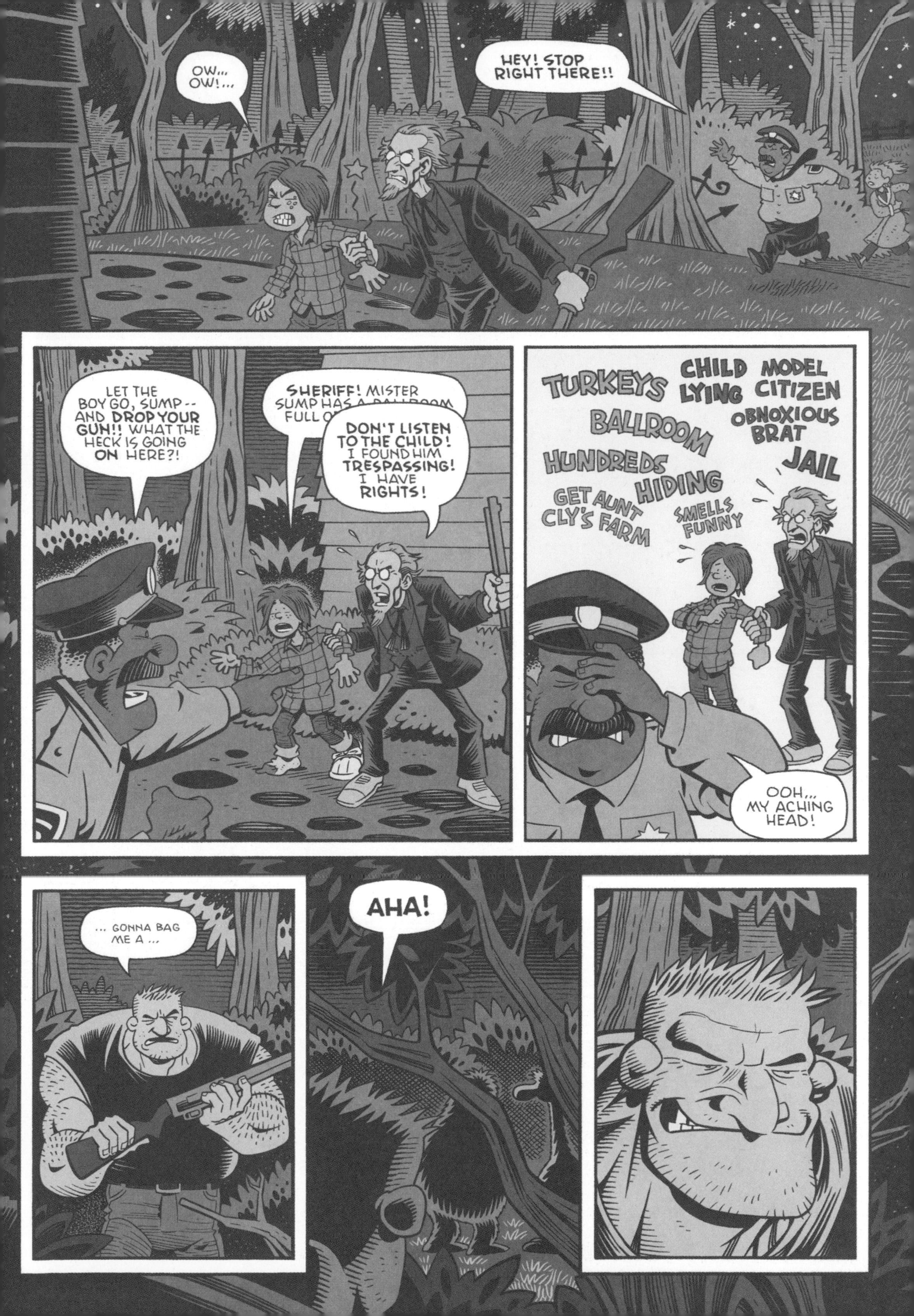
OW... OW!...
HEY! STOP RIGHT THERE!!
LET THE BOY GO, SUMP-- AND DROP YOUR GUN!! WHAT THE HECK IS GOING ON HERE?!
SHERIFF! MISTER SUMP HAS A
DON'T LISTEN TO THE CHILD! I FOUND HIM TRESPASSING! I HAVE RIGHTS!
TURKEYS
CHILD LYING
MODEL CITIZEN
BALLROOM
OBNOXIOUS BRAT
HUNDREDS
HIDING
JAIL
GET AUNT CLY'S FARM
SMELLS FUNNY
OOH... MY ACHING HEAD!
... GONNA BAG ME A ...
AHA!

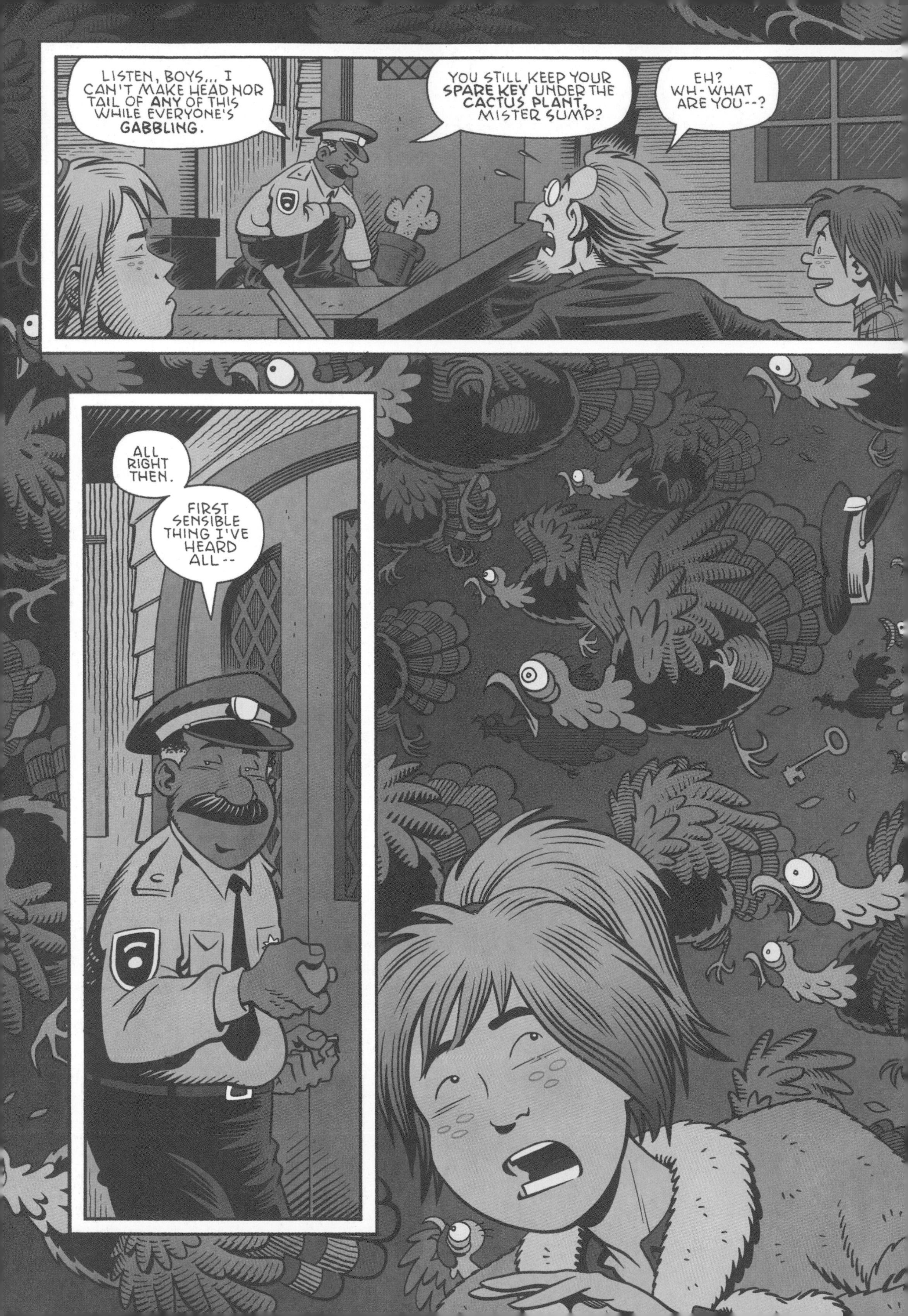

LISTEN, BOYS... I CAN'T MAKE HEAD NOR TAIL OF ANY OF THIS WHILE EVERYONE'S GABBLING.
YOU STILL KEEP YOUR SPARE KEY UNDER THE CACTUS PLANT, MISTER SUMP?
EH? WH-WHAT ARE YOU--?
ALL RIGHT THEN.
FIRST SENSIBLE THING I'VE HEARD ALL--

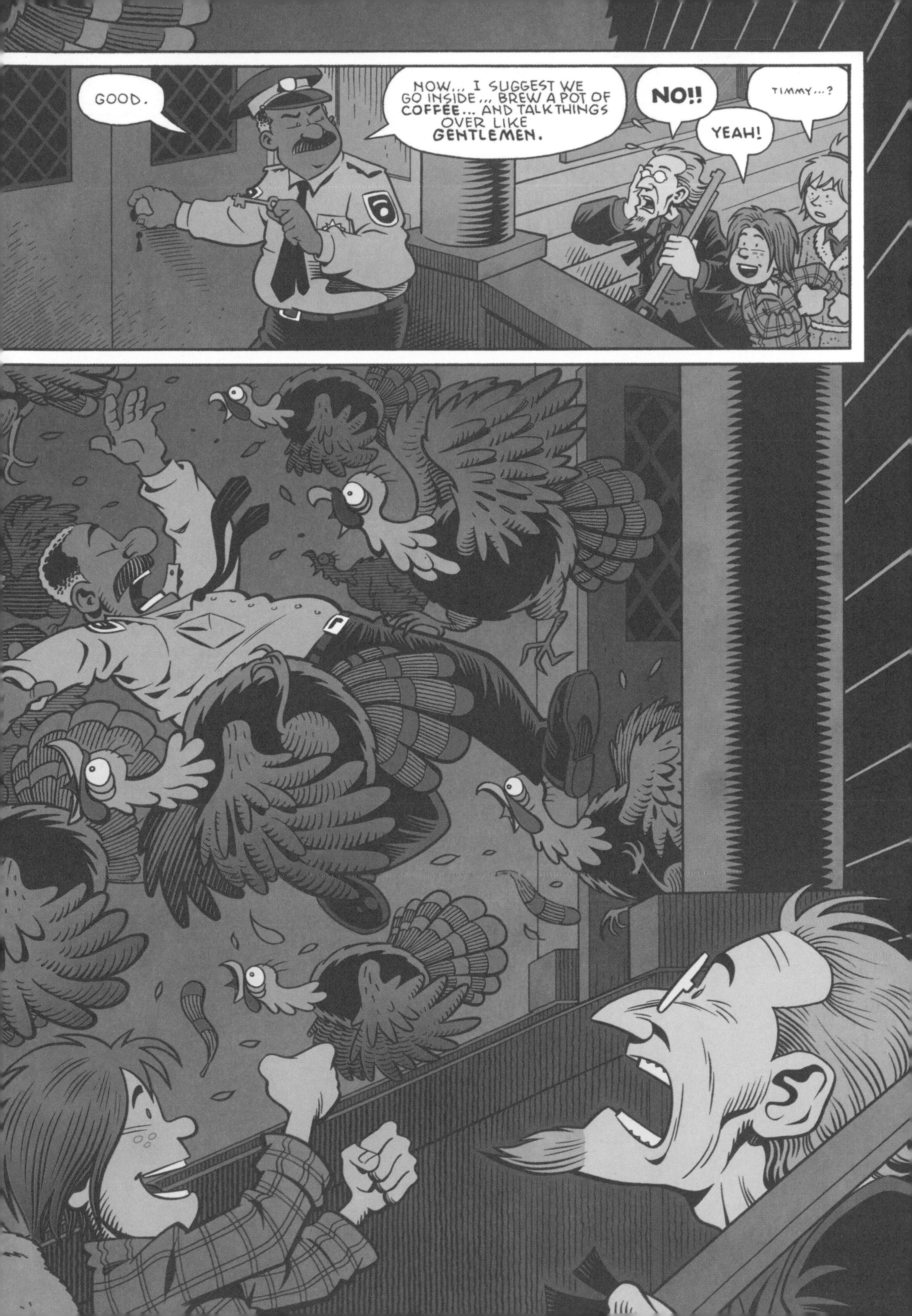
GOOD.
NOW... I SUGGEST WE GO INSIDE... BREW A POT OF COFFEE... AND TALK THINGS OVER LIKE GENTLEMEN.
NO!!
YEAH!
TIMMY...?

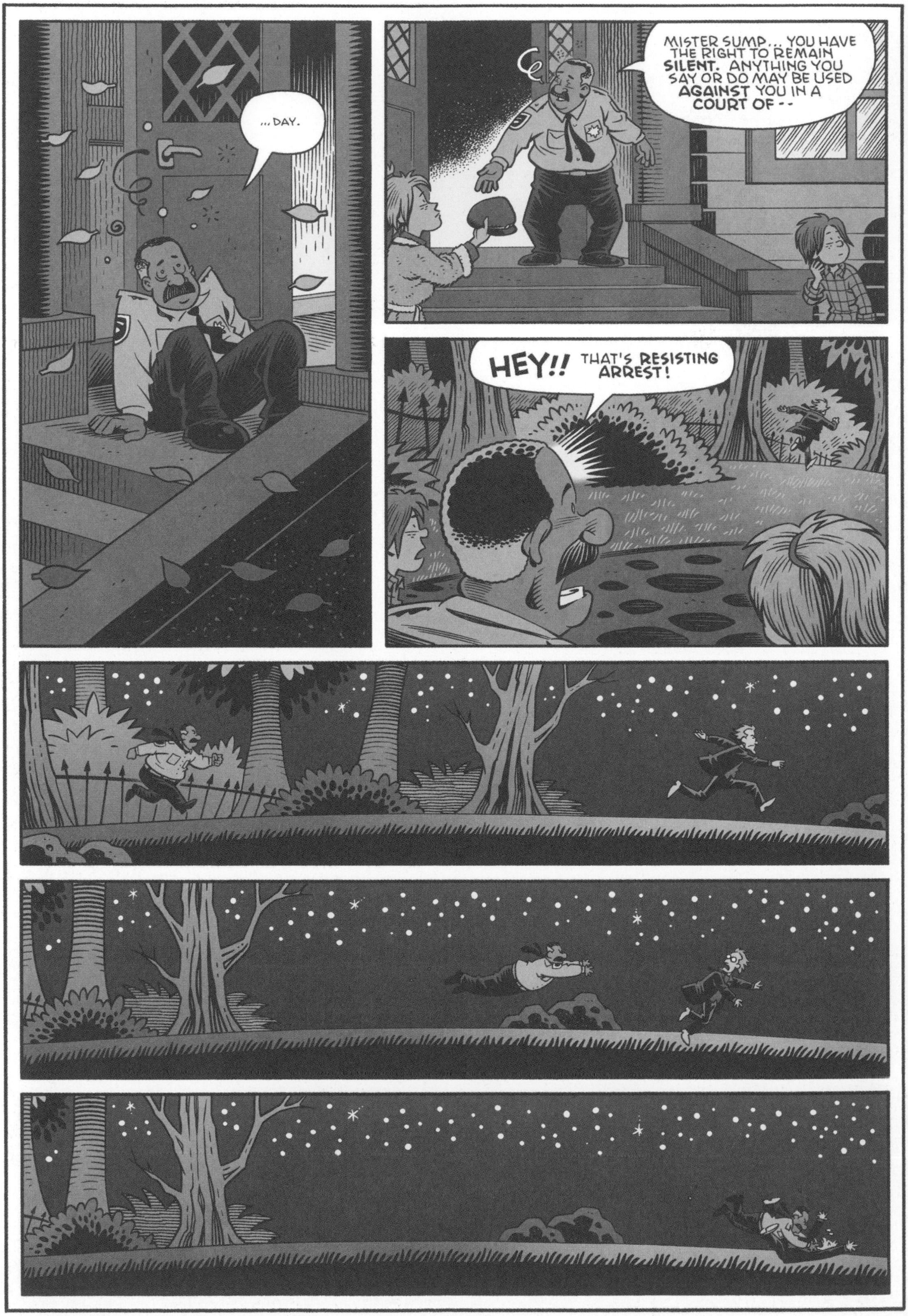
...DAY.
MISTER SUMP... YOU HAVE THE RIGHT TO REMAIN SILENT. ANYTHING YOU SAY OR DO MAY BE USED AGAINST YOU IN A COURT OF --
HEY!! THAT'S RESISTING ARREST!

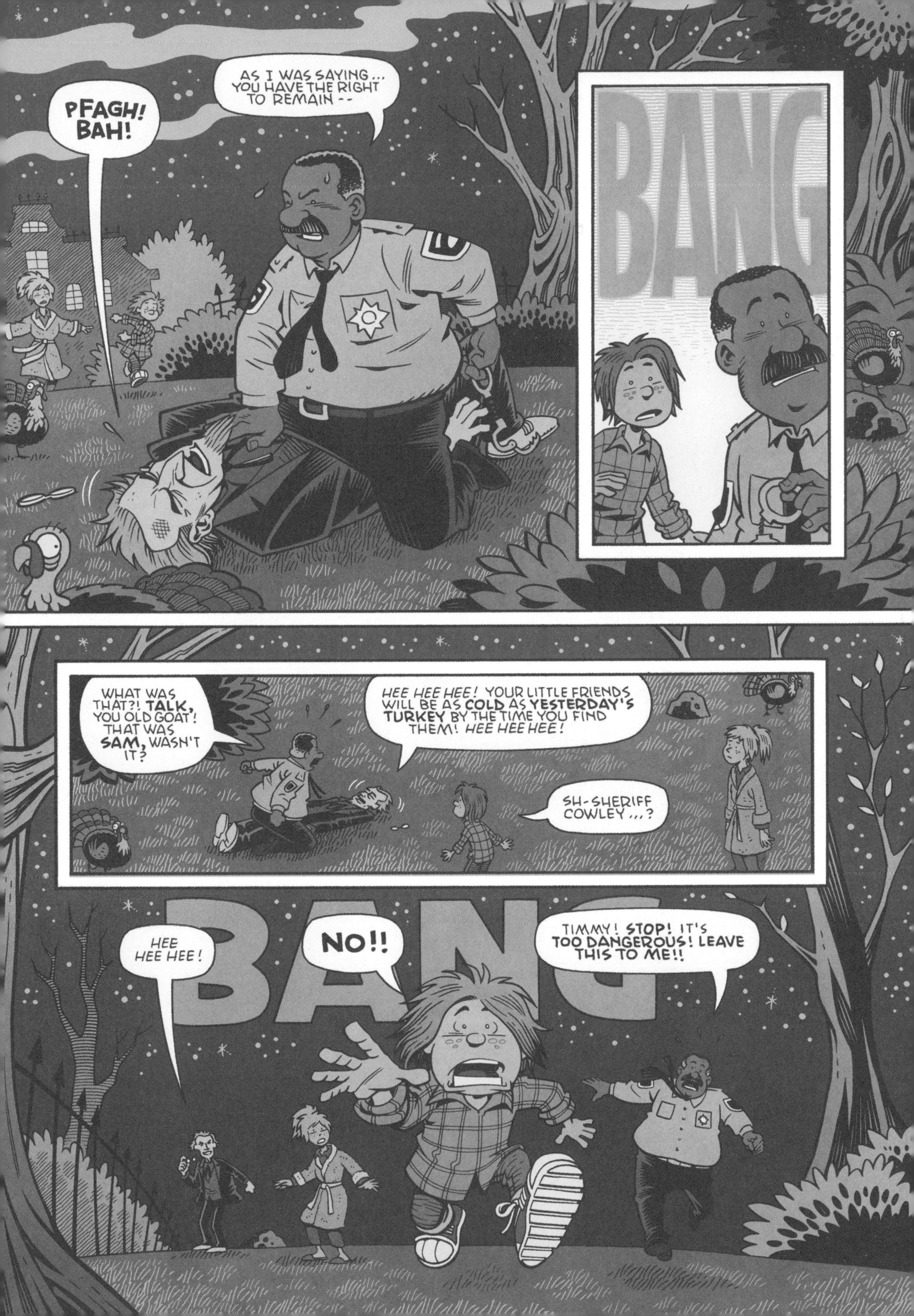
PFAGH! BAH!
AS I WAS SAYING ... YOU HAVE THE RIGHT TO REMAIN --
BANG
WHAT WAS THAT?! TALK, YOU OLD GOAT! THAT WAS SAM, WASN'T IT?
HEE HEE HEE! YOUR LITTLE FRIENDS WILL BE AS COLD AS YESTERDAY'S TURKEY BY THE TIME YOU FIND THEM! HEE HEE HEE!
SH-SHERIFF COWLEY ...?
BANG
HEE HEE HEE!
NO!!
TIMMY! STOP! IT'S TOO DANGEROUS! LEAVE THIS TO ME!!

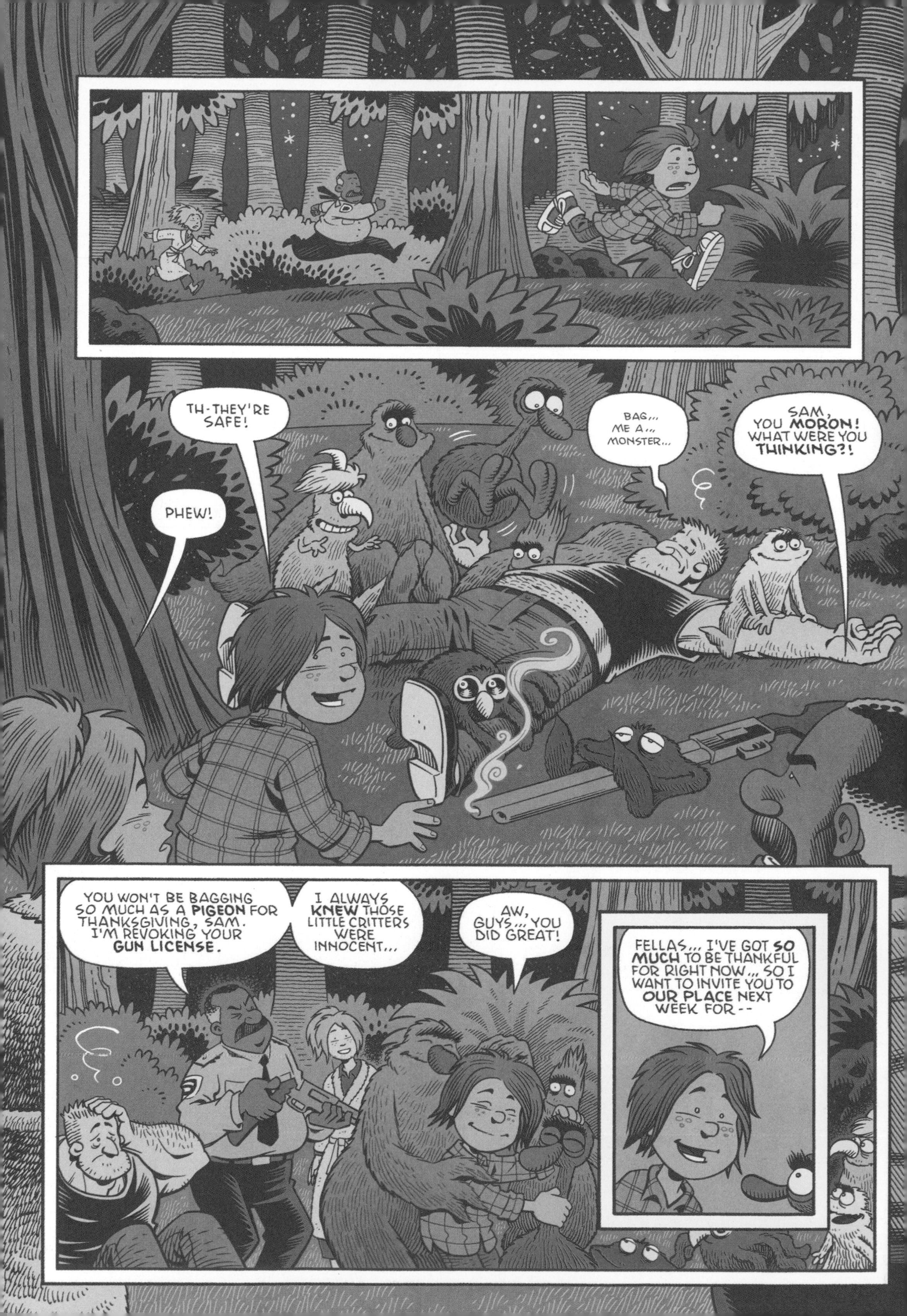
TH-THEY'RE SAFE!
PHEW!
BAG... ME A... MONSTER...
SAM, YOU MORON! WHAT WERE YOU THINKING?!
YOU WON'T BE BAGGING SO MUCH AS A PIGEON FOR THANKSGIVING, SAM. I'M REVOKING YOUR GUN LICENSE.
I ALWAYS KNEW THOSE LITTLE CRITTERS WERE INNOCENT...
AW, GUYS... YOU DID GREAT!
FELLAS... I'VE GOT SO MUCH TO BE THANKFUL FOR RIGHT NOW... SO I WANT TO INVITE YOU TO OUR PLACE NEXT WEEK FOR --

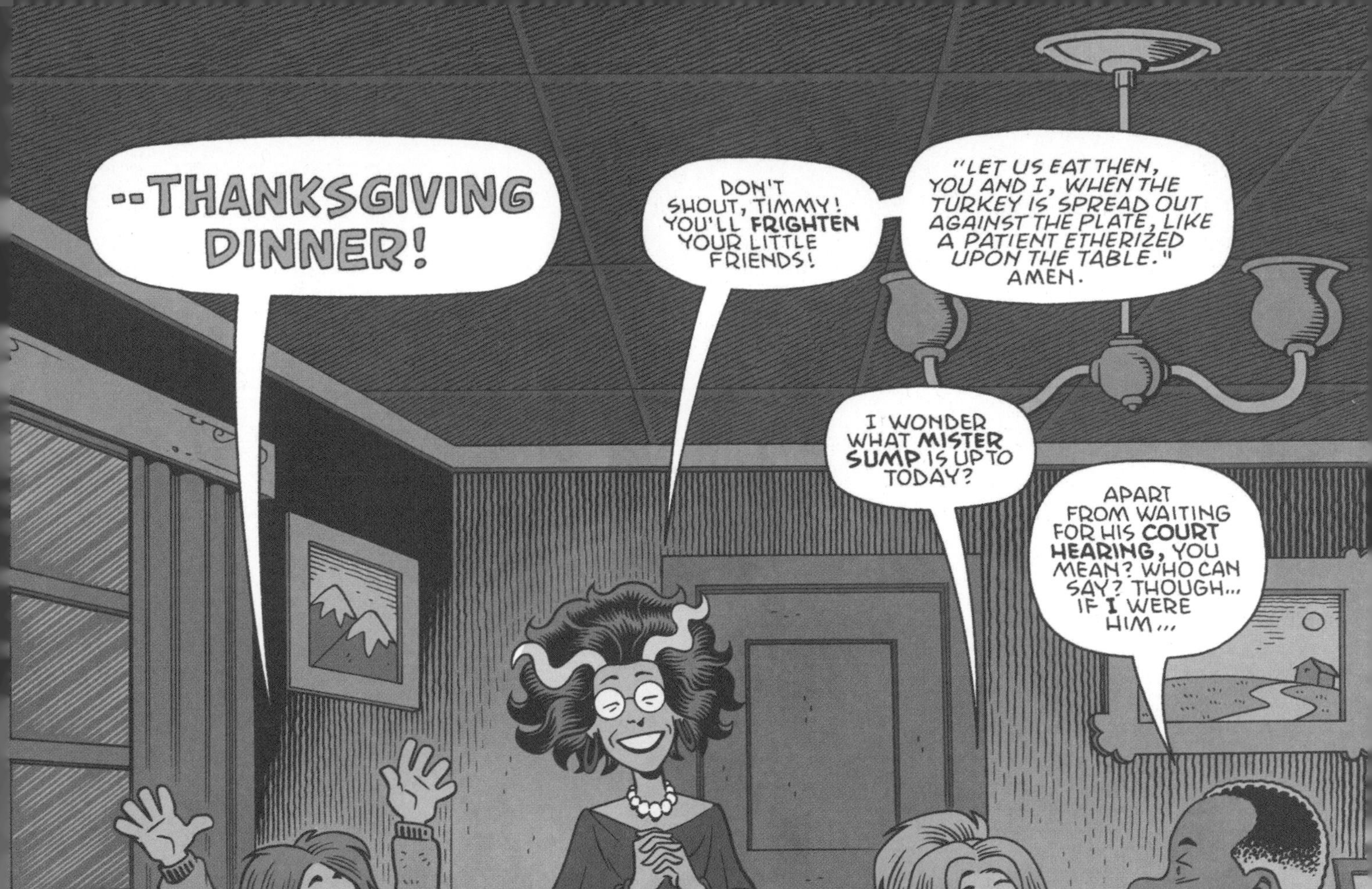
--THANKSGIVING DINNER!
DON'T SHOUT, TIMMY! YOU'LL FRIGHTEN YOUR LITTLE FRIENDS!
"LET US EAT THEN, YOU AND I, WHEN THE TURKEY IS SPREAD OUT AGAINST THE PLATE, LIKE A PATIENT ETHERIZED UPON THE TABLE." AMEN.
I WONDER WHAT MISTER SUMP IS UP TO TODAY?
APART FROM WAITING FOR HIS COURT HEARING, YOU MEAN? WHO CAN SAY? THOUGH... IF I WERE HIM...

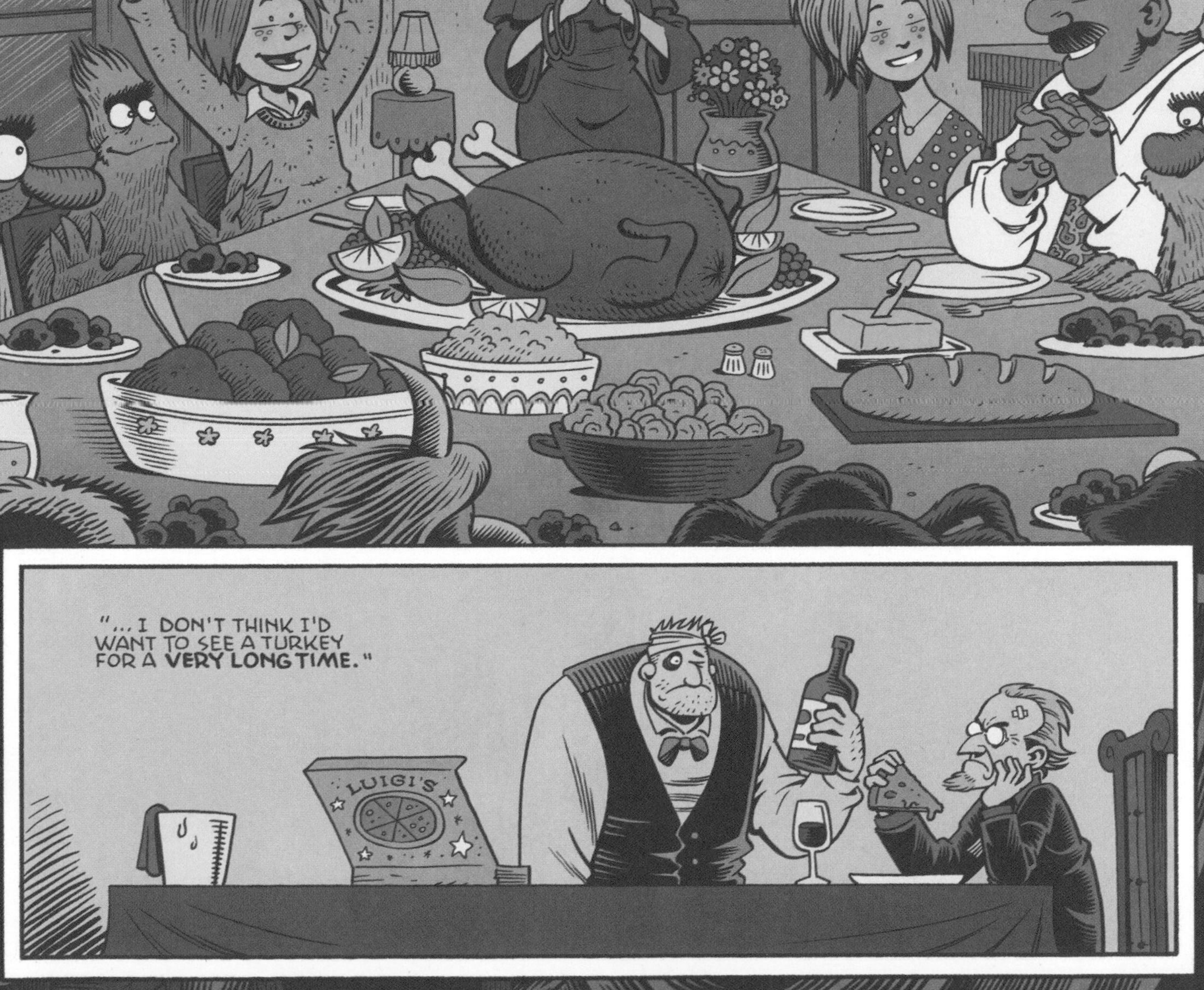
"... I DON'T THINK I'D WANT TO SEE A TURKEY FOR A VERY LONG TIME."
LUIGI'S

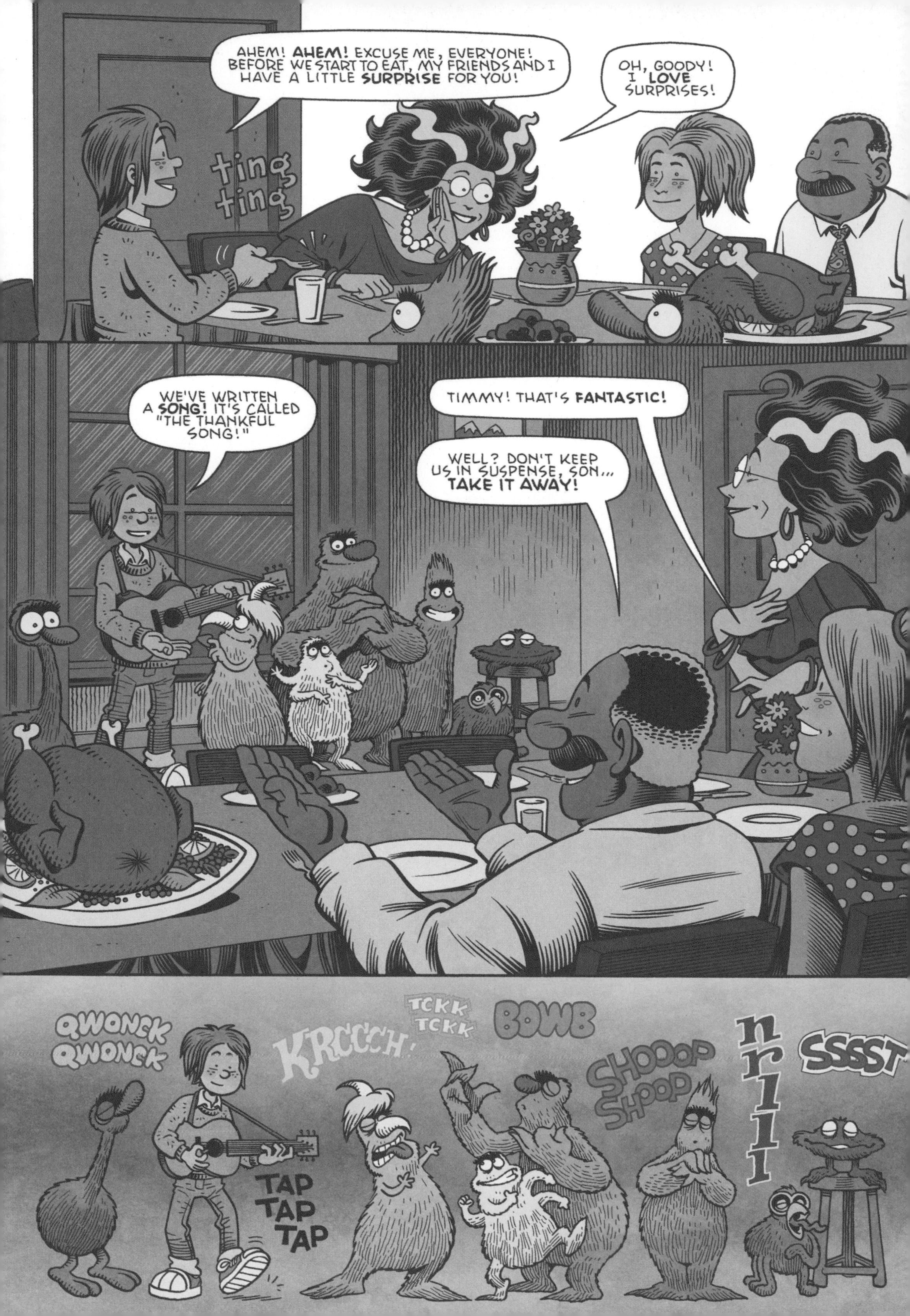
AHEM! AHEM! EXCUSE ME, EVERYONE! BEFORE WE START TO EAT, MY FRIENDS AND I HAVE A LITTLE SURPRISE FOR YOU!
ting ting
OH, GOODY! I LOVE SURPRISES!
WE'VE WRITTEN A SONG! IT'S CALLED "THE THANKFUL SONG!"
TIMMY! THAT'S FANTASTIC!
WELL? DON'T KEEP US IN SUSPENSE, SON... TAKE IT AWAY!
QWONCK QWONCK
KRCCCH!
TCKK TCKK
BOWB
SHOOOP SHOOP
nrlll
SSSST
TAP TAP TAP

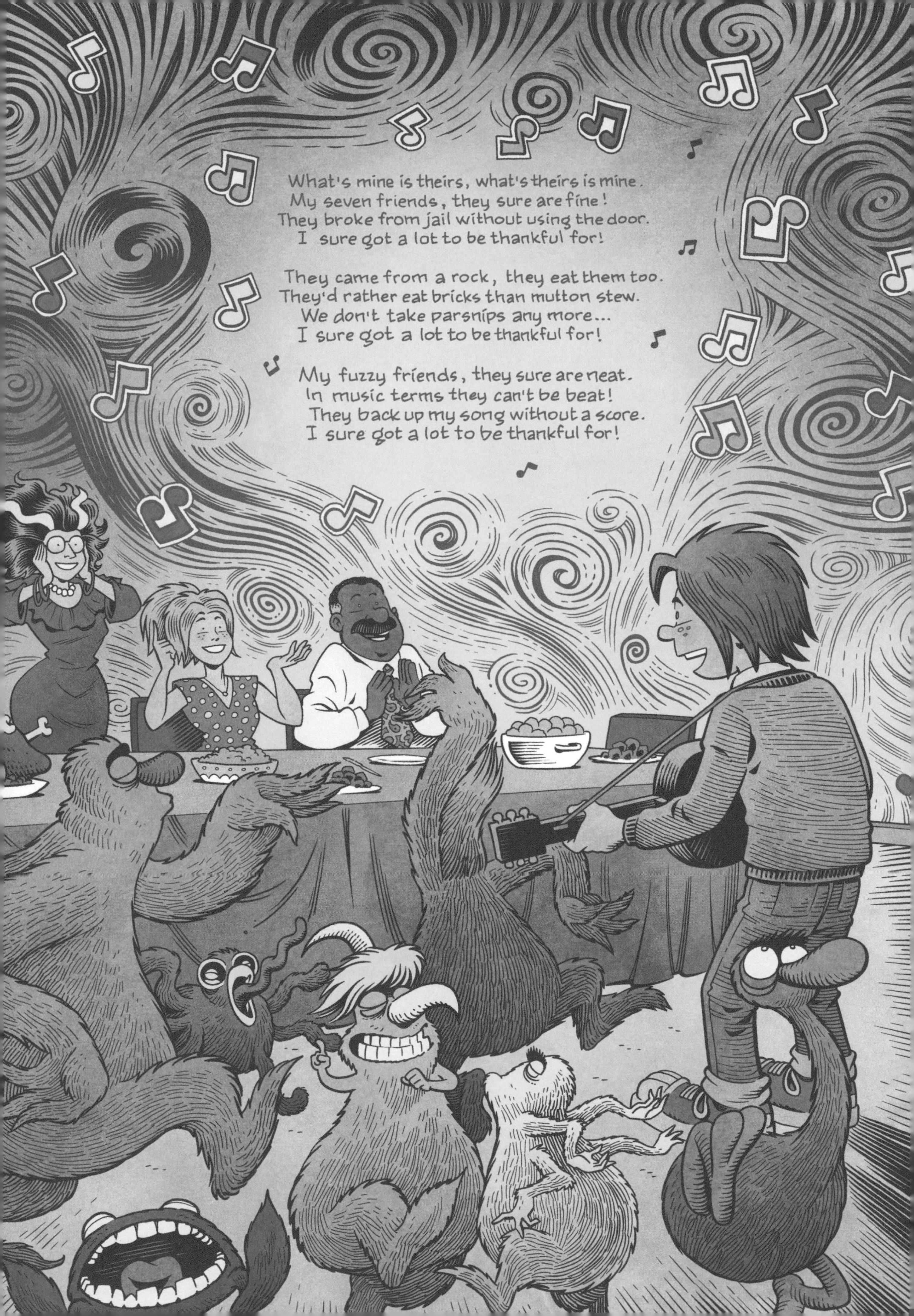
What's mine is theirs, what's theirs is mine.
My seven friends, they sure are fine!
They broke from jail without using the door.
I sure got a lot to be thankful for!
They came from a rock, they eat them too.
They'd rather eat bricks than mutton stew.
We don't take parsnips any more...
I sure got a lot to be thankful for!
My fuzzy friends, they sure are neat.
In music terms they can't be beat!
They back up my song without a score.
I sure got a lot to be thankful for!

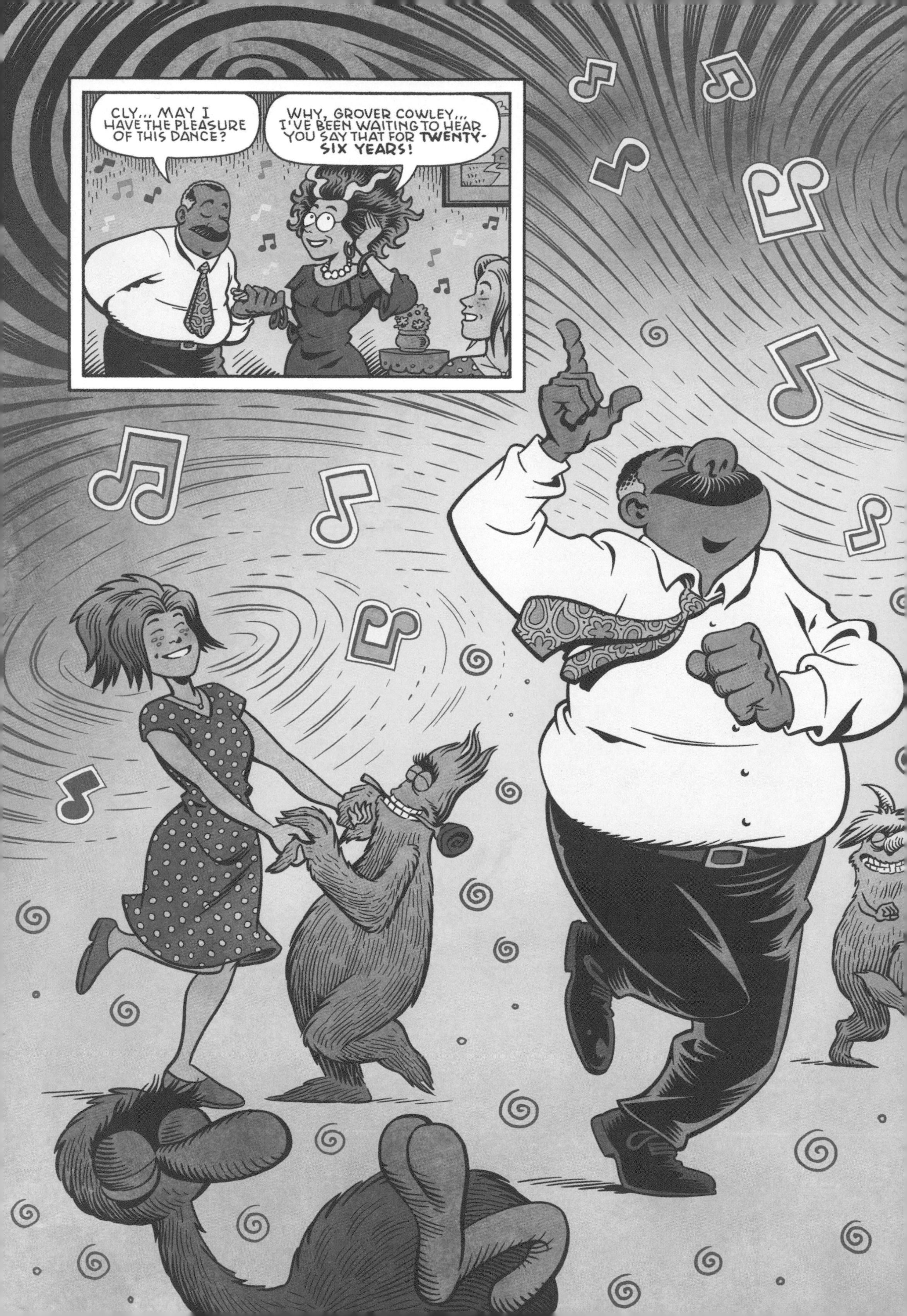
CLY... MAY I HAVE THE PLEASURE OF THIS DANCE?
WHY, GROVER COWLEY... I'VE BEEN WAITING TO HEAR YOU SAY THAT FOR **TWENTY-SIX YEARS!**

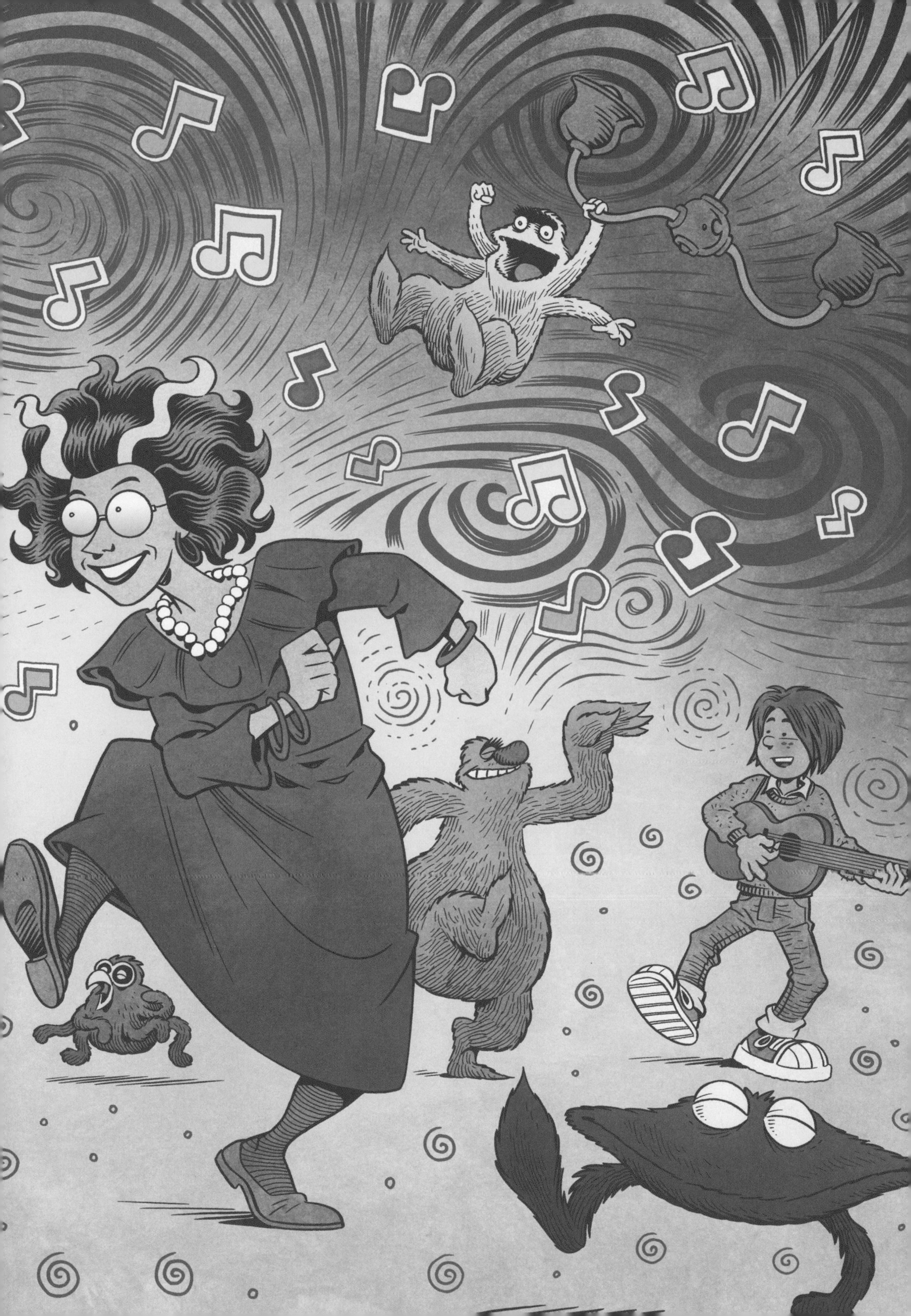

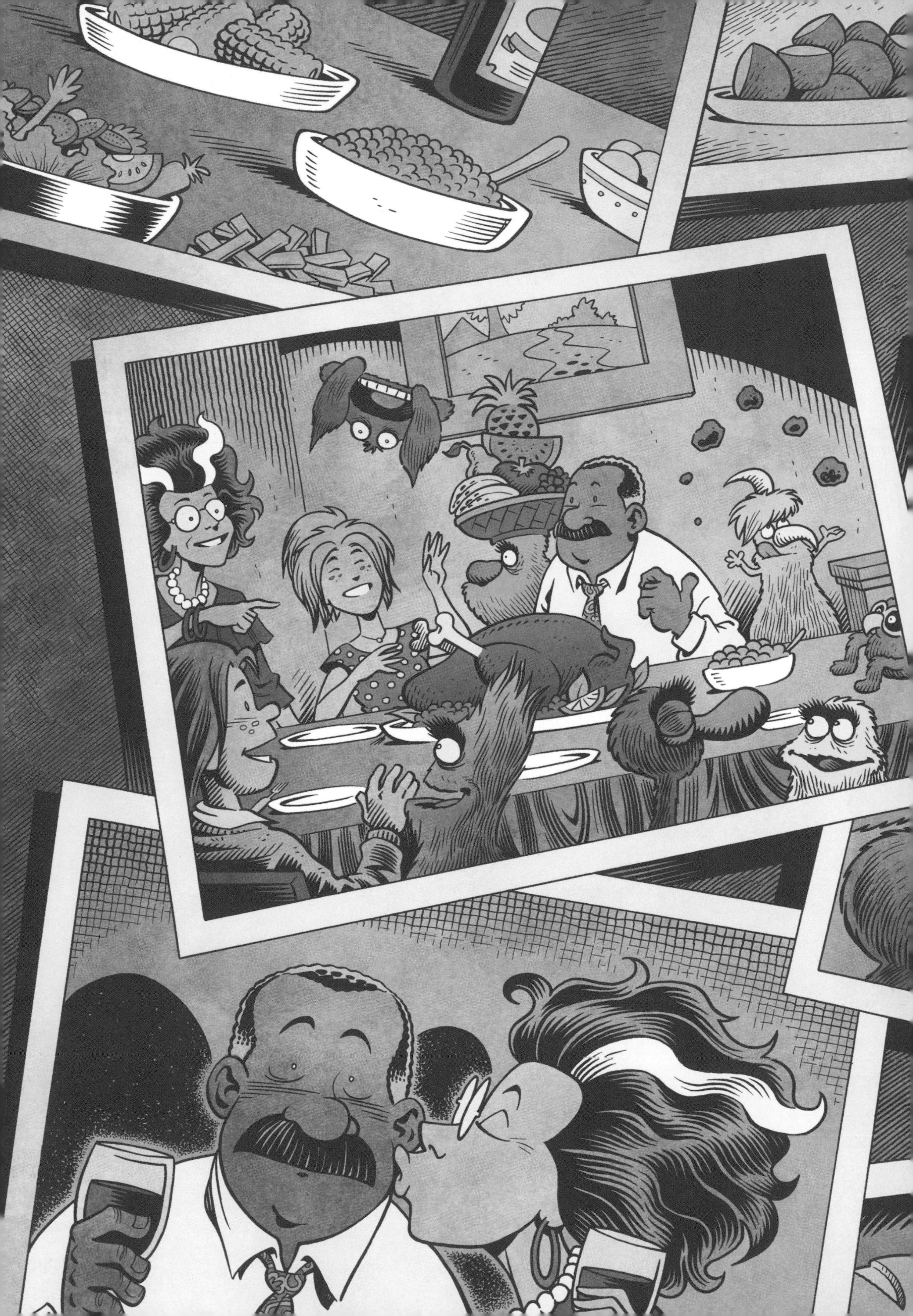

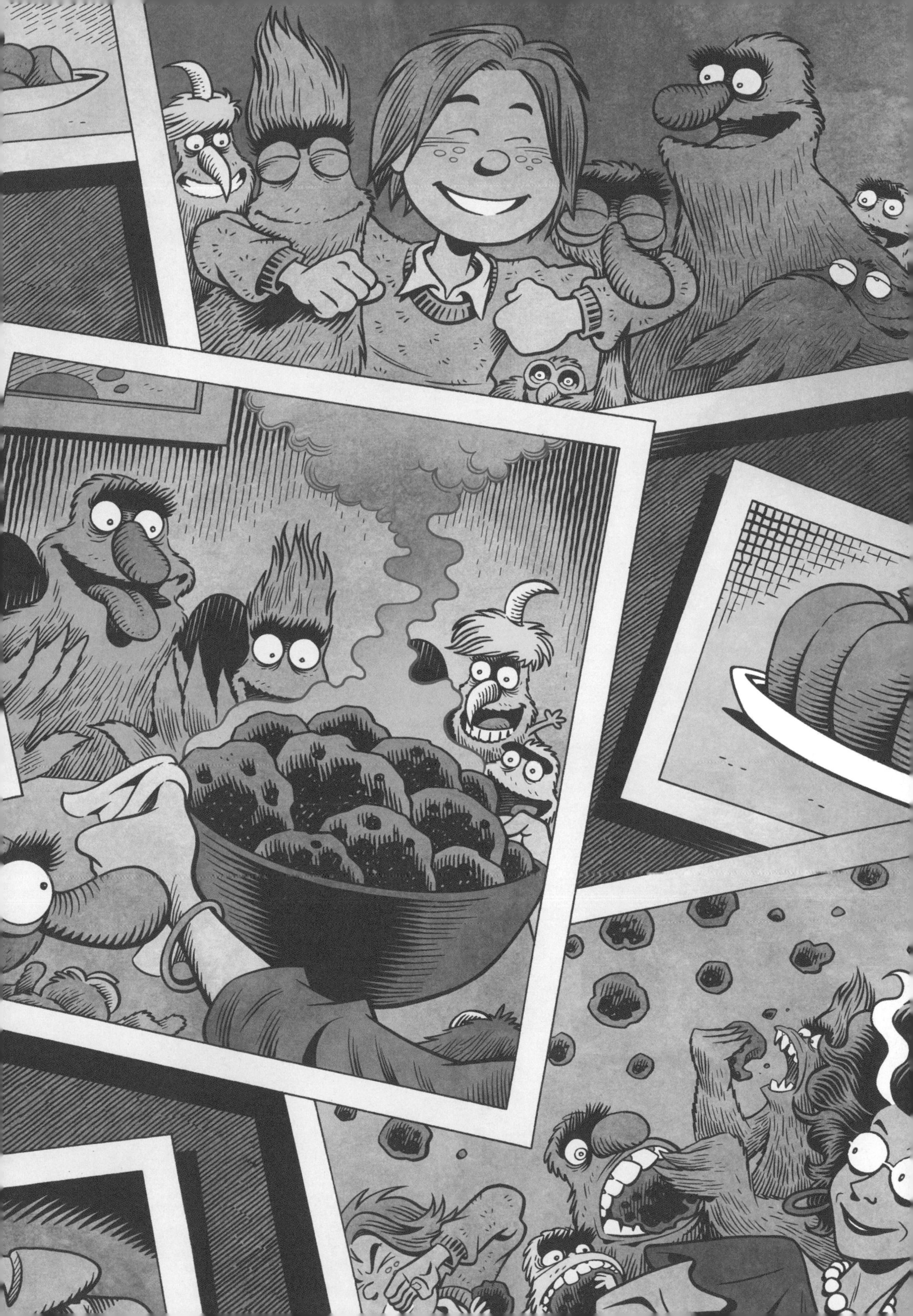

# THE END

# AFTERWORD

Well, that was fun. A lot of work in a very short time (as I write this, my hand is still sore from those last few weeks of inking!) — but worth it.

It's very flattering — incredibly so! — to be thought of as people's "go-to" cartoonist when anything Jim Henson-related comes up. From writing and drawing *The Muppet Show Comic Book* to opening the *Storyteller* anthology to this book you hold in your hands, every Henson-related project I've been involved with has been a privilege to be a part of. It's also somewhat daunting at times: because Jim Henson is thought of so very fondly by so many people, and because expectations of anything with his name attached to it are consequently so very high, I'm obliged not only to bring my "A" game to each project, but to strive to make my best effort noticeably better than whatever my best effort was the last time. Jim Henson's reputation really is an enormous one to live up to. If I made it even a fraction of the way towards that lofty peak, I figure I'm doing pretty well.

This particular book had some unusual challenges. Because music was such an integral part of the story as described in the initial treatment, I felt it couldn't really be avoided, despite my gut feeling that comics and music go together like chalk and peanut butter. Facing up to that problem required some creative thinking; I'm pretty happy with how we tackled that element in the end, coming up with a solution that took advantage of the unique graphic language of the comics medium. My thanks to Ian Herring, whose coloring expertise took my half-baked idea and ran with it, realizing it far beyond my expectations.

I don't claim to be any kind of expert on the life and work of Jim Henson, or to have any special insight into his creative world. I don't know all the minutiae about every project he was involved with; there are even *Muppet Shows* I still haven't gotten around to watching. I'm just a fan. So think of this book as a fan letter from someone whose life Jim Henson touched, in a small way, and made it a little bit brighter. Just one fan letter among the millions.

Hope he gets it.

**ROGER LANGRIDGE**
*London, 2014*

# FROM PUPPETS TO PANELS

## A BEHIND-THE-SCENES LOOK AT THE CREATION OF THE MUSICAL MONSTERS OF TURKEY HOLLOW

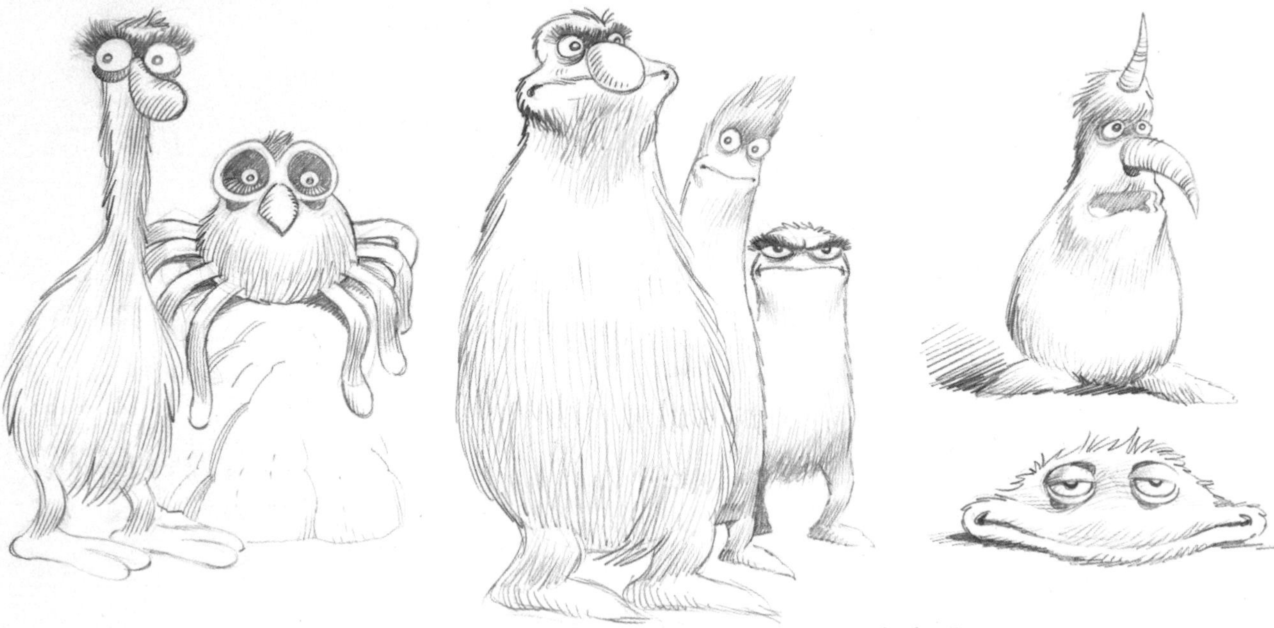

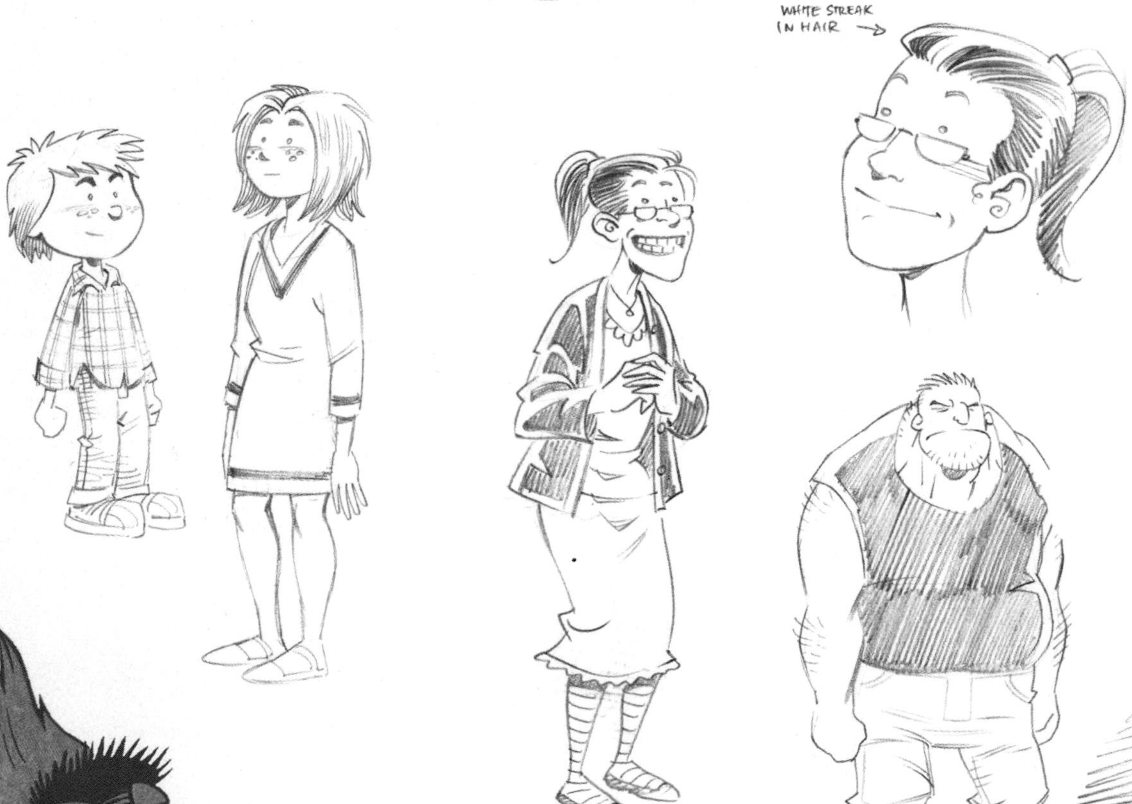
WHITE STREAK IN HAIR

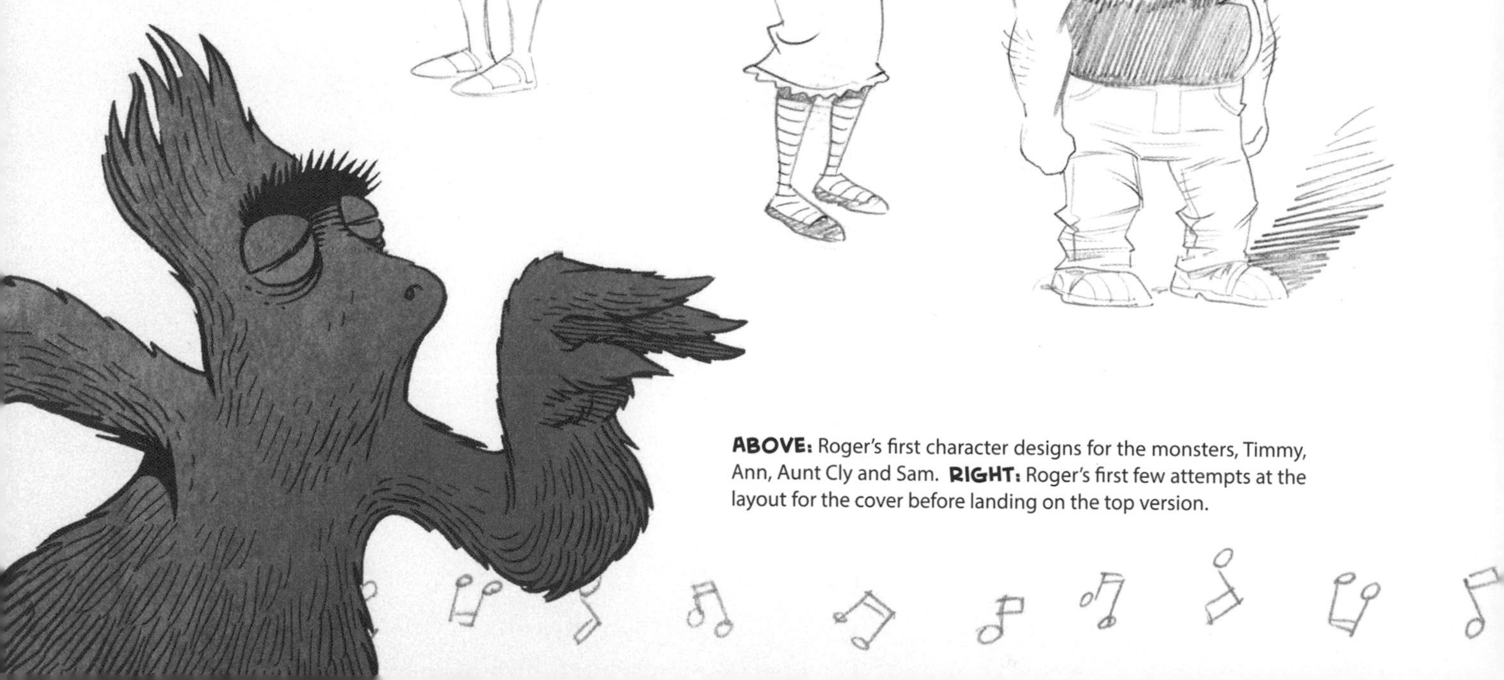

**ABOVE:** Roger's first character designs for the monsters, Timmy, Ann, Aunt Cly and Sam. **RIGHT:** Roger's first few attempts at the layout for the cover before landing on the top version.

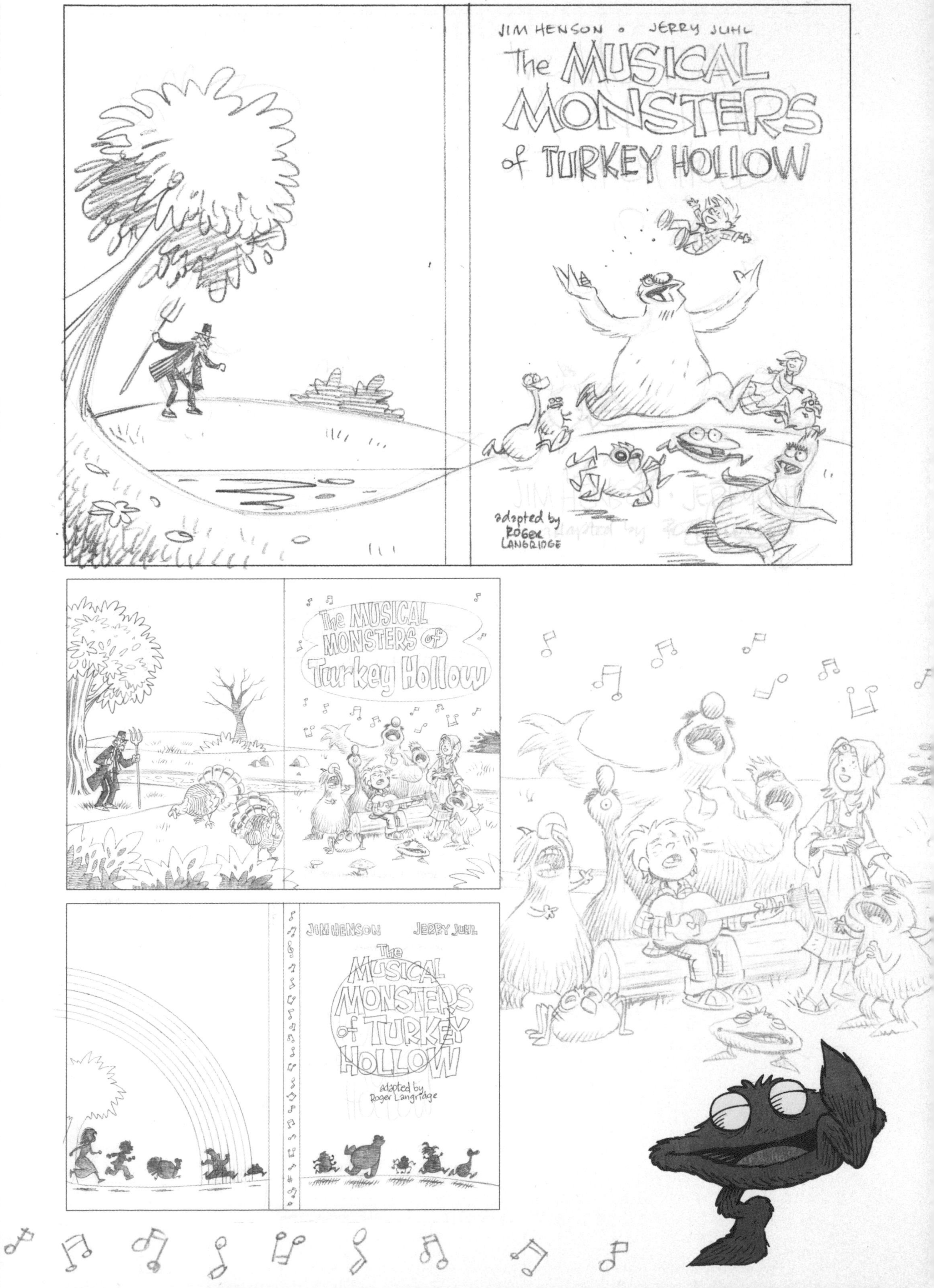

JIM HENSON • JERRY JUHL
The MUSICAL MONSTERS of TURKEY HOLLOW
adapted by ROGER LANGRIDGE
The MUSICAL MONSTERS of Turkey Hollow
JIM HENSON
JERRY JUHL
The MUSICAL MONSTERS of TURKEY HOLLOW
adapted by Roger Langridge

Sump then shakes a folded piece of paper under Cly's nose, announcing that he has unearthed a new piece of evidence which definitely establishes his ownership of her property. He is ready to take her to court if she does not pack up and get out. Grover Cowley, who is, you will recall, also the sheriff, allows as how that "new evidence" looks a lot like a folded gas bill. Eldridge Sump ~~steps~~ stamps out in a rage.

Aunt Cly laughs the incident off, calling the mean, grasping Sump "that silly old man", but Timmy looks a bit frightened as the two leave, headed for home.

Back at their farmhouse, Ann is waiting for them. Every afternoon, Ann, who is an accomplished folk guitarist, gives Timmy a music lesson, after which the boy goes out to his favorite place by the brook to practice. Today Ann begins to teach her little brother a new song. It is a ballad, a quiet, image-filled Autumn-in-New-England kind of song, and as she sings we time dissolve to Timmy coming out of the house with his little guitar slung over his shoulder. The song continues as he ~~traipses~~ hikes through a pumpkin patch, climbs a stone fence, and follows the fast running brook. When he gets to the clearing, filled with golden sun and purple shadows, Timmy ~~climbs~~ scrambles onto the log and begins practicing. Lying just next to him, unnoticed, is the mysterious rock which we saw split open.

As he plays, we are aware of a scurrying movement in the bushes. Then we hear an odd thumping, in perfect time to the music. Timmy stops and looks about. Silence. He plays again. The thumping returns, and now there is a pair of eyes, peering from the underbrush. Timidly Timmy investigates,

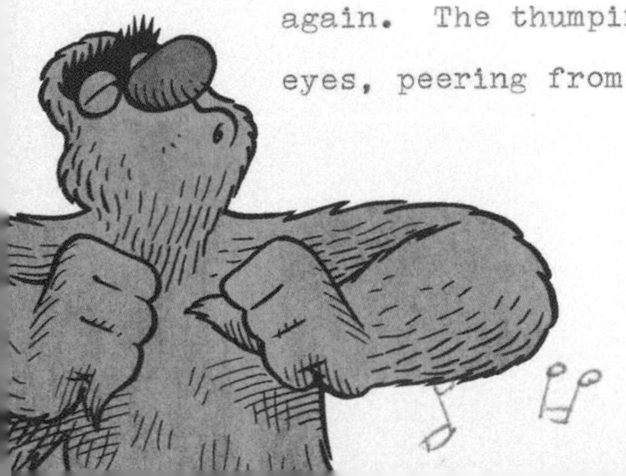

**ABOVE:** A page of Jim and Jerry's original treatment for the television special, including their own handwritten notes. **RIGHT:** Scans of Roger's original layouts from the same scene described in the treatment pages.

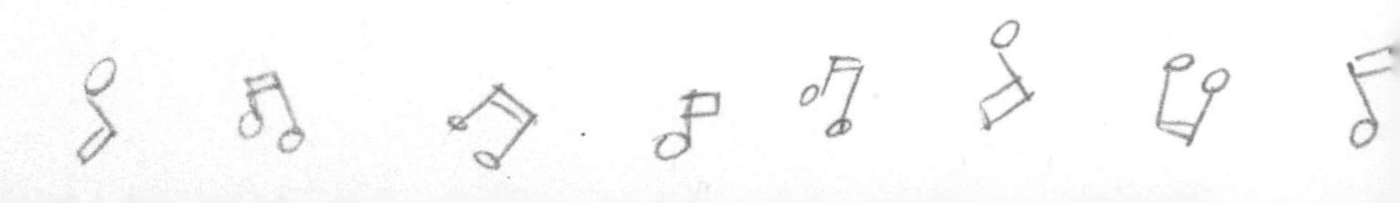

18

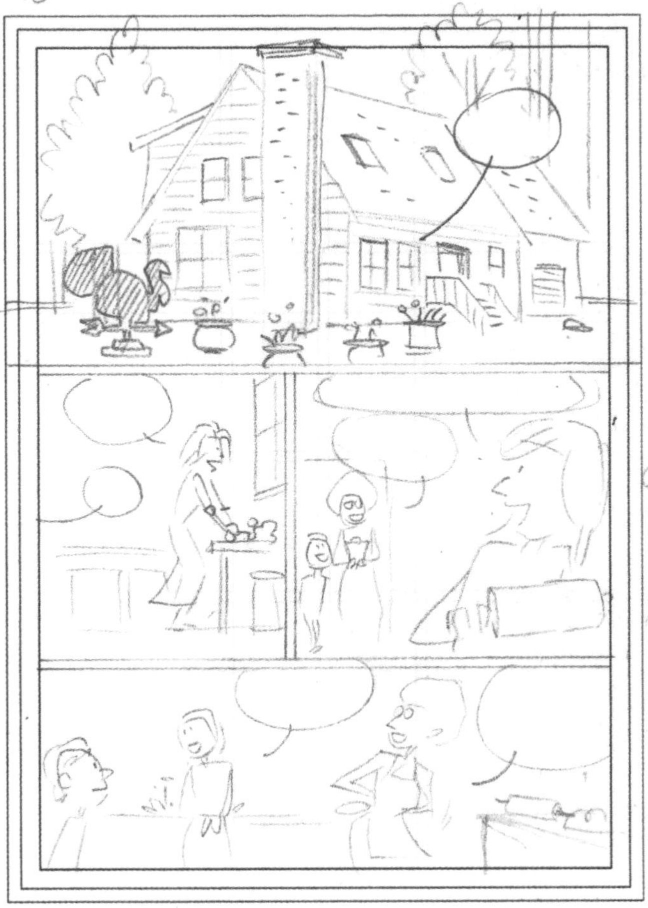

19

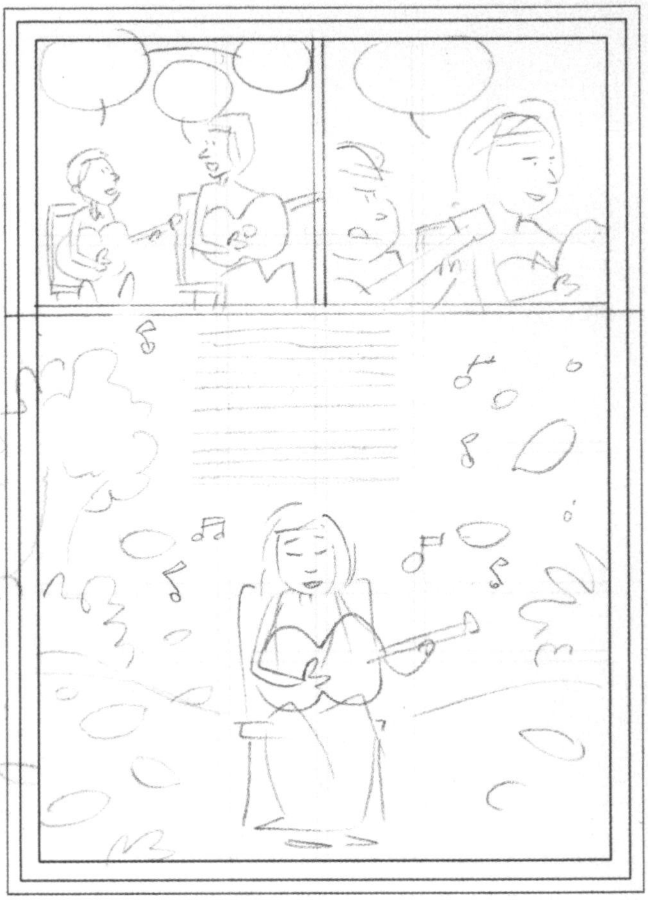

20

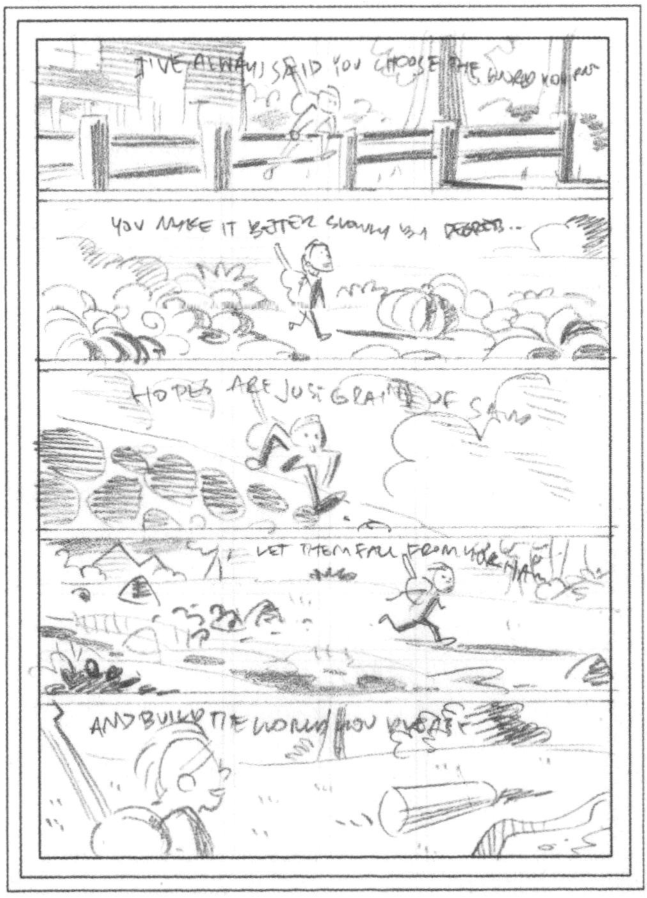
YOU MAKE IT BETTER SLOWLY BY DEGREES..
HOPES ARE JUST GRAINS OF SAND
LET THEM FALL FROM YOUR HAND

21

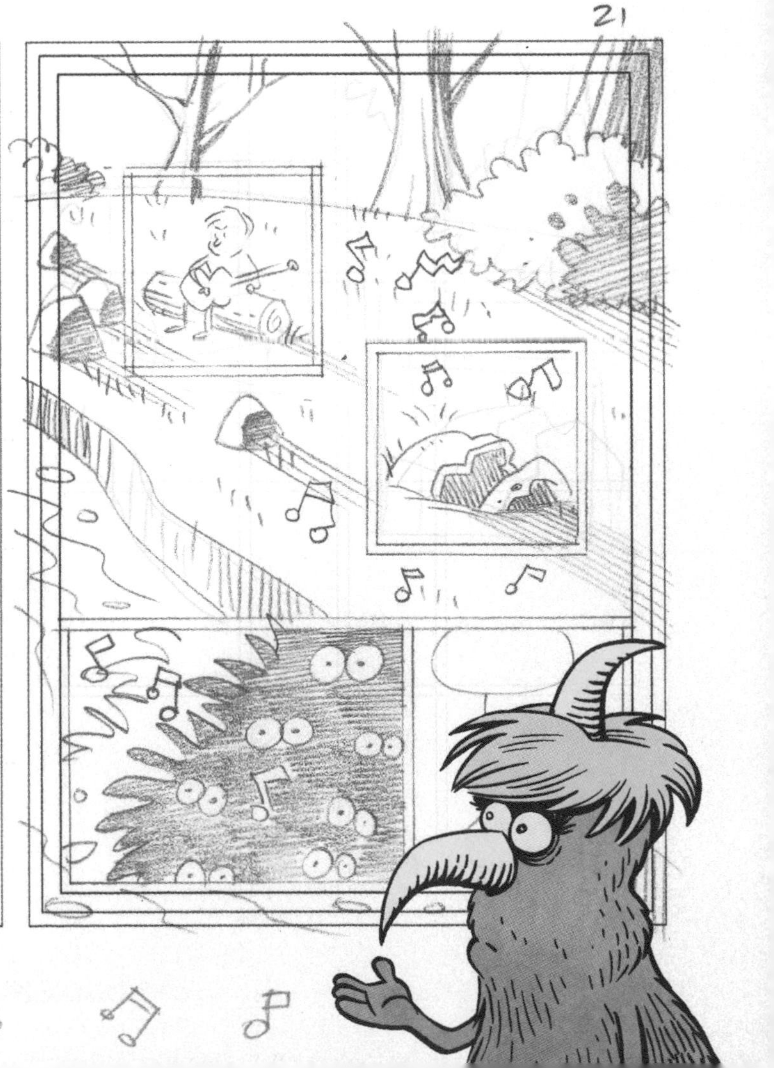

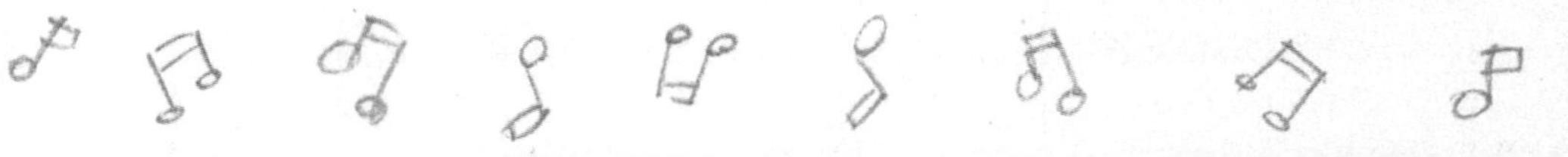

but finding nothing, returns to his music.  Slowly another
sound becomes noticeable, a strange hooting noise which
has actually picked up the melody of the song.  Timmy
whirls quickly to see several fuzzy creature vanish into
the brush.  Thoroughly shaken, the boy grabs his guitar and
runs for home.

That night he tries to ~~explain~~ tell Ann what he has seen and heard. ~~that he thinks~~
~~there are some musical creatures out by the brook, but~~ animals
~~S~~he thinks he's making it up.

returns to the brook. Both he
The next day ~~both~~ Timmy and the creatures have gotten
bolder.  Timmy keeps playing his guitar, and listens to
him.
strange sounds which accompany ~~it~~.  Gradually the little
music-making animals emerge into the clearing.  They are
like nothing anyone has ever seen before.  Perhaps they could
be called monsters, but they are certainly not frightening.
but not
~~There seven little~~  There are seven of them, creeping ~~without~~
~~being~~ creepy, furry but not ferocious, toothy but not at all
dangerous looking.  The sounds they make are equally
strange, altogether unearthly, but quite musical.  Timmy
gives a tentative wave and ~~x~~ says, "Hi."  The monsters
leap about in friendly fashion, and one actually rubs up
against the boys leg, like a cat.  Timmy explains that he
has to go ~~home~~, and bids them goodbye.  But the creatures
~~again~~ have taken a liking to him, and try to follow
him back.  ~~He I~~ It takes a good deal of persuasion to keep
home.
them from following the boy ~~into the farmhouse.~~

That evening, dark shapes can be seen scurrying across
the front lawn, and shining eyes peer from behind rose
bushes.  Very late at night, Timmy wakes from a dream to
find seven little monster lined ~~x~~ up at the foot of the
bed, watching him.

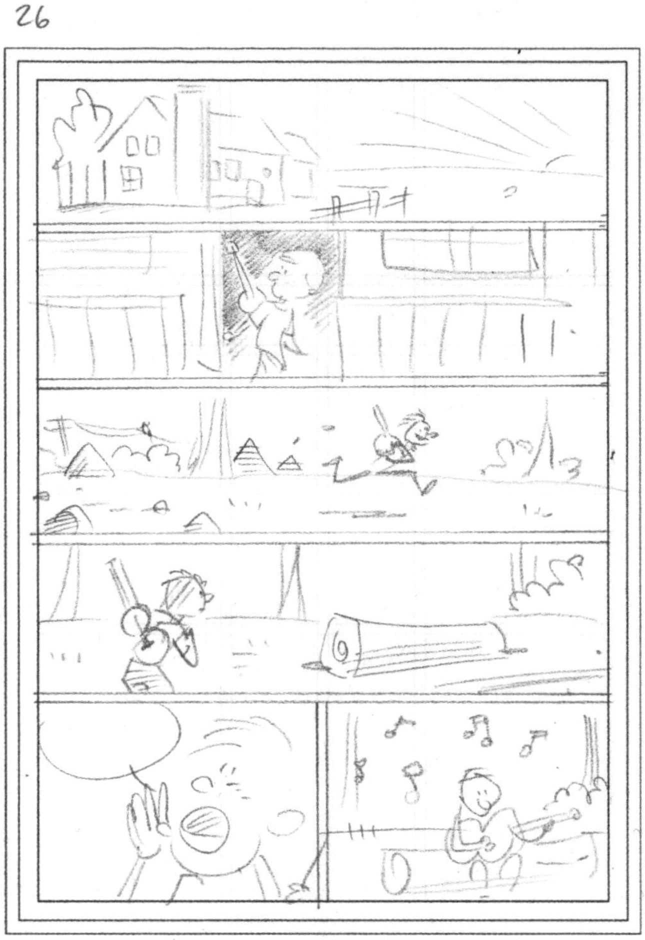
26

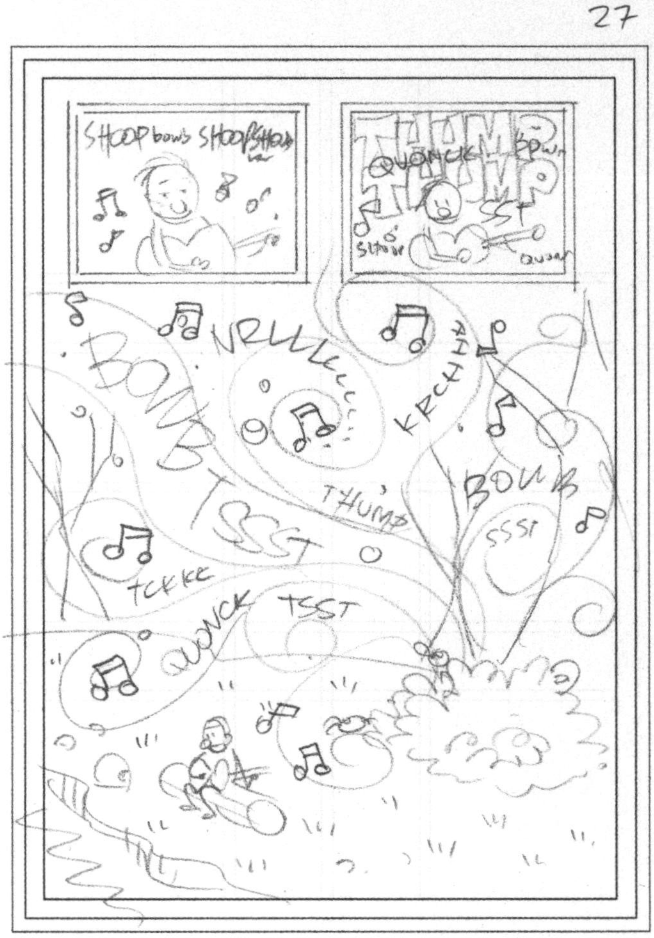
27
SHOOP bowb SHOOP SHOOP
THUMP THUMP
QUONCK
BOWB
KRCHHH
BOWB
TSSST
THUMP
BOWB
SSST
TCKKK
QUONCK
TSST

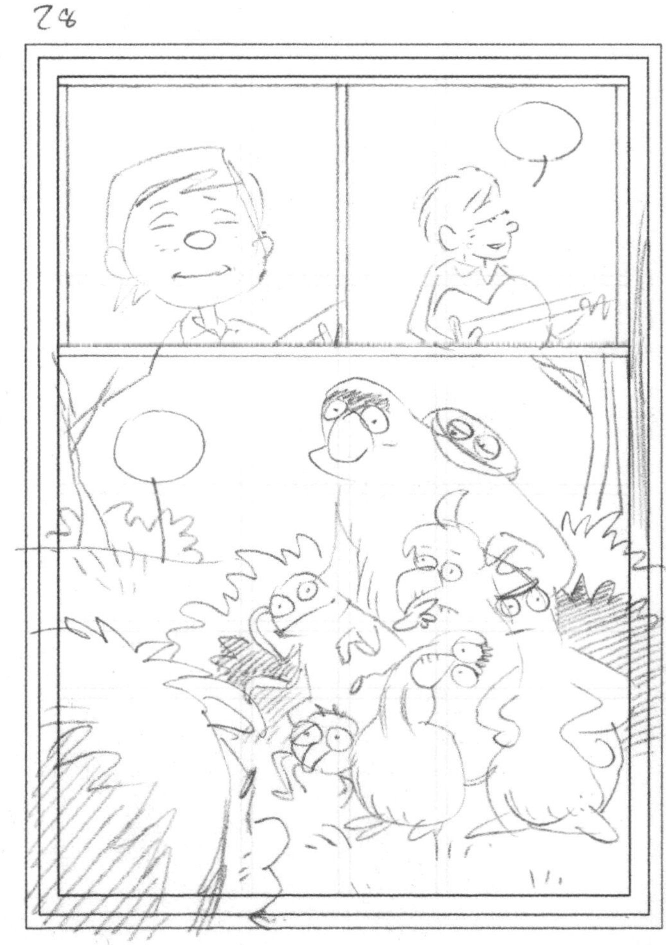
28

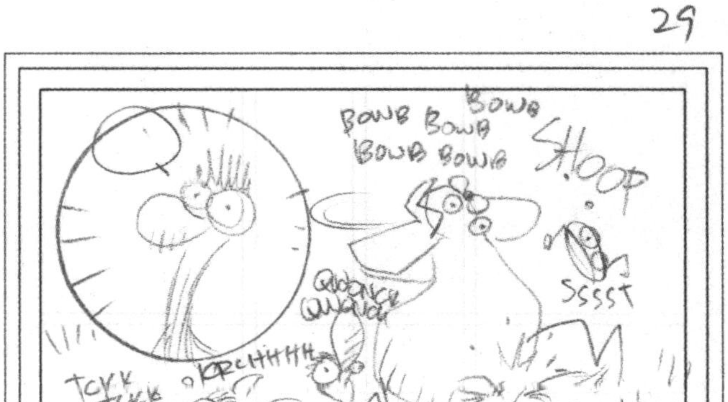
29
BOWB BOWB BOWB
BOWB BOWB
SHOOP
QUONCK QUONCK
SSSST
TCKK TCKK TCKK
KRCHHHHH
NRLLLL!

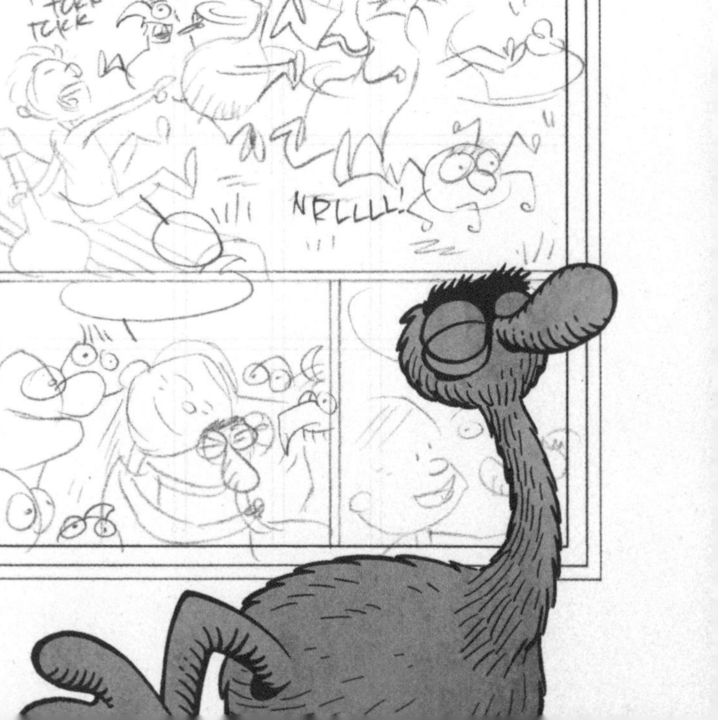

**THE FOLLOWING PAGE:** Photos of the original musical monsters, taken by Jim Henson in Connecticut in 1968.

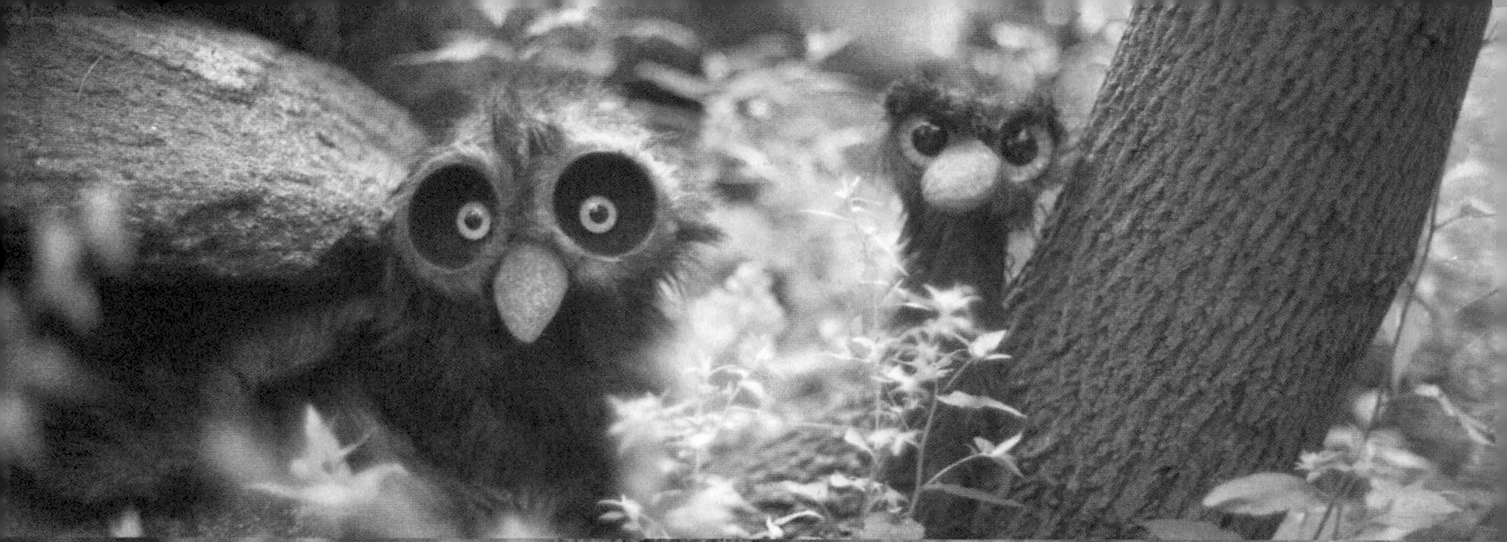

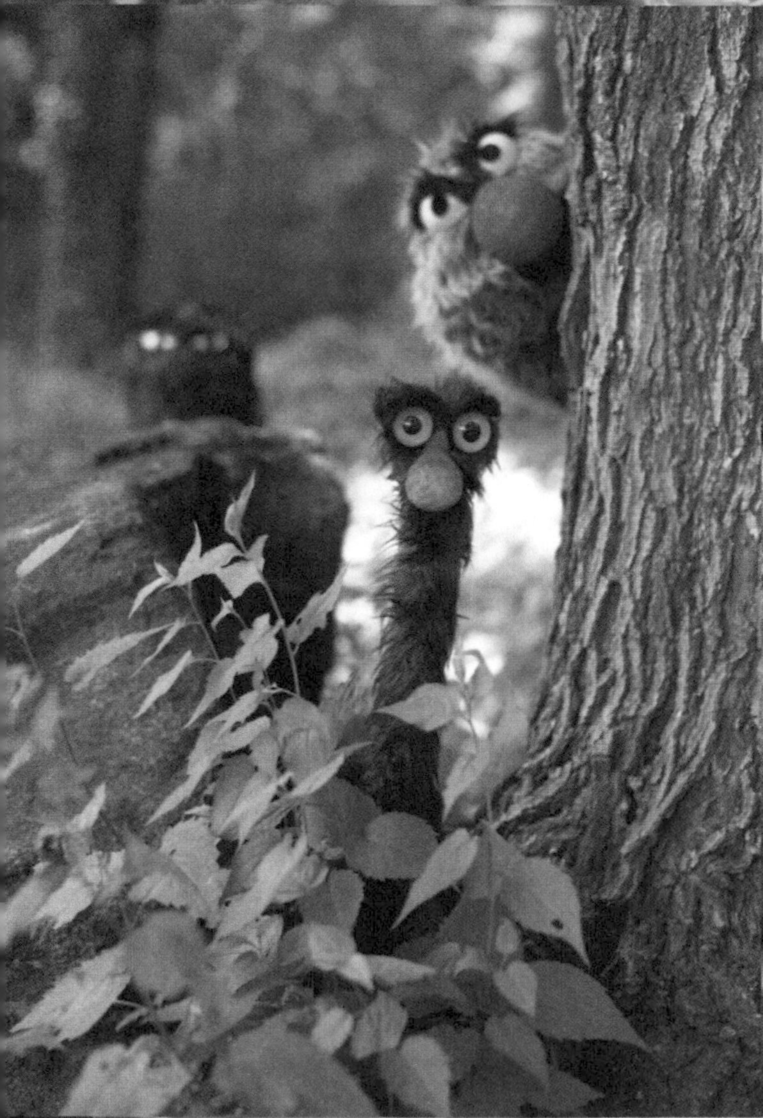

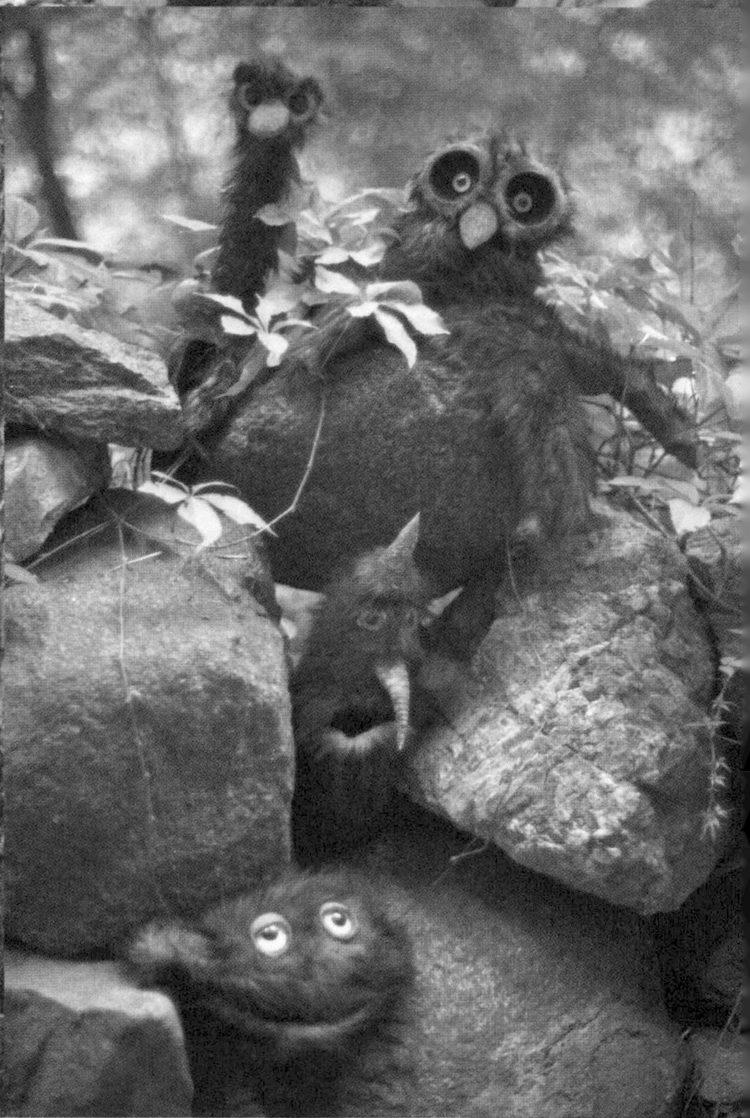

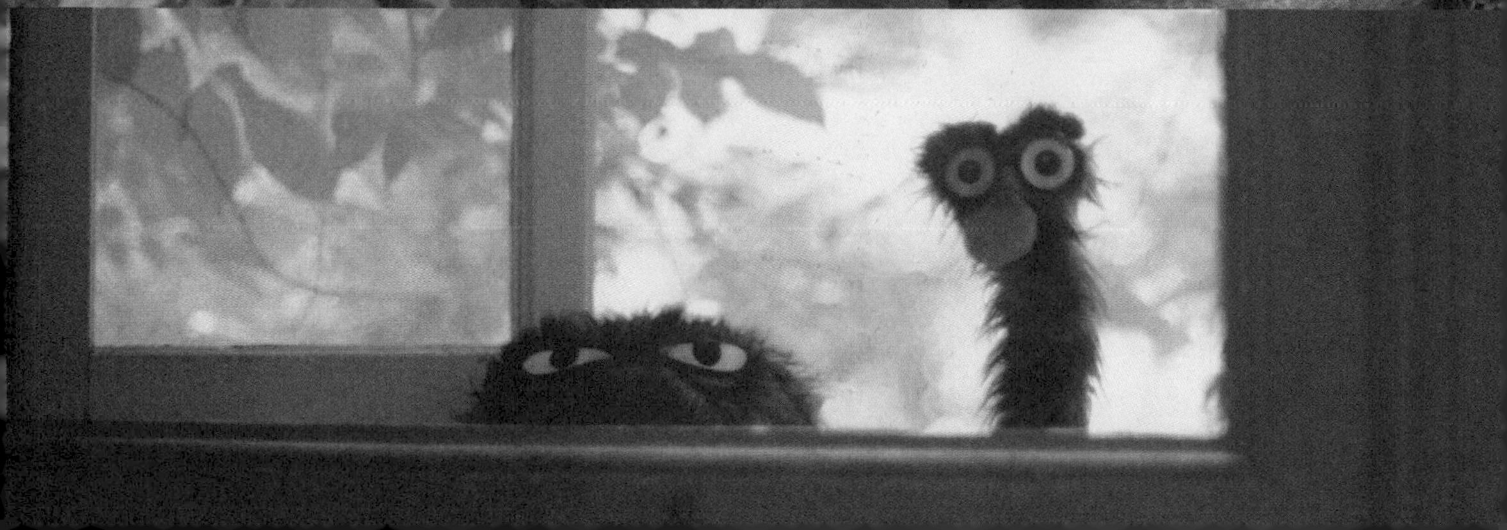

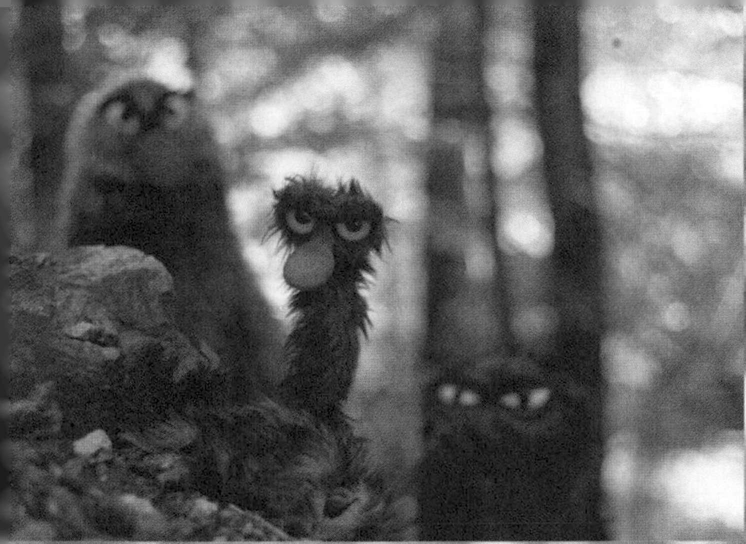
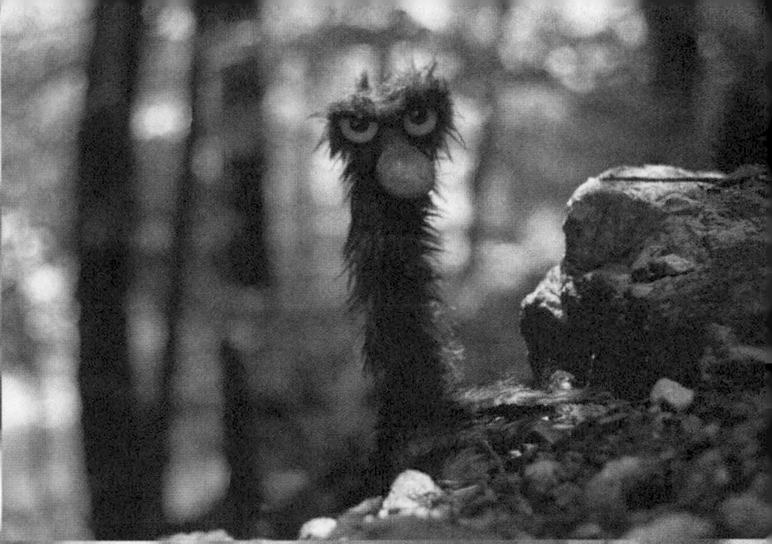
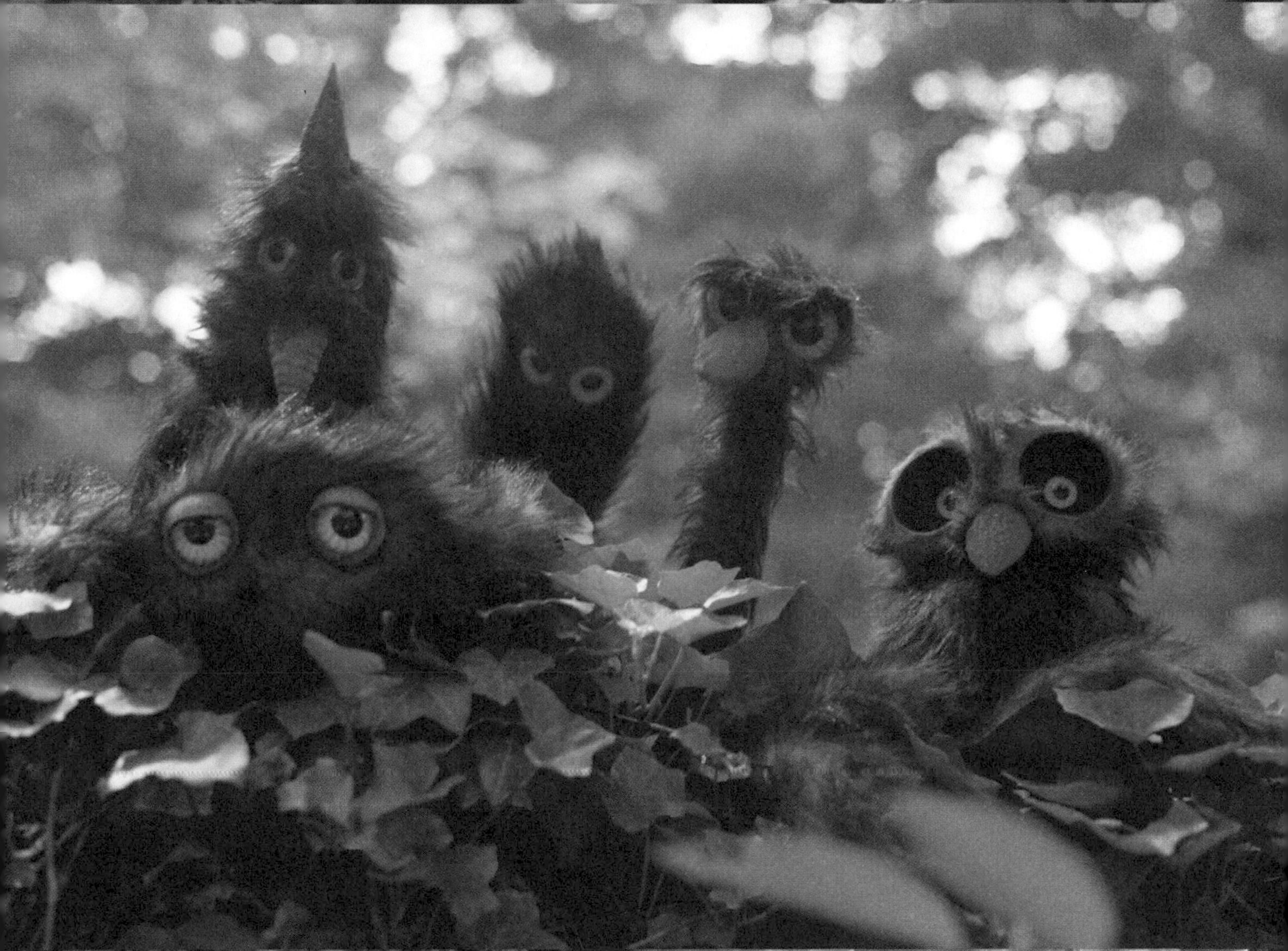
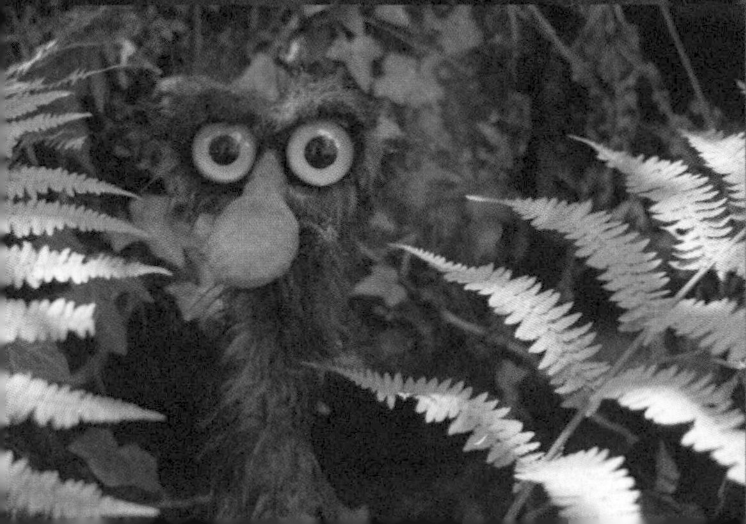
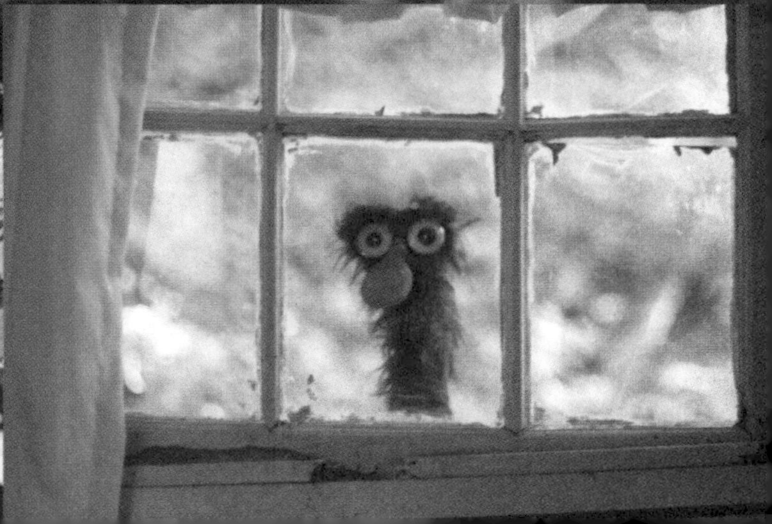

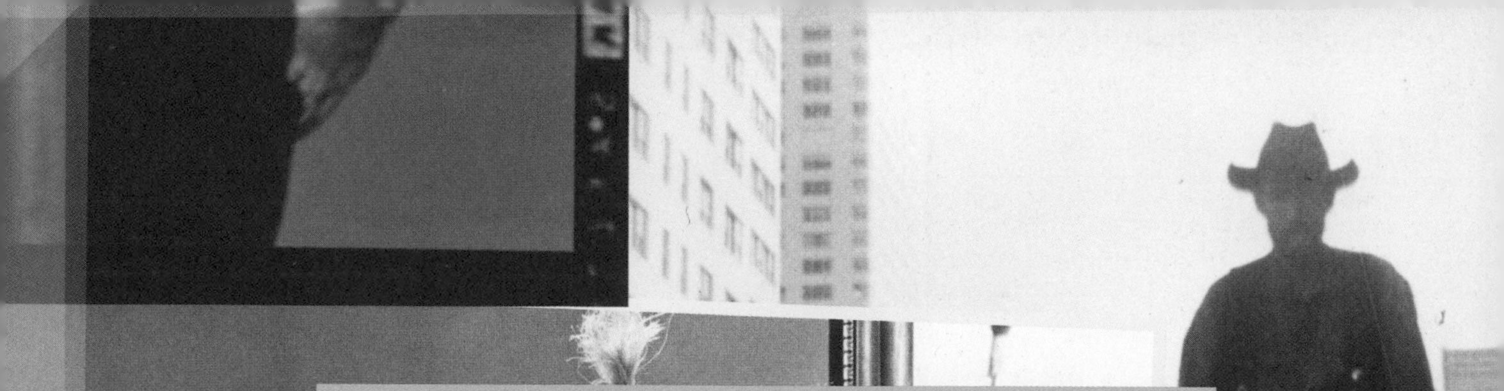

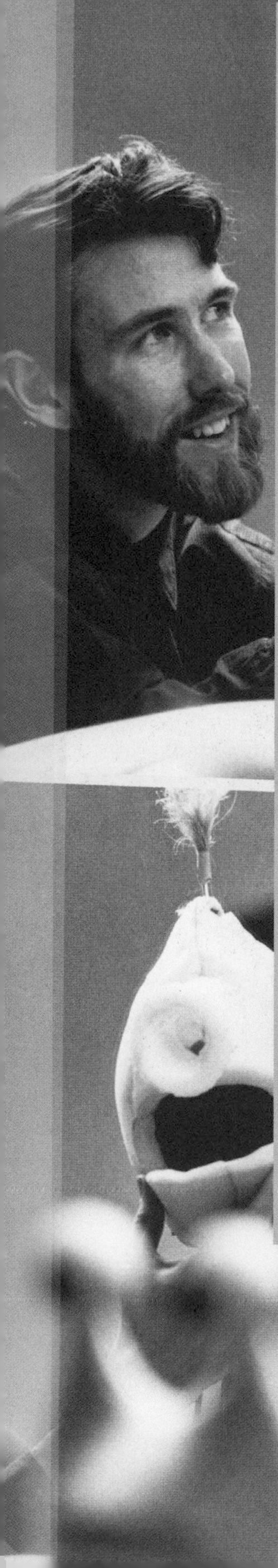

Early television intrigued young **JIM HENSON** and sparked his imagination and creativity. Seeing enormous potential for puppets in this medium, he began his career in local Washington, D.C. television. *Sam and Friends*, his nightly five-minute show on NBC's WRC, won Jim an Emmy in 1958 and introduced Kermit the Frog to the world.

During the sixties, Jim and the Muppets made many appearances on variety shows and were regulars on *The Today Show*, *The Ed Sullivan Show* and *The Jimmy Dean Show*. While the Muppets grew in popularity, Jim developed another career as a filmmaker. His experimental short film, *Time Piece*, was nominated for an Academy Award in 1965.

Jim's remarkable association with Public Television's award-winning children's show, *Sesame Street*, began in 1969. The humor and whimsy of his characters have continued to entertain generations of children over the past 42 years.

The introduction of *The Muppet Show* in 1976 was a phenomenal success, reaching 235 million viewers in more than 100 countries and winning three Emmys in its five-year run. The popularity of the show led to the feature films *The Muppet Movie*, *The Great Muppet Caper* and *The Muppets Take Manhattan*, as well as the animated television series, *Jim Henson's Muppet Babies*.

Throughout the 1980s, Jim explored new directions in both television and film. The series *Fraggle Rock* was developed specifically with an international audience in mind. He developed new characters and technologies for the award-winning *The Storyteller*, *The Jim Henson Hour*, *Dinosaurs* and for his groundbreaking fantasy films, *The Dark Crystal* and *Labyrinth*. Jim's final completed project, *Jim Henson's Muppet*Vision 3D*, continues to delight thousands daily at the Disney theme parks in Florida and California.

His untimely passing in May 1990 was met with a worldwide outpouring of love and renewed appreciation of his imagination and artistry.

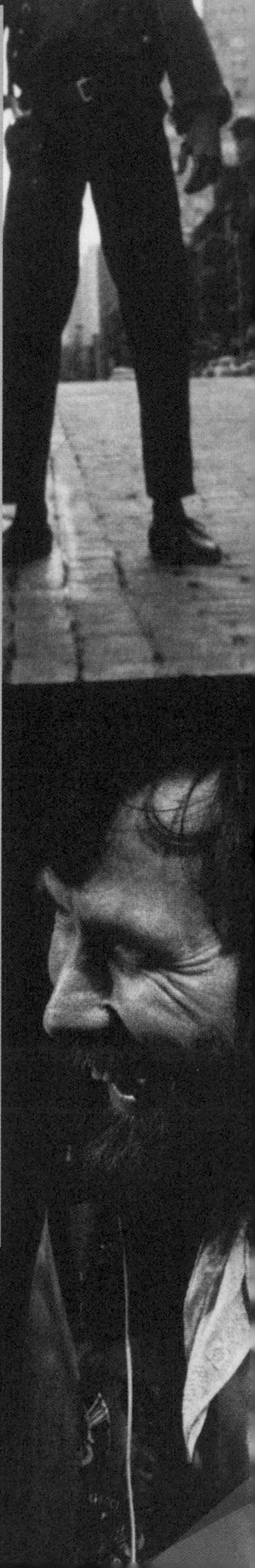

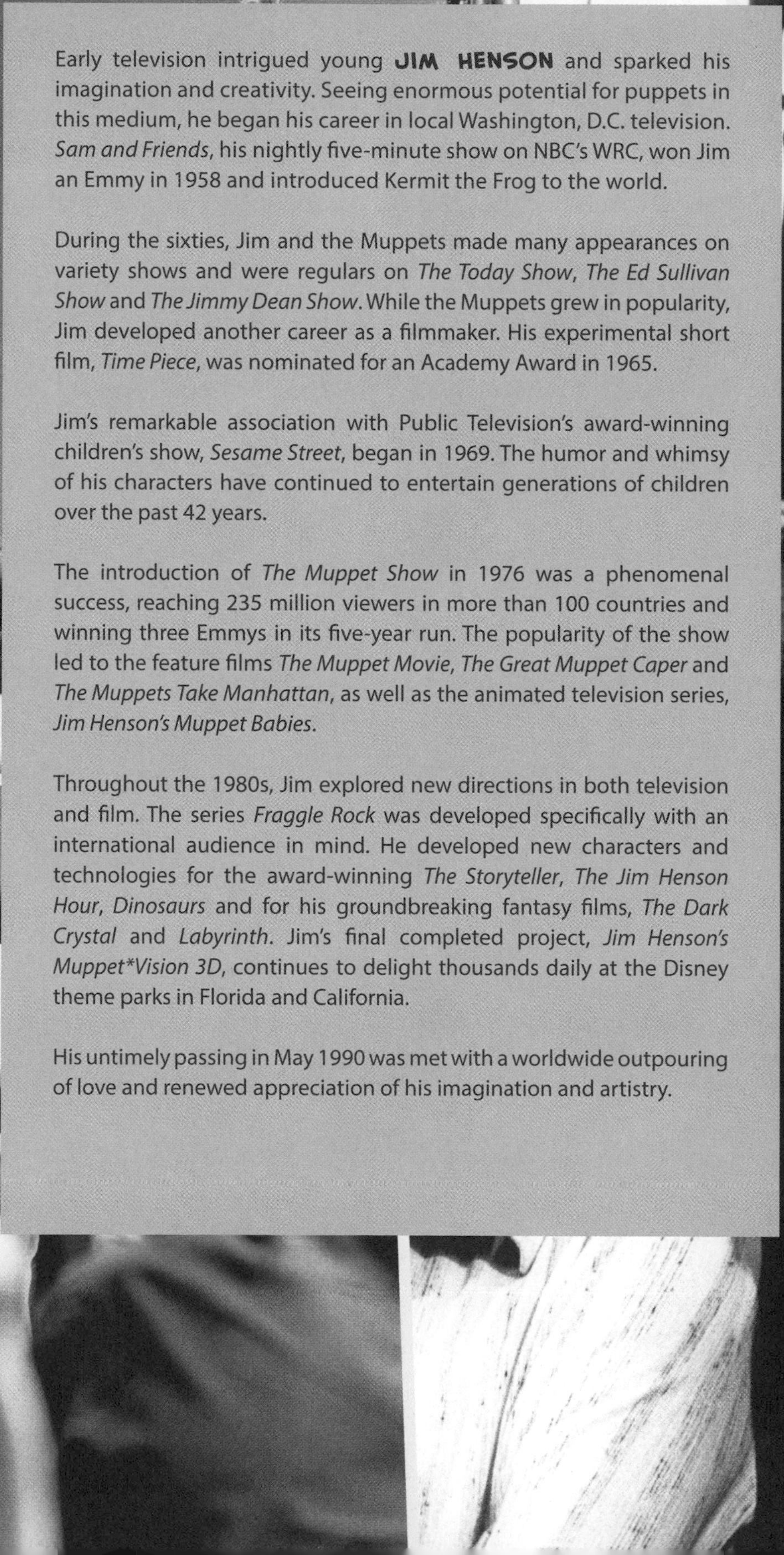

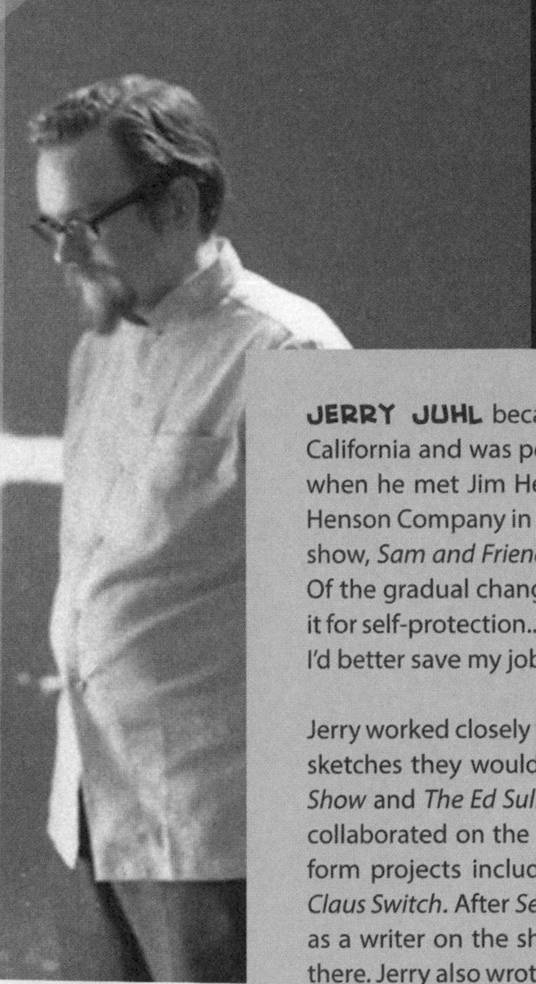

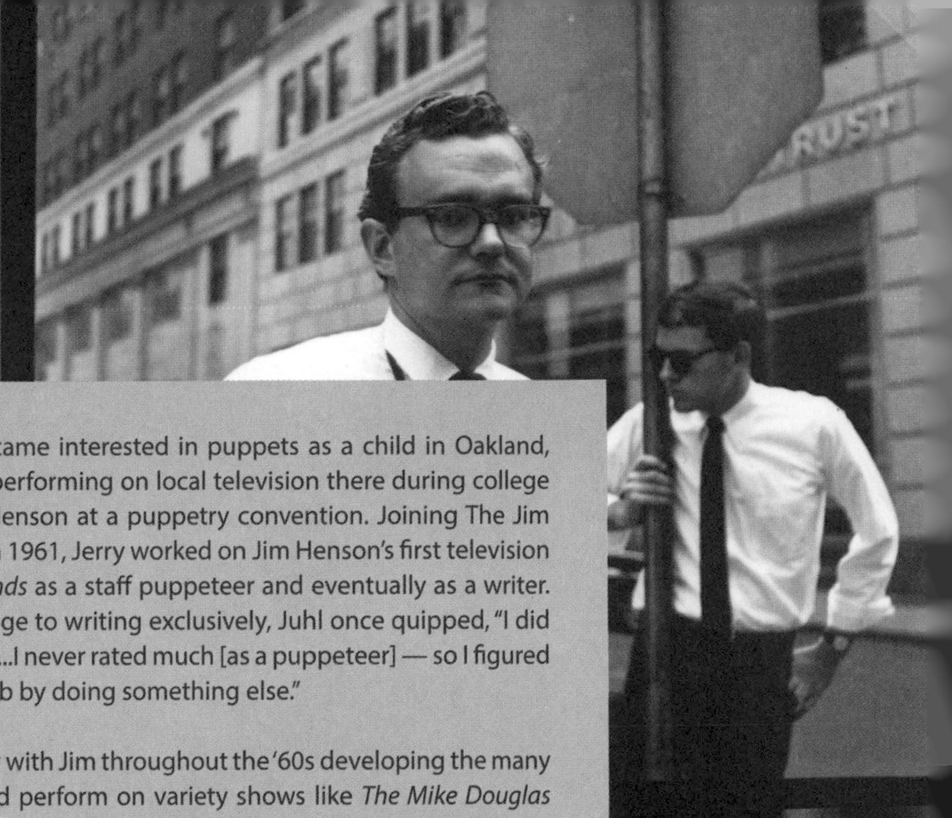
RUST

**JERRY JUHL** became interested in puppets as a child in Oakland, California and was performing on local television there during college when he met Jim Henson at a puppetry convention. Joining The Jim Henson Company in 1961, Jerry worked on Jim Henson's first television show, *Sam and Friends* as a staff puppeteer and eventually as a writer. Of the gradual change to writing exclusively, Juhl once quipped, "I did it for self-protection...I never rated much [as a puppeteer] — so I figured I'd better save my job by doing something else."

Jerry worked closely with Jim throughout the '60s developing the many sketches they would perform on variety shows like *The Mike Douglas Show* and *The Ed Sullivan Show*. During that period, Jim and Jerry also collaborated on the development of numerous experimental or long-form projects including *The Cube*, *Tale of Sand*, and *The Great Santa Claus Switch*. After *Sesame Street* began in 1969, Jerry spent six seasons as a writer on the show and received two Emmy Awards for his work there. Jerry also wrote extensively on every season of *The Muppet Show*.

And when the Muppets went to the big screen, Jerry was right there as well. He co-wrote *The Muppet Movie* (1979) and went on to co-write the Muppet features *The Great Muppet Caper* (1981), *The Muppet Christmas Carol* (1992), *Muppet Treasure Island* (1996), and *Muppets From Space* (1999).

Jerry was also instrumental in the 1980s television show that Jim Henson created "to make world peace" — *Fraggle Rock*. As head writer and creative producer, Jerry led the multiple-award winning series for five seasons, creating episodes and characters that continue to have devoted fans around the world.

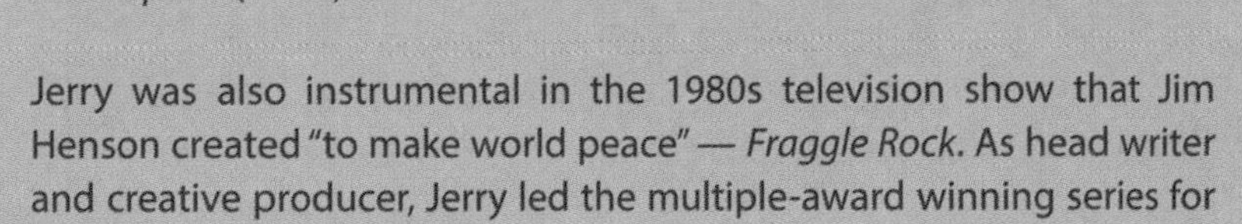

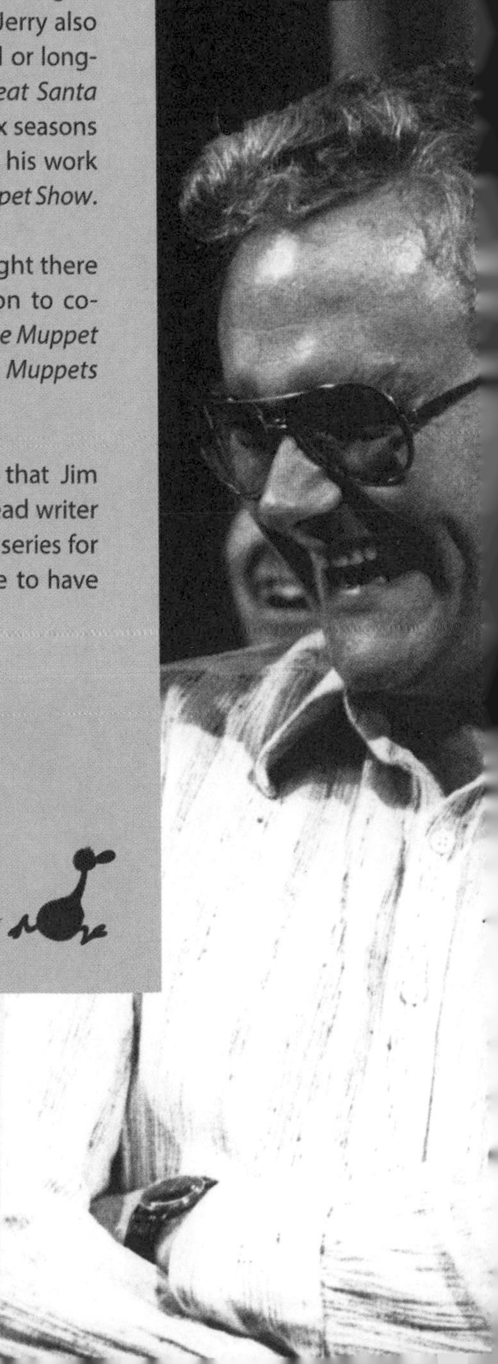

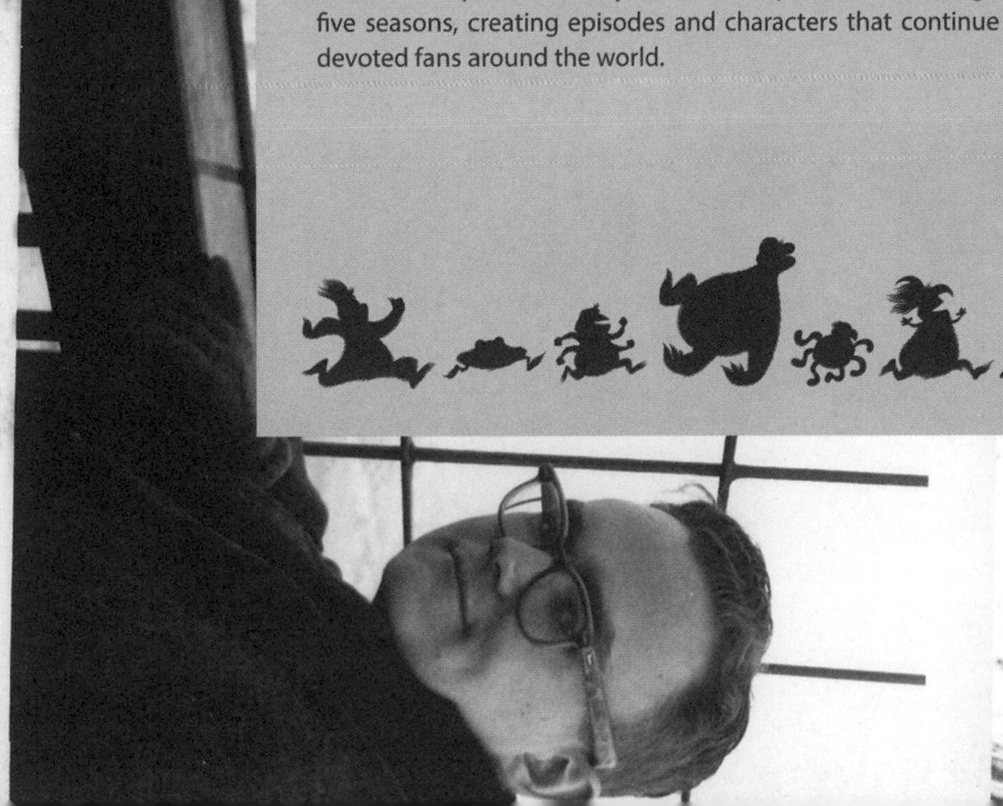

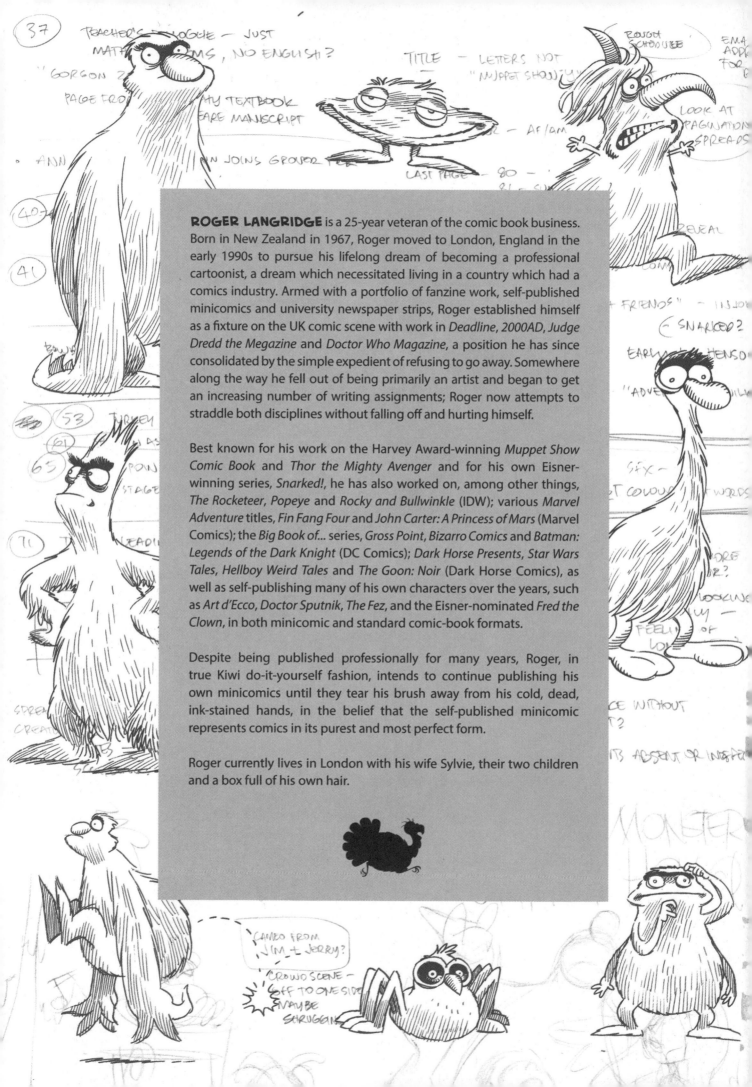

**ROGER LANGRIDGE** is a 25-year veteran of the comic book business. Born in New Zealand in 1967, Roger moved to London, England in the early 1990s to pursue his lifelong dream of becoming a professional cartoonist, a dream which necessitated living in a country which had a comics industry. Armed with a portfolio of fanzine work, self-published minicomics and university newspaper strips, Roger established himself as a fixture on the UK comic scene with work in *Deadline*, *2000AD*, *Judge Dredd the Megazine* and *Doctor Who Magazine*, a position he has since consolidated by the simple expedient of refusing to go away. Somewhere along the way he fell out of being primarily an artist and began to get an increasing number of writing assignments; Roger now attempts to straddle both disciplines without falling off and hurting himself.

Best known for his work on the Harvey Award-winning *Muppet Show Comic Book* and *Thor the Mighty Avenger* and for his own Eisner-winning series, *Snarked!*, he has also worked on, among other things, *The Rocketeer*, *Popeye* and *Rocky and Bullwinkle* (IDW); various *Marvel Adventure* titles, *Fin Fang Four* and *John Carter: A Princess of Mars* (Marvel Comics); the *Big Book of...* series, *Gross Point*, *Bizarro Comics* and *Batman: Legends of the Dark Knight* (DC Comics); *Dark Horse Presents*, *Star Wars Tales*, *Hellboy Weird Tales* and *The Goon: Noir* (Dark Horse Comics), as well as self-publishing many of his own characters over the years, such as *Art d'Ecco*, *Doctor Sputnik*, *The Fez*, and the Eisner-nominated *Fred the Clown*, in both minicomic and standard comic-book formats.

Despite being published professionally for many years, Roger, in true Kiwi do-it-yourself fashion, intends to continue publishing his own minicomics until they tear his brush away from his cold, dead, ink-stained hands, in the belief that the self-published minicomic represents comics in its purest and most perfect form.

Roger currently lives in London with his wife Sylvie, their two children and a box full of his own hair.

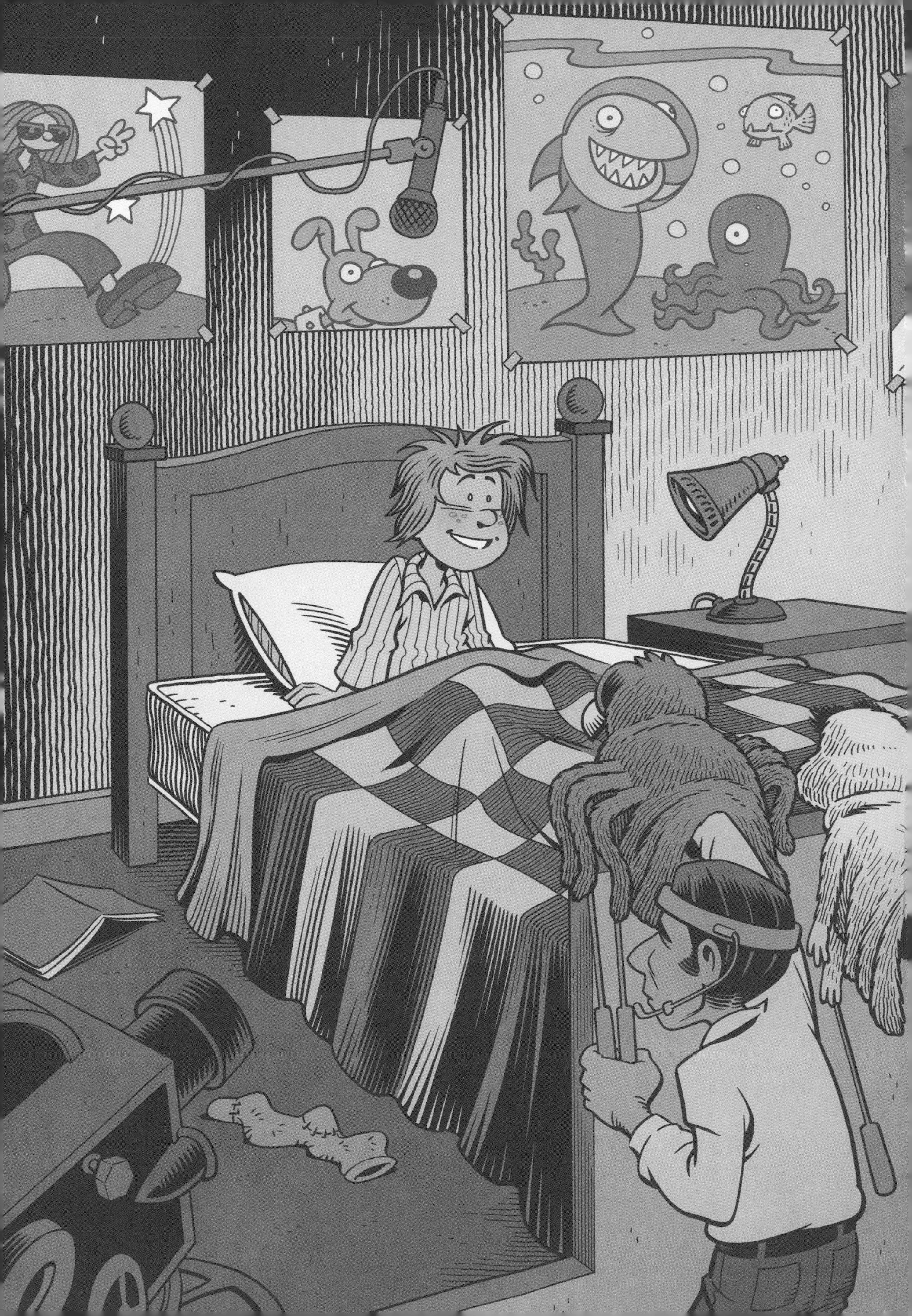